The Working Retrievers

The Working Retrievers

The Training, Care, and Handling of Retrievers
for Hunting and Field Trials

TOM QUINN

A DUTTON BOOK

This book was prepared for publication
by Hilltown Press, Inc., Worthington, Massachusetts,
and the Editors of E. P. Dutton
Color paintings by Tom Quinn.
Diagrams drawn by Jeri Nichols Quinn.

DUTTON
Published by the Penguin Group
Penguin Books USA Inc., 375 Hudson Street,
New York, New York 10014, U.S.A.
Penguin Books Ltd, 27 Wrights Lane,
London W8 5TZ, England
Penguin Books Australia Ltd, Ringwood,
Victoria, Australia
Penguin Books Canada Ltd, 10 Alcorn Avenue,
Toronto, Ontario, Canada M4V 3B2
Penguin Books (N.Z.) Ltd, 182–190 Wairau Road,
Auckland 10, New Zealand

Penguin Books Ltd, Registered Offices:
Harmondsworth, Middlesex, England

First published by Dutton, an imprint of New American Library,
a division of Penguin Books USA Inc.

10 9 8 7

REGISTERED TRADEMARK—MARCA REGISTRADA

Library of Congress Cataloging in Publication Data:

Quinn, Tom.
    The working retrievers.

    Bibliography: p.
    Includes index.
    1. Retrievers.   2. Retrievers—Training.   I. Title.
SF429.R4Q56   1983   636.7'52   82-21088
ISBN 0-525-93287-9

Printed and bound in the United States of America
Color insert printed by South China Printing Co., Hong Kong
Designed by Earl Tidwell

For Nakai

Field Champion and Amateur Field Champion Nakai Anny
(*Bill Hillmann Photo*)

Contents

Preface

Hunting with my keen young Lab, sharing with her the serenity of the salt flats and closeness with wild things, is one of my earliest and fondest memories. Since those days, I have owned and trained many retrievers. I've discovered the satisfaction of seeing my dogs excel in both wetland and upland hunting as well as field-trial competitions and, from the vantage point of a judge in these trials, witnessed the extraordinarily high levels of retriever performance. I've bred, trained, and hunted over Field Champions and Amateur Field Champions, National Derby Champions and National Open Champions, dogs whose titles denote worthiness and trust above and beyond the status of winner. In short, I care deeply for these dogs, enjoy their companionship, and admire their capabilities.

These sentiments are, I believe, shared by many people who own or would like to own retrievers, whether as a pet, hunting dog, or competitor. Much of the information and advice in this book, therefore, pertains equally to the man who spends his Saturday in a duck blind, the woman who regularly loads her Lab into the back of a van for field trials, and the family who want nothing more from their dog than devotion, good behavior, and an ability to retrieve a thrown stick.

Chapter 1 affords a glimpse of my own early hunting experiences. Chapter 2 discusses the history and lore of hunting and field trials, their British origins and American practice. In chapter 3 is advice about selecting a dog that is appropriate to your needs, whom to consult in buying and what to look for and/or avoid. Chapter 4 defines the terms used in training and outlines various methods and tools that may be used. (Here I have brought under consideration certain training devices that I do not wholeheartedly endorse, although they are employed by other responsible and reputable trainers, and which many owners would like to understand better. If one wishes to use certain means of force, I hope my discussions of them will make it possible to do so humanely.)

Chapter 5 addresses basic Derby training, lessons fundamental to the education of any dog. The essential next steps, force-fetch training and teaching your dog to be steady, are discussed in chapter 6. Chapter 7 continues the Derby training, bringing your dog to the level where he may enter the Derby Stake in field trials or accompany you in the field. Between these two phases of Derby training is the concise section on force-fetch, a stage of training which not everyone will endorse, but which is vital for any serious working retriever.

Chapters 8, 9, and 10—each concerned with more complex tasks than its predecessor—outline exercises and drills for bringing a dog to increasingly higher levels of achievement. The reader who would train his animal to obey only basic commands (and stay out of the laps of guests) may not perceive the need to educate his dog to such a fine degree—but I hope that many such dog owners will employ these exercises if for no other reason than that they show the remarkable skills their pets can develop, and at the same time give these pets the pleasure of achieving what they are bred to accomplish.

Chapter 11 provides information about the health and care of a retriever, and chapter 12 discusses the procedures of buying, selling, and breeding.

Finally, in chapter 13, I have written about issues that pertain not only to anyone who owns a water dog but to anyone concerned about the welfare of retrievers, their roles in our culture, and the way our society regards—and might regard—them and their reasons for being. I do this because I love these dogs deeply, and because I hope I can persuade others who share my feelings to think a bit harder and longer about the responsibilities that these wonderful animals entail.

—TOM QUINN

Northern California
September 1982

The
Working Retrievers

1

First Exposure

ALERT DRAKE SPRIG AND KILDEER

Walking the dark miles home down the shoulder of the two-lane highway, our breath shows in the cold yellow headlights of the oncoming commuter traffic. We take turns lugging the heavy string of ducks. A sinister black-and-white California Highway Patrol Olds disengages itself from the stream, makes a U-turn, and comes snuffling and crunching up behind us.

"Evening, boys."

"Hi."

"Where you headed?"

"Home."

"That gun you got there loaded?"

"No." We show him the slide is open—even shake it nervously as further proof.

"Who's it belong to?"

"It's ours."

"Hop in the back, I'll run you home."

We pile in, trying to be cool about the muzzle of the shotgun. The air is stale and hot inside the car, and the rear door handles are missing. The meaty patrolman induces some wheelspin for our benefit. We roll, unsure whether we're going home fast or to headquarters. Either way, we've been captured.

"Nice bunch of Pintails you got there. Where'd you get 'em?"

"The Flats."

"Yeah? Where are they?"

"Oh, out on the edge of the bay. South of the third P.G. & E. tower."

"Yeah?"

"Yeah. We never get skunked there. We call it 'The Channel of Plenty.' "

The car is flying—passing knots of traffic at will. Dan and I grin at each other in the darkness of the back seat. Why should we tell *him* where we'd gotten the birds? Why get the real Channel of Plenty raided and wrecked by a horde of hungry cops?

"This where you live?"

"Yep." Our birds and muddy gear are dumped on the lawn.

"*Adios,* boys. You guys take it easy." Again he floored it, streaking the lane with rubber.

Those black-and-white rides occurred frequently during winter. We fancied the cops liked us because we were free and wild and enterprising, but most often they stopped when we were laden with game.

I was fourteen and my brother Dan was twelve. We had a good Model 12 Winchester between us. We tried to make the ducks fall on solid land; if one of us nailed a duck and it dropped into the chop of San Pablo Bay, he forfeited the gun, stripped, and swam for it.

Our swims were exhilarating at first, and a source of amphibious pride; but raw exposure finally drained us as the bleak day waned. Hauling clothes on and off for every bird became such a chore that we sometimes skipped dressing and simply camouflaged ourselves under lumps of wet coats and rusty-rose pickle-weed. With each successful shot, the shooter then slithered, shivering, into the deep blue mud and gray water, and struck out toward the bird and mile-long rafts of resting Canvasbacks that rode the cold bay swells. If new birds whipped into range, the gunner ashore might hammer down another as the gatherer swam. Retrieving our ducks this way seemed noble work; we felt hardy and useful. We had no teachers.

Once home, we carefully drew and plucked our birds and tried to guess their identities from steel engravings in an ancient dictionary. After stripping them of their fabulous plumage (and saving samples for a feather collection), I often examined the viscera and major organs, comparing heart sizes, fat content, and the food in their crops. As the last of the birds' down was singed away over the stove, thereby laying a stinking pall on the household, a platoon of nude bodies gathered in final formation on the drainboard. Dan and I continued to pat and heft them, admiring them in death as they awaited apple, onion, celery chunks, and then roasting. We wondered how these birds talked and how they knew danger; how they could fly and navigate in dark; how their small eyes could be so much better than ours. Visions of the storms and great distances they had flown through touched us as we debated which were the strongest and fastest by their shapes, and finally, which ones were our favorites.

Sunday mornings we hit church pretty damned early in order to get to the Channel of Plenty at a decent shooting time. With the Winchester in two pieces and wrapped in a coat, we trundled into a back pew and waited. Weather or the black hour discouraged most of the faithful, but occasionally a Dunlin-like string of nuns fluttered in—none of whom cared to kneel near us. We were grateful. Before the Last Blessing we were out on the frozen road, scurrying toward dawn and the Channel.

As we neared the Flats one morning, other shotguns were already barking at the lifting lid of heaven. I reckoned these were in the elaborate floating blinds anchored deep offshore. The incoming tide was planning to make itself very high very soon as we sloshed and leaned our way into a cutting northwind and neared our spot on the great serpentine channel. We were almost there.

"Sons of bitches!"

Somehow some hunters had set up a pair of huge wine barrels on stilts and scattered their decoys all over *our* goddamned channel. Quacking and calling to the ducks aloft, they stood up in their barrels and shot *our* ducks. The strangers used a small over-and-under and a heavy humpback Browning Auto that spat out used shells like a bum emptying his nose in the street. Their shooting was incredible; sometimes they seemed to have three birds tumbling in the air at once. They matter-of-factly sluiced their cripples and lowered into their wine barrels to wait for more.

We crawled closer and watched the spectacle unfold across the channel from inside a large tide-perched plywood packing case . . . and waited too.

During a lull, a most astonishing thing occurred: one of the hunters yelled something and a thin red Irish setter traipsed out from under the barrels and casually began collecting ducks. The dog dragged each bird to the blinds and went to fetch another; first, those on land, then reluctantly, *the ones in the water!*

The hunters, dressed in real camouflage outfits and honest-to-God hip boots, climbed out of their barrels laughing and drinking from a thermos. As the dog pulled more ducks to them, they nonchalantly hung the birds like laundry on straps rigged between the blinds. Eventually, as the tide began its turn, the hunters withdrew, altogether pleased with themselves, their purloined ducks, and their dog—and suddenly it occurred to us: those slick invaders were completely *dry!*

The channel was changed forever. I was changed. Within an hour, I managed to down two elegant little Buffleheads; it was a fine double shot, but somehow I was embarrassed that they weren't Greenheads. I went into the water after my birds, swimming to *their* side of the channel through *their* floating shell casings, almost to *their* footprints. When I got back, Dan and I whispered together rather than talked. Maybe those heavy hitters would return and find us, pathetically naked, trying to retrieve. We cussed them every way we knew—but we had to admit we *liked* their dog.

OUR OWN DOG

A honey-blond named Joanne was the most memorable of all the high school cheerleaders—for more reasons than one. Her Labrador had a litter of puppies, stashed under her mom's front porch. She gave me the last black female.

At three months our pup pulled crippled coots and ducks out of the bay, stuffed her head under for divers, and shifted her tiny grip and hung on when they flapped and pecked her. She was delighted and eager despite the report of a 12-gauge. Regrettably she was spayed at six months—to save her from rape by my father's Irish terrier; I never picked up her registration papers.

Our bitch swam with skill and gallantry, even as a nipper. One day I repeatedly threw a tennis ball into high storm surf for her; after a dozen exhausting retrieves she refused to enter *any* more water. The following summer we managed to revive her fondness for water by launching ourselves in inner tubes to the center of a small, warm pond. There we languished like muskrats, eating and brandishing lunch; teasing, calling, tempting her in. She became one of the wettest retrievers I've known—easily navigating the forbidding wakes of oceanbound tankers, and disappearing under the surface in brave pursuit of diving cripples.

She could be disciplined by voice, mockery, and twists of her sensitive ears. Sometimes she was spanked with a green switch; she'd calmly accept three blows, then retaliate. She understood visual hand signals and sometimes pointed game. She could never be cured of running occasional jackrabbits, because we could never be cured of occasionally shooting them.

Difficult bird work became her specialty. Eventually, she taught her bosses some field manners, and gained a towering reputation among other hunters—leading many of them to acquire Labradors of their own. Old-timers asked us to hunt with them, deliberately leaving their own dogs behind and reminding us to "bring that black bitch of yours along." She was rarely deceived into staying home from a hunt—especially if she whiffed the smell of Hoppe's No. 9 in a shotgun.

At fourteen years, she was arthritic, tumored, deaf, and blind but could outhunt most younger retrievers if we set her into a proper breeze. Rewarding herself, she ate one bird for every one delivered to hand.

She died in a sunny chair in a cow barn after blindly working quail one morning. She was sixteen. We buried her on a hillside, carpeted blue with lupin, in the finest quail country we knew.

QUAIL RITES

Rounding the shoulder of the slope I caught the clear questioning call of the sentry—"Chicago birds" the old Italians called them, for the three sweet gurgling notes of the valley quail. It was always a cock bird, the jaunty protector of twenty or thirty of his brethren who fed below, while he scanned the world, like a fleet admiral on his bridge.

"Wait," Dan whispered. "They're right up ahead, but I want to show you something new."

An intense "pit-pitipitpitpit" guided us. There was no wind, but the chatter telegraphed out from a tangled whorl of blackberry vines atop a chalky ravine wall. The sentry was suddenly quiet, and we could see him melt down through the branches to his flock. They sat tight.

"Here, you take the gun and watch this," Dan said. He waved the small Lab toward the hanging fortress of thorns and called "Get in there." The bitch dropped into a gap on a fair heading for the covey. Then Dan stopped her briefly by whistling through his teeth, and pointing inaccurately at other cover adjacent to the birds.

"What's so great about that?" I demanded. "You've got the wrong patch!" After all, we had both practiced pointing out promising cover to her, and she appreciated the rewards.

Dan ignored me. "Now get ready to shoot," he ordered, "but look at me first."

He whistled again. The dog was sitting thirty yards opposite us and about ten away from the covey. I expected Dan to flick out a horizontal left arm, indicating the target to her. He didn't. Instead, he slowly raised his right hand in a fist until it was almost in front of his heart. Then from the fist came an extended, waggling index finger that tentatively pointed to the covey.

Into the berries the dog slammed, and down the draw boiled the birds. I managed to concentrate enough in the scattering rush of wings to down two with three pops. When it was over and the last bird had hummed down the gully to safety, we entertained each other with more obscure little clues and gestures, directing the bitch toward the fallen game. *Finger signals!* Unknown to me, Dan had discovered and refined a new and subtle art; one our dog understood and seemed to have completely mastered.

In half an hour we hit another covey on the ridge and dropped several birds. The new art of finger signals was employed to pick them up. With quail stuffed into every pocket of our Levi's jackets, we rejoiced by collapsing on our backs in the high, wild oat hay, and complimenting the black dog, who recognized our rough praise with small quick tail slaps. Across the still meadow a Great Blue Heron was methodically stabbing gophers. Above us, two Red-tailed Hawks cut compass arcs in the cobalt air. We decided we were all hunters.

After a long spell of serious sky study, I glimpsed three tiny delta shapes, dropping fast.

"Did you see those?"

"Yep. Ducks."

"Going in over the hill."

"What's over there for them?"

"I dunno. Only the prison."

The only thing over there was San Quentin Prison. Even from here, we could feel the malignancy of the place.

On a foggy afternoon the previous year, we had trudged up to where we now lay admiring the hawks. Hurrying against the fading light, we chewed up the miles with a quick, rhythmic gait. The dog was along, but we ignored the likely cover and trotted on toward the deep, open pits of a shale quarry. My arm cradled a short, solid 30-30 lever-action Winchester, and my brother carried a Purple Royal Triton motor oil carton and a black crayon to make a target. We wanted the little deer gun finely sighted in by dusk. Thirteen burnished bottle-neck bullets clinked sweetly in my chest pocket.

"Hold it right there!"

We slowed and almost stopped, looking up the sidehill. Standing in the waist-deep buckbrush, a wiry middle-aged figure clad entirely in khaki work clothes hollered again:

"I said *you, hold it!*"

I felt a numbing scalp squeeze, and discomfiture that in our haste we hadn't scouted anything ahead. This s.o.b. had probably escaped from the prison, spotted our carbine, and figured to have it. I couldn't see a weapon on him, but our gun was empty, so it might amount to a standoff; then again, maybe we could slice off and vanish into the scrub oaks below—outrunning winos from a nearby hobo jungle was one of our outdoor joys.

"Where you headed with that rifle?"

Oh, shit! "Up to the quarry to sight it in. Deer season opens Saturday."

Slowly he shook his head, doubting us, then gestured with one arm and the whole texture of the hillside seemed to shift and raise. We were locked in a circle of thirty men with scoped rifles, shotguns, and Thompsons. Some stared down their sights at us; others just looked and smoked. Some were in guard uniforms; others wore suits and ties under hunting garb.

"We lost two blond guys from the prison this afternoon. They'll be dressed in blue dungarees, same as you."

We were blond, didn't consider our Levi's the same as dungarees, but weren't about to argue it.

"I suggest you forget today and take yourselves and that rifle the hell out of here."

The light was weakening and so were we. The afternoon was shot. Wilting down into the descent, I looked back after a couple of hundred yards. They stood there still, speckling the slope, watching us. I realized it was only the black Labrador that made us different from the hunted.

Dan interrupted this reverie of the year before. "You want to gut these quail? We could eat a couple for lunch."

"I'd rather go on up to the top of that hill and see if we can spot those ducks from there."

"That's the Prison Land," he guffawed, remembering our scrape with the posse.

"What the hell do we care? We're just hunters. We're also under eighteen—what can they do? Those redtails hunt in there, don't they? Damn right they do!"

We lifted the bitch over the shoulder-high hog wire and barbed strands of the outer prison fence, then poked the Model 12 through and climbed over. The ground felt different. A huge stand of eucalyptus trees draped the spine of the tawny ridge ahead and below us. No water and no ducks yet.

"We could sit down under those eukes and wait for Band-tails," Dan suggested.

Now that we had the dog, it was not uncommon to be carrying ducks, quail, snipe, Band-tailed Pigeons, doves, and possibly a rail by the end of a good movable hunt.

We entered the towering grove. What had seemed to be a typical high windbreak revealed itself instead as a long rectangle of trees enclosing an area larger than a football field, as still and dark as the nave of a Gothic cathedral. My eyes adjusted to the gloom and focused on the damp floor between the soaring walls of sickle-shaped leaves. The ground was stabbed with rows of flat wooden shakes, thousands of them, like bedding plants in a giant nursery. They were hand-split redwood shakes, and each was deeply branded with numbers. We were in the burial place of San Quentin's unclaimed dead. I watched for the dog's hackles to rise along with my dread, but she just sniffed about in normal reconnaisance. In collapsed adobe banks, washed-out graves appeared, revealing loose and delicate bones. Downhill we drifted, through fallen strips of bark and pods, keeping our voices soft. The oldest markers had very low numbers; others were fresh. There were no names. The grove was ancient, and haunted. We found no bird sign. No ducks yet.

Where the guardian circle of trees gave out, a dirt road dropped steeply away. Below could be seen the hulking walls of San Quentin. It squatted, old and huge, half in the bay and half in the hills, its high walls washed in sickly yellow. Through the shimmering light we could see fishermen in tiny boats, drifting close in and trolling for stripers. An electric warning rasped from the manned parapets: "You in the aluminum boat . . . come no farther!" The fisherman meekly waved and putt-putted into retreat.

On the land, miniature men and cows moved slowly in and out of long tin milking sheds. They were convicts and Holsteins. The rolling pastures were spiked with lighthouselike machine-gun towers, each painted with a numeral. Nearer still, between us and a large white hay barn, was their water supply, a medium-size earth-dammed stock pond. Rainwater fed into it from a high brush-filled cleavage that connected threadlike to the burial place. On the pond's surface we counted nine ducks.

"Well, we've come this far, what the hell," Dan said.

Calling "Heel!" to the dog, we sprinted downhill and spilled into the drainage cut. We dove and rolled, sweating, gasping, dry in the mouth, then rested in the last poison oak clump before a final crawl across open territory to the base of the dam.

As we lay there, a fine clean whistling came from above. Six mature Pintails were pumping heavenward from the prison pond.

"I don't believe it!" I moaned. "Our stalk was perfect!"

We were so close to San Quentin now, we could hear radios in the cells. Chuck Berry's "Maybelline" spanked cement walls. Feedback hissed and screamed through the public address loudspeakers. We knew Caryl Chessman was up there waiting, somewhere on Death Row.

"There should be three left in there," Dan reasoned. Flat on our bellies, heads down, we elbowed slowly out into the open. I could see ripples.

"Heel, heel!" I squeaked. The bitch was crawling between us. Once under the brow of the dam we tried to predict their range and where they'd jump. I chambered a 7½, to be followed by a 6 and a number 4 in the magazine.

"Hold the dog," I commanded, and scrambled to the top of the dam. Three wary birds, necks extended, were centered in a slash of molten gold. Backlit silhouettes sprang off the surface while I squinted into the blinding glow. I smashed out three of the loudest shotgun blasts in history; they rang through the metal barns and echoed off the brick and concrete galleries. One duck fell backward into the pond and two sizzled away into the glare. The dog hit the water, steaming for the cripple. Flattened on the dam, I watched her trying to round up the poorly hit bird. Silence hung on the disbelieving prison walls; though later, Dan insisted he'd heard sirens.

"Come here, come *here,* damnit!" I tried to whisper the dog out. No deal. I heard a truck motor cough, then voices.

"Screw this stuff!" I picked up my empties, as if we could be traced by them.

"Come out of there!" We were whooping at the bitch now as we bolted for the safety of the drainage ditch. Halfway up the ridge we halted to watch and listen for her. In minutes she appeared with the duck in her mouth, having tracked us to our hiding place.

"A Widgeon!" The bird was examined with disgust. "Eight sprig and one Widgeon, and we have to get the goddamned stinking, *grass-eating* Widgeon!"

We slapped the dog's wet ribs in happy relief at having her back; then scuttled toward the cover of the solemn eucalyptus grove. Once there, we heard more yells and held like quail down between the graves, and didn't move anymore. Finally, when it became blue-dark, we got up, tripping over the markers, and retraced our steps to the fence. The moon slowly rose too, and approved as we marched our dog, quail, and duck homeward.

We eventually managed a few more good dry shoots near the wine barrel blinds on the Channel of Plenty. Sadly, though, all hunters were to be expelled from the paradise of the marsh; we were chased, hazed, warned, and finally ushered out by deputy sheriffs who told us they had "noise complaints" from the residents of encroaching subdivisions. Our shotgun was silenced. Soon the marsh itself was annexed and rezoned. Birds, migratory and local, were the next to go, banished in exchange for manicured lawns and barbecue pits. The rich alluvial plain, where ducks sheltered and rail crept, is now an enormous "rustic" shopping mall, boasting stores stocked with tapes of bird calls, songs of the humpback whale, and decorative prints by J. J. Audubon. All that remains of the hunt are antique shops where young matrons buy old decoys for their husbands' dens.

One afternoon, years later, I found myself locked in a New York skyscraper, gazing out a nineteenth-floor window at the filth of the East River. I was trying to construct a cover painting for *Field & Stream* and remembered the lovely brown corduroy of the pickleweed flats and the slanting autumn light filled with fast birds. My wife was pregnant and nearing her time. If the child was a boy I would wish him many things—especially the wide, wild spaces and a dog, like my Lab of yesterday.

2

Other Days

VALLEY QUAIL PAIR

As I labored at my drawing board one July morning, a gentle bluebird day, I could make out spaced, muffled gunfire rolling evenly down the fingers of nearby Drake's Bay. The cadence of shots and the season seemed wrong for poachers. I phoned a ranger friend at park headquarters and asked him to check on the source. He reported that the gunning came from "some kind of dog trial."

I struggled to work as the *whump* of distant shotguns drifted into my studio, but curiosity finally halted my progress. I grabbed my field glasses, wife, young son, and Hobbit—a borrowed black Labrador bitch. We hiked the buckskin-colored hills in the direction of the sound. Three miles later, just as we drew close, the shooting abruptly ceased. Dust plumes from far-off vehicles were visible as I crested the final hill, my weary son on my shoulders. As I stood there catching my breath, I witnessed a strange and amazing scene. Across a deep, water-filled draw was a large assemblage of cars and trucks and curiously quiet people. At the perimeter, a small figure in white was blowing a shrill whistle and signaling with outstretched arms to a huge Labrador shouldering through the low brush close to where we stood. The dog spun in a spray of pebbles and sat down squarely, his eyes fixed on the white-clad figure two hundred yards away across the draw. The man gestured, the dog reached down, snatched up a dead pheasant from a bush, and bore it proudly away.

From somewhere in the crowd a bullhorn boomed. "You on the hill! You'll have to leave or come down here to the gallery!" I knew I wanted to see more. Slowly and self-consciously we began to descend toward the crowd. About halfway down, a leprechaun of a man, looking absurd in an Abercrombie & Fitch costume, rudely accosted us.

"Hurry, for crissakes! And tie up your dog. Oh, hell, it *would* be a bitch!"

"She's trained to stay with me," I answered.

"I *said,* you will have to restrain that bitch somehow. Sit down over there and be absolutely quiet," he directed. From out of his shooting jacket he fished a length of used boot-lace. With clenched jaws I tied this around poor Hobbit's neck, and prepared to watch my first field trial.

The people sitting in the wind-whipped grass seemed utterly incongruous on these remote summer hills and with such magnificent animals. Who were they, some in safari garb, some in flapping English tweeds, and others perched on shooting sticks? What were they doing on a California cattle ranch overlooking the Pacific?

I watched as thirty or forty handlers took turns steering their dogs across the flooded canyon and up the opposite hillside, using whistle blasts and arm signals to guide them. Sometimes their efforts prompted applause, but even the ones who didn't merit a hand looked splendid to me. The spectators kept consulting copies of a slender booklet. I mildly inquired of a woman nearby where I might get a copy of my own. She looked me up and down, regarded my tethered animal, and sniffed, "I'm afraid we don't have enough for everyone."

What did I expect? They made me tie up my dog on a shoelace—why should they let me see their book?

We watched transfixed until the last amazingly skillful dog was run. The dog people loaded up their trucks, motor homes, and station wagons and slowly moved off through the dusky fog toward the main ranch roads. There were many out-of-state license plates—some from as far as New York.

Finally left to ourselves, we released Hobbit and loped around the deserted site, picking up crumpled programs from the ground, which revealed the names of these remarkable dogs, their lineage, and where they lived. I brought a copy home, pinned it to my studio wall, and studied it carefully.

The people gathered on that hillside, I kept thinking, were apparently very interested in the same things that were so precious to my youth: dogs, dogs that rejoiced in gunfire, wing shooting, and falling game; dogs that swam as cheerfully as otters to haul in ducks and pheasants; disciplined dogs that delighted in their bird work and handlers' signals; dogs that proved themselves by vying with each other in huntlike showdowns.

To raise funds, I sold my fine L.C. Smith double with its tight English barrels, bought a bitch puppy from field-trial stock, and a plastic bumper to throw for her. I replaced my nimble Porsche Speedster with a clumsy 4 x 4 Ford pickup to carry us. Two years later, my young Nakai Anny—her name means Dark Anny in Navaho—was a Field Champion and we were competing in the Nationals.

Several years went by before I understood or even cared about the connection between tweedy apparel, shooting sticks, and the dogs I love. I gradually discovered that a long and eventful history underlies the sport of retriever contests—history that helps explain why vestiges of British customs still tinge our competitions and hunting behavior today.

The first record of a British field trial appears in 1899 at Little Green, near Havant on the south coast of England. English trialing has remained remarkably unchanged since the turn of the century. That first field trial took place eighteen years before the first Labrador was registered with the American Kennel Club, and thirty-two years before the first U.S. trial was held on Long Island in 1931.

The traditional British retriever trials closely reflect that country's own approach to hunting. In fact, these trials are hunts. A day's shooting can generally take one of two forms. In the first, the invited gunners, with their servants and dogs, occupy concealed stations called *butts* and shoot birds that are driven over them by beaters. This is classic pass shooting. The downed birds—from twenty to sometimes as many as one hundred grouse and pheasant—are eventually retrieved by patient dogs, who aren't allowed to leave the butts until the drive is over; they finally locate the birds by scent alone.

The second method is the *walk up,* a moving skirmish line of gunners and aides (including dog handlers) that formally extends itself across each promising field, with the retrieving dogs walking at heel. Flushing dogs, cockers and springers, are occasionally used in combination with beaters (workers who ha-

Gallery and contestants at the fifth field meeting of the Labrador Club on R. Stuyvesant Pierrepont's estate at Bedminster, Pennsylvania. (Edwin Levick Photo; courtesy the Labrador Retriever Club)

Gunners and handlers prepare for an early field trial. (Edwin Levick Photo; courtesy the Labrador Retriever Club)

rass the game into movement). Game is anything with feathers or fur—from pheasant and grouse to hare. As the walking gunners drop game, it is retrieved at the command of the dog handlers and bagged. The dogs are judged on their handling ability, steadiness, endurance, and on their chief asset: their nose.

It must be added that hunting and hunting dog competitions in England are largely confined to the landed gentry due to a lack of space, physically and socially, on their small island. Her Majesty Queen Elizabeth keeps a stout line of trial Labradors. In America, too, open land or access to it is essential.

English gamekeepers are similar to our professional dog trainers but are retained exclusively by a single patron to propagate game and to keep, teach, and develop his dogs for his hunting and sometimes for trialing. These trainers teach most of their employers' retrievers in the course of several days' wild-bird shoot. Unlike our American dogs, the British animals are trained to recognize blood scent rather than body scent. A young prospect is sometimes taken into a huge, two-acre game pen, roofed and fenced in. The enclosure is alive with an assortment of grouse, pheasant, hare, and other game. A single, pinioned pigeon is scratched or cut along the shaft of one leg to produce a drop of blood, then released into the ground cover and the throng of scurrying, flushing occupants. The pup is urged and disciplined to ignore the able-bodied game and follow with his sensitive nose only the wounded bird's blood scent.

An English field champion might look like a preoccupied fool in our trials today; likewise most American field champions would appear as incompetent renegades in the heather of Scotland—simply because trial practices and customs in the two countries have differed so much over the years. The rootstocks of the dogs are the same (with the exception of the Chesapeake Bay Retriever), and were brought across the Atlantic by a cluster of eastern outdoor aristocrats in the 1920s, men who had savored shooting over retrieving dogs on grouse hunts in Britain. These retrievers were imported not only for their skill and beauty but to compete in the infant stages of American trials. The kennel prefixes of early American breeders ring with the enchantment of the empire they modeled their own after: Glenmere, Earlsmoor, Arden, Meadow Farm, Blake, Kilsyth. "British-bred, American-whelped" was the practice of the period here.

The list of American trialing people who fancied and supported these dogs reads like a "who's who" of eastern power and wealth: Franklin Lord, Gerald Livingston, Jay Carlisle, W. Averell Harriman, Mrs. H. S. du Pont, Daniel Pomeroy, Marshall Field. They imported not only the dogs and the manners of the sport but also at least one English judge, to assist each field trial in recog-

A dapper Marshall Field stands with Odds On at the fourth field-trial meeting at Meadow Farm, East Islip, Long Island. (Edwin Levick Photo; courtesy the Labrador Retriever Club)

Field-trial judges (from left) Charles B. Lanier, Charles L. Lawrence, and Harold B. Johnson. (Edwin Levick Photo; courtesy the Labrador Retriever Club)

nizing the "real" retrievers in America. More important, they brought over a platoon of gamekeepers from Scotland to care for and train their dogs. Dave Elliot was one; he trained sheep dogs as a boy in Scotland, then retrievers for J. F. Carlisle at Wingan Kennels. It was Elliot who first succeeded in teaching a string of Labradors to accept hand and whistle signals in picking up difficult fallen birds. So stirring was this feat that rival owners wondered why their trainers couldn't cultivate the same skill in their own dogs.

Elliot's work was pivotal, leading to the demanding, sophisticated blind retrieves that are mastered by American retrievers today. A blind retrieve is a hidden bird whose location is known only to the handler; it is discovered and retrieved by his dog through a system of hand signals. Yet fifty years after his first displays of handling virtuosity, Dave Elliot said he felt a sadness for those modern champions undergoing the immense pressures of advanced training.

There is concern in some camps today that we are eroding some of our dogs' natural retrieving virtues by demanding too many extraordinary training frills. Others believe we have just scratched the surface of dog potential and performance. In the earliest days, the real pressure training was in the single area of "staunchness," that is, sitting and staying quietly while birds were shot. The crime of "running in" or "breaking" before being sent was a genuine hazard. As in the English practice, dogs sat in an obedient line with many other competing dogs and watched several birds fall. They were sent to retrieve *only* when the judge gave permission by calling out that dog's drawn number. If the preceding dog failed to find the birds, another dog along the line could be given the opportunity to "wipe his eye" by successfully retrieving the same birds and thereby distinguishing himself. The emphasis was clearly on the ability to mark fallen game as a natural and unassisted gift, rather than to execute blind retrieves. These marks may have been fundamentally more difficult than many we see today. No attempt was made for consistency in these falls, and if a bird fell in a high stand of cover such as woods, and the working dog buried himself—rooting invisibly for five or ten minutes—it was considered an honorable and praiseworthy effort.

For a long period, land blinds required little more than a general directional line of no great distance, no diagonals, and no obstacles. And water blinds were often just a cast into the drink and another cast downstream, sometimes to a picket with a dead bird attached. This was cursory stuff, quickly dispensed with before getting back to the serious business of shooting birds and seeing whose dog could mark and whose couldn't. Water marks were shot over live decoys, since hunters of this period still employed "live" setups.

Americans once held to another British tradition: a strong appreciation of the field-proven bitch. The English have always placed greater value on the credentials of the bitch than those of the male when breeding their future working dogs. We did too, for a while, but as American values evolved we forgot this principle and focused our expectations solely on the large, athletic male retriever. In the tradition of a pro football camp, bigger, wilder, faster, and tougher males became the aim of the breeders. Owners sought the excitement of association with huge, rippling, powerful dogs. When breedings were made or discussed, it was always the dominant male that was assayed. Little room was left for the "papered" ladies, who mostly stayed home and stayed pregnant. Unfortunately, stampede breeding to this or that sire has limited the directions and dimensions of our present bloodlines.

The culmination of this "invincible dreadnought" trend probably came with the 1955 National Field Champion, Cork of Oakwood Lane, an enormous charger of a dog, well above 110 pounds. Patrons and galleries of fans felt thrilled and itchy-palmed at the sight of him, and of similar memorable males like the 1956 National Field Champion Massie's Sassy Boots. But very few people knew how to train such creatures when they finally had one. In following generations, huge, rambunctious dogs were competitively thrashed by a smaller, more intelligent, and cooperative kind of male, and even more recently, by bitches. In a renaissance parallel to the Women's Lib movement, females have become very assertive. Wild Hearted Dinah, Dairy Hill's Michikiniquia, Kannonball Kate, Nakai Anny, Michelle, Ornbaun's Diamond Lil, Risky Business Ruby, Euroclydon, and Wanapum Darts Dandy are some of the contemporary Field Champion bitches that have made shambles of the males-only theories. As a group they are probably faster and more efficient than males; recent studies indicate that the bitches in wolf packs may be superior to males in hunting pursuit and finesse.

The evolution of the relationship between patron and professional dog trainer is noteworthy, too. As in Britain, trainers in service to the early American kennels were thoroughly aware of their occupational stations and limitations. They traveled, ate, and drank separately from their employers, who in turn rarely worked directly with the dogs. Patrons and their friends were addressed as "Mister" and "Sir" at all times. Any social mixing at dinner parties, receptions, and balls that accompanied early trialing was out of the question. This tradition eroded in the late 1950s, once the less formal western dogmen began traveling east with their own retained professionals (and some sensa-

1950 Canadian National Field Champion
FC Rip of Holly Hill with handler Roy
Gonia. (Courtesy Roy and Wanda Gonia)

Professional trainer Rex Carr and his dog
string at home in Escalon, California.
(Photo by Harold Mack, Jr.)

tional retrievers), and insisted that "their man" be allowed to drink and eat with the other guests, or their dogs would be withdrawn.

In 1939, a variant of the traditional procedure appeared in the form of a gentleman named Paul Bakewell III and his Deercreek Kennel in the Midwest. He insisted on personally running his own Goldens and Labs against the best professionals of the day, and became the first amateur to win an Open stake and the first to win the National Open Championship. His dogs, Rip, Shed of Arden, Marvadel Black Gum, and Little Pierre of Deercreek, are legendary.

In 1957 amateurs in field trials finally won formal recognition, although they had always paid the bills, with the first National Amateur Championship, open only to amateur handlers. Many pros still refer to it as the "Little National."

During World War II, some of the finest young retriever trainers in this country were pooled in San Carlos, California, to work with U.S. Army war dogs. They became some of the most influential professionals in the sport: Cotton Pershall, Roy Gonia, Charlie Morgan, Billy Wunderlich, and Dave Elliot.

Today's outstanding professional is now engaged by several amateur clients, who often compete for his attention, skill, and remedial advice for their dogs. These keen amateurs have no social problems in associating with the trainer; each is motivated by a common desire to succeed at this subtle, fragile, difficult, and deceptive sport—a desire that increasingly obliterates class barriers.

Perhaps the most significant change in trialing tradition came in the 1960s. The pleasant, unblemished realm of merchant princes, captains of industry, Wall Street bankers, and several old-line aristocrats was infiltrated by a new element: professional people. Wealthy physicians and attorneys, followed by tooth and oil drillers, lumber barons, and cattlemen, became afflicted with trial fever. Some were old hunters who would have given up the fields long before but for the singular pleasure of watching good dog work. To a few newcomers, these dogs represented an upward rung on the ladder of social mobility, but to most it was simply a chance not only to own these fabulous animals but to shoot over them, scratch them behind the ears, pet them, and encourage them into action.

This group was followed in the seventies by fascinated hordes of like-minded tradesmen, housewives, firemen, bartenders, veterinarians, even a few artists—people who neither wanted nor could afford professional help. They availed themselves of the same great heritage of bloodlines (and even concocted new ones of their own) and banded together in small groups to train their dogs to hunt and trial well. The West Coast, with its forgiving weather and ready supply of fanatics, soon became the seething hotbed of the smitten.

Ironically, several old-guard easterners whose peers originally imported great dogs to this country from Britain now purchase splendid stock from right here at home. And I like to think that somewhere in Idaho a grocery boy may have his hands on a retriever that could send quakes of envy through the likes of a shooting earl.

3

Finding a Good One

MUGS

Carefully and candidly, the first question you should ask before saddling yourself with any kind of pup or dog is "What do I want it for?"

What do you expect of a retriever in particular—and of yourself, once you acquire one?

Do you understand your responsibilities to a good pup, and to your neighbors, through obedience training? Will the dog simply be a companion for you or your kids, or one that can be well hunted for two or three months a year? Do you need a gorgeous specimen for bench showing, or to decorate your fireside, or are you looking for a dog that can be competitive in field, obedience, or tracking contests?

Perhaps you're unprepared to undertake a large sporting dog; without a sound reason, these dogs can be a burden. Maybe you really need a sparkling little rat terrier, or a parrot.

These questions and aims should be thoroughly resolved before you approach buying a dog. Once you are sure you need a retriever pup, carefully consider which breed is best for you, which sex, and what kind of breeder you should approach.

It is no genetic accident that retrievers are friendly and attractive. They have been specifically bred to work closely with man—in small boats, tight duck blinds, and teamwork hunting situations.

Within the general category *retriever* are several distinct breeds. You should know the major strengths and weaknesses of each.

THE CHESAPEAKE BAY RETRIEVER

Much of the respect for these dogs was established during the market-hunter period of waterfowling. Stamina and rough-water hardiness were functional values in bay gunning, and these brown dogs could retrieve hundreds of ducks daily without so much as a head pat. Legends have sprung from accounts of Chesapeakes swimming for hours in cold currents, hauling bird after bird to the punt or sinkbox, simply tossing the bird over the gunnels and swimming out for another retrieve.

The Chesapeake Bay Retriever was also a dominant figure in early field trials. Sadly, this is not the case today. One theory holds that when the American Kennel Club decided to recognize these eastern American water dogs as a distinct breed, they called for owners to help establish a standard by registering their own dogs and supplying data on their physical characteristics. Formal registration was the goal, but some old-timers insist the best of the breed were never inventoried because their owners were too busy making a living market hunting with their dogs to bother, or because outstanding dogs already glowed with such local renown that registering them seemed frivolous and unnecessary.

Chessies are often considered independent, perhaps because their ancestors were chosen for performance and results that were not based on praise, and also because they prefer to work and identify with one man or one family. These rugged dogs often make good protective watchdogs, probably because of their heritage of guarding the dinghies, ducks, decoys, guns, and gear of their masters. Their coarse coats are thick, and vary in color from rich roan and teak to taupe or the color of dead grass. Their coats carry a heavy waterproofing oil that is forgivingly described as a musky "perfume."

THE LABRADOR RETRIEVER

Labs have long been considered the "retriever's retriever." Descriptions penned by naturalists and sportsmen of a small, short-coated Newfoundland dog filtered into England during the early nineteenth century—these invariably noted that the dogs showed "sagacity" and "bravery," and "were easily managed." The writers had watched these black dogs work for fowlers on New World upland birds, as well as on ducks, geese, and swans, and with cod fishermen, merchant sailors, and salvage workers in the howling North Atlantic. The dogs assisted seamen and fishermen by retrieving lines, nets, and floats.

Whether the Lab sprang from a Newfoundland-setter cross or a St. John's breed-spaniel union, or if it was imported to British soil by fishermen or simply jumped ship, makes little but romantic difference. More important was the fact that sporting English gentlemen immediately recognized the dog's qualities and ushered in a century of admiration for the breed. Resources and time were lavished on the Labrador as breeders worked to refine its great talents through discreet experiments with Setter and Flat-Coated and Curly-Coated Retriever blood.

The Lab's overwhelming field-trial records speak well for it, as does its popularity in the duck blind. Its speed and alert, obliging nature have earned it scouting jobs in the military, and its discriminating nose has won the breed detective jobs on bomb and drug squads. Its greatest value, away from birds and water, is its ability and intelligence in guiding the blind.

THE GOLDEN RETRIEVER

Sir Dudley Marjoribanks, First Lord Tweedmouth, in 1868 bred a *sport* (the term used for the yellow dogs known to occur in strains of black Flat- and Wavy-Coated Retrievers) to a Tweed Water Spaniel and produced four yellow (Golden) puppies. The Tweed Water was used by the professional hunters of the rugged coastal area by the River Tweed because of its agility and first-rate nose.

To many, Goldens are the most handsome of the retriever group. Golden owners are quick to assert that their companions are not *right* for everyone, adding that they tend to develop and mature emotionally somewhat less rapidly than Labradors, and can be disappointingly "washed out" too quickly as a result. They especially resent heavy-handed training methods. Nevertheless, many of the best field-trained Goldens have a reputation of toughness. The Golden's long, beautiful coat carries extra water into the duck blind and boat, reduces swimming speed, and collects mud, burrs, and other field debris.

Goldens did very well in the infancy of field trialing, and at present are enjoying a renaissance as truly competitive retrievers. They still retain the remarkable scenting ability of their ancestors, and have compiled an outstanding record in obedience contests. Because of their brightness, grace, and tractability, Goldens, too, are often chosen to serve as guides for the blind.

I have been fascinated by the appearance of a few Curly- and Flat-Coated Retrievers in training and competition. Although they are always welcome at field trials, their numbers are so small in this country that they are considered rarities. Unfortunately, this is also true of the stylish Irish Water Spaniel.

Whatever breed you select, if you are primarily interested in a beautiful dog, seek a reputable bench (show) breeder: one that consistently produces standard, handsome, and well-formed puppies. Do not be disappointed, however, if this Clark Gable or Liz Taylor of the show retriever world cannot accomplish the work of a specifically bred field athlete. Each time I've helped a stymied owner of a show-stock pup with hunting ambitions, I've been astonished at how far such pups lag behind trial-bred examples of the same age. Much "show-stock," no matter how blocky the build or finely chiseled the features, is unable to move well, doesn't exhibit exceptional intelligence, courage, or "heart," and lacks that special appreciation of feathers that sportsmen call *birdiness.* These traits, so important in hunting and field-trial work, are seldom necessary for success in the show ring. In fact, many canine authorities regard "conformation only" standards as the ruination of any working breed. There has been some recent interest in *function* for show retrievers; but peer pressure among bench people rather than function has raised the level of concern regarding such dog disorders as hip dysplasia and congenital eye diseases.

A fine-looking field champion can occasionally be fattened and groomed into a bench champion, thereby making him into a *dual*-purpose champion, but a fine-looking bench dog is rarely made into a winning trial retriever or a good hunter. So different have the aims of each group become that many dog people worry that the exaggerations inherent today in breeding goals are creating subspecies, or two completely different breeds of dog.

If you live in an apartment, an extremely physical dog—especially one out of hot field-trial blood—may well be unsuitable for you. A dog from bench stock will probably cause you the least dissatisfaction. But if you hunt, your best chance of getting a satisfactory bird dog lies somewhere in the direction of field-trial stock.

Whether you choose a bench or trial-bred puppy, make sure the dog exhibits good conformation and an ability to move soundly. Investigate the parents and grandparents of litters that most interest you, and watch the dogs in action if possible. Ask questions, and visit the breeder more than once. Is he offering any guarantee against poor eyesight or hip dysplasia, which is malformation of the hips? Do the parents have a good disposition and temperament? Does the pup have a sound jaw structure and an even bite? And what are the dog's overall proportions compared to the breed standard?

Trial- and hunting-oriented people may consult the *Retriever Field Trial News,* or their current record book of performances in championship stakes, or review the pedigrees in the *AKC Stud Book.* Bench-minded people and those with a general interest in a satisfactory dog should contact the American Kennel Club for the name of the current club secretary for the particular breed.

Keenly interested breeders seem to have a computerlike aptitude for storing pedigree data. Do your own homework, examine the qualities of the parents and grandparents, but bolster this with a firsthand look at a number of dogs (at shows, club trials, and Nationals), and cross-reference your impressions by talking with veteran knowledgeable, practicing dog folk at every opportunity.

Some breeders feel complete *outcrosses* of families are the most stable and wholesome approach. (An outcross is a mating of two completely separate family strains, which introduces a fresh mixture of blood in the offspring.) I think that, before any match is made, each member of any union should be examined on that particular animal's merits and attributes, not simply on the tendencies shown in his litter brothers and sisters. In the match-up, attempt to compensate in one mate for specific deficiencies of the other, as well as to align positive attributes. It is preferable if these attributes are inherited rather than results of training.

Example:

MALE:		BITCH:
Good marker, sensitive	X*	Good marker, tough, stubborn
Bold, rugged, thick-coupled, good bone, light in the water	X*	Fast, well-angulated, shy, highly aquatic

* Symbol for "combined with."

A notion surrounds the breeding of dogs that a repeat breeding after a successful litter never matches the quality of the first. This belief has always seemed to lack supporting evidence. It is true that older bitches—from five or six years on—being bred for the first time risk more maternal complications than younger dogs, and older males may not produce as high sperm counts as they did as younger dogs. But would human parents have more than one child if this belief were true? Thoroughbred horse breeders obviously don't agree with this idea either. I bred my own favorite bitch, Field Champion and Amateur Field Champion Nakai Anny, on an outcross to a natural athlete named Super Powder. This union produced the highest-scoring Derby litter in retriever trial history. The litter scored 178 points and included the 1977 National Derby Champion Dr. Davey Ph.D., high-point Derby bitch FC AFC Amazing Grace of Ornbaun, AFC Rip Snortin' Good Times, and National Field Champion CFC AFC Risky Business Ruby. I repeated the breeding and, again, the litter was collectively stunning. These same parents produced Sunday Hawkeye, the 1979 National Derby Champion, an unprecedented feat!

Many hunters come to the breeder with the idea that they need a huge, tough dog to shoot over—one that can handle itself in a fight. They're wrong on both counts; size is of little or no working advantage and has no connection whatever with birdiness or mental toughness. If you insist on size, get a Newfoundland—but remember that a small, keen bitch can outperform him in field efficiency. Oversize or "overstandard" dogs often break down skeletally (see chap. 11) and are in crippling arthritic pain well before their smaller counterparts. Further, in their discomfort, they risk going mean.

A fighting retriever is an unforgivable, disruptive kind of character who should be shunned. Aggressiveness can be an inherited behavioral trait in a dog, and one that is compelled to assert himself against other dogs may next turn to man-fighting. After all, if you really admired fighting dogs and dog fights, you would forget retrievers and buy yourself a pugnacious Staffordshire terrier and teach him how to fetch. You'd have a "winner" at fighting, and the two of you could rule your duck club—if the other members didn't shoot you both!

Two of my own Labrador males have been repeatedly attacked by smaller street dogs during road work, without defense or retaliation. Although temporarily incensed, I'm proud of their refusal to disturb the peace. Their reluctance to brawl is due to their breeding and training—but I know that if they are someday attacked by a larger, vicious dog, I'll have to help defend them. These congenial retrievers are my bird dogs and my friends; they are not bred for battling, but for picking up game.

Trainers gather with famous litter mates—all offspring of the author's FC AFC Nakai Anny—for the 1977 Derby in Portland, Oregon. (from left) Carole Lane with Pistol Packin' Mama, Joe Beitler with Poker Face, Barbara Ornbaun with AFC Rip Snortin' Good Times and FC AFC Ornbaun's Amazing Grace, Ed Minoggi with Black and Blue, and the author with Dr. Davey, Ph.D. (left), and NFC AFC Risky Business Ruby.

Try to select an alert pup that looks you in the eye.

The instinct to retrieve is often present by five weeks of age

Another trait I dislike in certain retrievers is an inability to *relax*. "Kennel-walkers" are antsy, nervous dogs that constantly pace and wear out the pads of their feet. They seem ready for any action, any time, but once in the field they're usually too pooped from constant pacing, or too frivolous to concentrate. Most great athletes, whether human or canine, have an ability to relax and sleep well, to turn it on, then turn it off.

If you are a serious hunter or would-be trialer, you will want to do more than discuss pedigree and the confluence of bloodlines. You will want to see some performance. I have often turned a litter of month-old puppies loose on a flock of experienced domestic mallards in order to scout early talent. A five- to eight-week-old tyke may be willing to watch and chase a tossed white clipped-wing pigeon. How long is his bird-interest span? Will he attempt to retrieve? Will he enter gentle, warm water with you?

Many dog people believe in a "forty-nine-day-old theory" for removal of a puppy from his litter mates and bonding him to his new human companion. While forty-nine days may indeed be the optimum period for behavioral imprinting in many dogs, the rate of maturity is variable, and I've seen great dogs grow up without strict adherence to this schedule. Different pups—even from the same litter—can range from tough to weak, physically as well as mentally, or be precocious, or slow, or sensitive, or shy, or spooky. "Runts," which are not necessarily inferior, are sometimes the result of a second impregnation by the same sire, and may be as much as a week behind their brothers and sisters in development.

Try to select a well-formed, well-coordinated pup that is quick, aggressive, curious, birdy, alert—an active water nut that looks you in the eye. But don't forget that these tendencies can reverse themselves a month after the seventh week.

Bitches mature faster than males. A bitch may radiate very pleasing attributes, but you and she will experience her heat cycles, which occur roughly from six to eighteen months apart. The lost time—about twenty-one days—and trouble caused by a bitch in heat is probably counterbalanced, however, by males that write endless love letters on trees and power poles and exhibit periods of stubborn assertiveness and "studdiness."

Finally, try not to be so intent on getting reassurance from a piece of pedigree paper, from a bloodline or a kennel name. Owners too often forget that they're going to have to *work* and teach the animal in order to get results. Far too many young dogs are hurried through early training, then trashed in disappointment because they couldn't convince their anxious owners of their "greatness" before they matured.

COLOR

Obtaining desirable coloring has not been a big problem for show breeders, as color can be genetically isolated and is largely determined by esthetics. Field breeders in England and America have tried for generations to produce fine working qualities together with desirable color—a yellow, apricot, gold, liver, "dead grass," chocolate, or russet, for instance—and the results compared with the effort have seldom been brilliant.

Some experts believe that pursuing a recessive color gene, such as yellow, disregards all the virtues that accompany the dominant gene direction. Others go even further and claim that large doses of foxhound blood were purposely laced into the Labrador by old breeders to secure light color—and that this accounts, in the yellow, for a diminished retrieving capacity but a superior nose and scenting ability.

Many horsemen steer clear of colts with light-colored or streaked hooves, believing this indicates a soft, sensitive foot. Certain dogmen share this color/foot theory, equating the light Labradors with easily worn, sensitive foot pads. As an insurance edge against deficiencies, field dogmen who are intent on a light-colored Lab often choose light puppies that are the product of solid-black parents.

An eager market awaits the "different" or fashionable field dog, and some colors in retrievers are truly pleasing and rich. However, color bias may blind you to other qualities more important in a talented retriever pup—pretty is as pretty does.

Occasionally I hear a duck hunter insist that a black dog at the duck blind flares or alarms the birds before they reach the decoys. They add that camouflage is their reason for employing chocolate dogs or those colored butterscotch, caramel, or whatever. This is difficult to swallow. The sprig and mallard I shoot don't seem to be dog color-minded, though they do react to gross movement, noise, silliness, and other poor manners in a retriever. Many hunters solve the dog-flares-bird problem by rigging their blinds with a separate, covered-box blind and a tie-down leash for the retriever, whatever his color.

I've found that dog people who keep an entire litter in order to find the best dog in it are seldom better off than those who just grab the puppy that seems most talented.

Some behaviorists maintain that the most promising pups in a newborn litter are those that have the highest rate of heartbeat. Those with 170 per minute (at rest) and above are thought to be the quickest to learn, the least timid, and best able to accept new experiences. This theory is new and may be absolutely true. However, I have raised and trained dogs who were mortally afraid of dairy cattle (without previous bad experience with them), and another, who as a youngster, was terrified of sneezes. They grew into superb and dauntless retrievers, reveling in the blasts of shotguns and the feel of feathers and cold water. I never checked their heartbeats!

Color-coding my litters with dabs of acrylic paint at the base of the tail has always been my practice. (Others use colored ribbon collars.) For each retriever, I keep a simple report card on the whelping room wall that records such traits as aggressiveness, willingness to explore, appreciation or fear of shallow water, and birdiness. Canine behavior experts believe early physical handling, socialization (petting and stroking), and environmental diversity will maximize trainability. At three to five weeks pups may be taken into the house, out to a field, and to other new worlds, which may include significant temperature change. Many a fine pup is deliberately exposed to early stress in order to create pressure tolerances as he grows and matures. Such experiences, which need not necessarily be harsh, are intended to stimulate adrenal activity that increases the pup's stability and resistance to stress. Methods for inducing puppy-size stress include turning them on their backs, rotating them over and around in the hands for slight disorientation, light pinching of the skin over the shoulders and hips, and brief abandonment.

When your puppy arrives at his new home, be sure to have him physically checked by your vet and "socialize" him—handling, befriending, reassuring him. I begin this process with my own litters at a week of age by letting them "nose read" me to imprint my scent, even before their eyes and ears are open. Because they have more time available, amateurs are better suited to socializing puppies than pros. Feed your pup yourself and praise with "Good dog" when he eats. Entertain each other. Touch your puppy often.

A naturally talented working dog flatters his trainer and makes him look smooth and knowledgeable. A good dog *does* benefit from good help, but great dogs are often good *in spite of* their human partners. The professionals know this better than anybody. They don't rely on their training expertise alone; they seek out the naturally talented ones as keenly as the amateur. Good dogs simplify their work and enhance their reputations.

As you seek responsible breeders and breedings, remind yourself that skimping on the outlay for a decent puppy is usually misplaced thrift. If the dog you *really* want is higher in price than a less desirable offering, shoot high. Remember that this is an animal you may love and support for a dozen years. Your initial outlay may have much to do with whether these years are good times or a tiresome, sour drag.

4

Training and Gear

"WING-STRETCH" CANADA

Chilling gray tule fog seeps over miles of level Sacramento Valley. Knee-deep, eerie stuff, it erases ditches and all familiar landmarks. Pheasants rattle the stiff, cut rice stalks beneath it; a lot of them. I drop half a box of shells into my vest pocket and two into the Parker.

Wading toward me through the vapor is Calhoun, my regular gunning partner's brother-in-law, whom I've just met. Tying one end of a long rope around his waist, he turns to his station wagon and cautiously cracks open the door. A scuffle begins, a scrambling, frantic body bursts out into the mist, bowling Calhoun over. Regaining his feet like a game calf roper, he manages to fasten the end of his rope—to his "bird dog." The undaunted dog rallies by spinning fast loops around Calhoun's boots, dumping him again.

I whistle my Lab to heel, edging away to the outermost point position, before our party strings out to sweep the stubble. Most of the birds are quickly warned and vanish as Calhoun's dog advances, jerking and dragging him forward through crop rows and barbwire, presumably demonstrating his "stamina and remarkably fine nose." At each opportunity to shoot, Calhoun's "companion" assists by yanking his gun barrel askew. Chancy gunfire rakes fog and earth, clods are punched up in showers.

In other attempts to control canine ambition, I have seen strong retrievers lugging twenty-five pounds of heavy-link chain around their necks during pursuit of fleet-footed pheasants. "In order to teach that sonofabitch to slow down!" one owner explained. Pumping iron like this simply made the dog's muscles bigger and a hell of a lot stronger. Had the weighted dog misjudged jumping a water ditch, or tried to retrieve a fallen bird from a slough, he would have drowned. Maybe he has by now.

Then, too, I have often suffered watching some hunting friend (an otherwise mature, knowledgeable, and rational person) gradually raise his volume of dog cussing to yowls as his speeding speck of a dog set every possible bird to wing, then broke out into the next field and the field beyond. Succumbing to temper, the hunter rains shot at the dog who "refuses to listen to reason," "has no respect," or "won't come back."

What a pleasure it is to work through the same fields half an hour after the circus has departed, with a tight quartering dog who moves up more birds in gun range—birds the rank predecessors failed to notice. It is difficult to explain to an enthusiastic retriever that he won't be allowed to go to the fields or the Duck Club anymore if his behavior doesn't improve. Using a whistle instead of scalding language doesn't help much either if the dog has not been given thorough *previous* instruction in your conception of the work.

Most hunting retrievers require a less fanatical degree of field training than trial dogs. Yet, every bit of law and order you *do* put into your field dog is usually returned in improved performance, greater satisfaction, and more hunting success for you.

The conveniences and rewards of good dog control are not limited only to success in the fields, but appear in the home as well. The large sporting and working breeds, when uncontrolled, will invent jobs for themselves. These commonly include packing with other dogs and running livestock and wildlife. "Pack mentality" in domestic or feral dogs is disgusting and dangerous. Small children especially are unsafe in the face of it. Retrievers, despite their graciousness, are not immune to it. The legal answer for most ranchers, farmers, park rangers and other law enforcers dealing with free-roaming packs is to shoot them.

We seem quick to admire big, rugged male retrievers. This stems from a wish to identify with power, and a pride in strength. Some individual animals are surely stronger than we are. I have a friend, an accomplished dog trainer, who contends that the real reason for all the troubles and triumphs of dog work is rooted in man's ancient wish to dominate beasts—the more difficult to dominate, the greater the achievement. Is the man who carefully sits a rippling, powderkeg stallion more respectable than the man who easily sits a mare or a graceful gelding?

The difficulties of training a tough, assertive dog should be a consideration in your selection of a dog. These physically dominant dogs are called Alpha types. (If they were wolves, they would likely be pack leaders.) As you attempt to furnish a role of leadership, an Alpha may be the last to serve you and your wishes. While such a dog might be stylish, he may be a nightmare to train and control—he may, in fact, contest your authority his entire life. These dogs are often described as "defiant," "contrary," "back-stabbing sons of bitches," and "counterfeits." As a starting trainer, you may not be prepared for the heartache and force necessary to break and train one of these strong ones. Bitches can also be pack leaders, according to studies of wild dogs, and surliness, stubbornness, and "bitchiness" can equally test the trainer's mettle. Owning the toughest stud or bitch on the ranch is no privilege, especially if you are truly interested in accomplished dog work. I prefer a dog that might be described as "stylish," "pleasing," "brave," "willing," and "honest"—a dog that can easily pick up my birds, sometimes with finesse, sometimes in adversity, and still be my friend.

We admire a guide dog as he steers his blind charge through thick traffic, or the Budweiser Clydesdales' ballet of giants, or a Kentucky Thoroughbred moving at full stride, drawing on his reserve and heart, even when the jockey goes to the whip. We also are warmed by the sight of a sheep dog craftily moving a flock, often using only his eyes to keep them under control, as his boss leans on a gate and dips snuff. In almost every case, these animals have experienced some form of force training in order to emphasize or deemphasize certain natural gifts or tendencies.

Two words—*force* and *pressure*—are kicked around at training sessions and trials by professional and amateur trainers. For years, I have asked various people to define what those words mean to them and their dogs. The answers have ranged from dire blacks to forgiving whites, with a pearly grayness in between. The purpose of this chapter is to define the terms and to address responsibly the subject of punishment and discipline.

Force is the physical means and ability to discipline a dog and compel him to perform tasks—some of which may be unpleasant or boring and contrary to his natural choice, inclination, and will.

Pressure is the trainer's insistence on task performance through methods of force or implied force.

I have found that most available literature omits or only obliquely alludes to this area of teaching and control. Some sources casually dismiss the subject of discipline by announcing, "If a dog must be beaten into doing the job he was bred for, then the relationship between man and dog has only succeeded in failing." This and similar sweeping pronouncements and disavowals are misleading to serious beginning dog trainers. They imply that if your dog doesn't mind you, then you don't love him enough, or his breeding is inadequate.

Why bother with any kind of force and pressure? Why be unpleasant to a young and willing retriever who is doing his light tasks cheerfully and naturally? Some force training seems unnecessarily barbaric and emotionally draining, yet the purpose, ultimately, is to define your dog's work obligations and strengthen his skills. If you are interested in training your dog for hunting or for trial work, it is important to bear in mind that very few high-achieving animals have been bribed or seduced to their level of work with cookies, marshmallows, or love alone. It is not impossible—but it is very rare indeed.

Here are some axioms to consider before stampeding down to the hardware store or tack shop to arm yourself with an array of hell-raising devices:

• Decide what you expect of your dog. Effective hunting companion? Bench show dog? National Field Champion? Obedience specialist? Hearth ornament? Tramp?

• The methods, tools, and approaches to force training must be matched to each dog's individual capabilities and character.

• Defining and communicating the task or specific work details are the first responsibilities of the trainer. The handler must understand the reason and components of the lesson *before* he attempts to influence the dog. Show, tell, then correct.

• Stupid force—the first tactic many hunters use after a period of total permissiveness—is to "beat the living bejesus out of him." It may seem gratifying after a succession of crude, embarrassing field "sins," but usually teaches nothing. This is a clumsy, pointless handler response and a poor imitation of training.

• Temper, frustration, and vindictiveness are the number one enemies of any pressure lesson. Avoid a physical conflict if the dog is not understanding your wishes.

• No severe punishment should be dished out until you are sure the dog understands your intention and is clearly in defiance. Use the least painful methods first. Give him the benefit of the doubt, although you may eventually have to demonstrate your full capacity for physical punishment and imprint your authority.

• The word *No* is generally used too often for too much. Introduce consistent alternative cues and commands.

• Emphasize positive reactions and encourage successes by praise and reward (petting, food, or birds) in drills and yardwork, completely away from the hunting or trial situation. Negative reaction is discouragement through punishment. Positive plus negative response and reinforcement are necessary to define the job for a dog. Remember that many very willing and honest dogs resent being set up to commit mistakes and errors for the sake of correction.

• Repetition, pattern, drill, and familiar responses are all integral to impressing a lesson. Be alert to physical and mental fatigue, although you are trying to instill a lasting impression. Extreme heat or cold must be considered in any session. A dog that is cross-eyed from overheating, or a bitch in the ebb of her season, may not make an ambitious student.

• Nagging or begging for a desired response usually produces boredom and disrespect. Chip away with short, quick, simple, assertive lessons.

• Canine intelligence differs greatly. If you truly have a slow or stupid dog—one you can't respect—get rid of him and find a dog that *you* want to spend time with.

• Stoicism: all dogs have different pain thresholds. Crying out and yelping may or may not indicate the dog is yielding to influence and pressure; although this should be regarded initially as communication, many tough dogs quickly learn that noise reduces punishment. Be aware of submission signals: eye aversion, head and neck turns, lip licking, and ear and tail positions. Read up on canine psychology, behavior, and wolf language. Writers on these subjects include David Mech, Durward Allen, Stanley Pimlott, Michael Fox, and Barry Holstun Lopez.

• Expert help: get advice from an experienced dogman, amateur or professional, whom you respect. If possible, see similar dog work done well by others before beginning. A good pro may cure a problem for you and get "blamed" for the pressure by the dog, but he may also be rewarded by the dog's allegiance. The respect imprinted may not be extended to you.

• There are several "right" ways to train retrievers to do an identical task. Learn to read your dog.

• Good and great dogs can and do recover from trainer mistakes involving use of pressure and force, through their strong desire to retrieve or to please, or through their love of birds—an amazing trait that simplifies the lives of trainers.

· *Timing* is essential: time of day; timeliness of location (where, how often, what distance?); timing and smoothness between dog and man; timing of lessons dovetailed into similar lessons; time in life: when and what to teach, from puppyhood to maturity.

The key question is: Where am I in the progress of this dog?

Some very fine trainers adhere to a deliberate, planned system for all dogs. Others of equal skill propose training whatever way it takes to get the job done. The "system" group runs a real risk of squashing the ambitions of a sensitive and intelligent dog. The "intuitive" group, on the other hand, may omit critical segments of work or insufficiently impress its candidates with the importance of a lesson or the trainer's willpower.

THE TOOLS

I am listing the following tools because many of them are routinely used by a large body of dog trainers. My aim is to dispel the notion that field retrievers are commonly trained with a pocketful of cookies and a rolled-up newspaper. Many of these training aids or "problem solvers" can have serious, sometimes damaging mental and/or physical side effects. This is not a recommendation or a condemnation of any of them, as each raw retriever is a responsively different individual. I do not include this list as a recipe, neither do I include it subversively, as a blueprint for a pipe bomb. Many state, county, and local agencies have statutes and ordinances that vary widely in their consideration of what represents humane behavior by a man toward his domestic animals. You should know your laws.

Corrective-force tools fall into three categories: some are used for stopping the dog, others for making him proceed, and others for changing his mind.

— *Sticks* —

Carrying a stick is a primal symbol of authority to men and dogs. Many trainers use sticks and switches—cane, fiber glass, wood, and so on—as disciplinary tools, and to enhance their authority image.

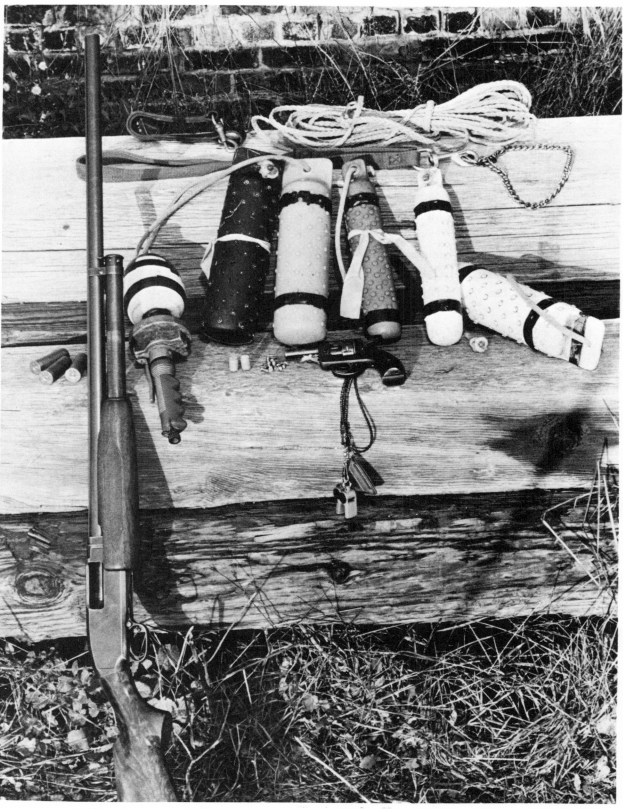

Ordinary training gear includes a .12-gauge popper gun with ammunition, a gas-powered bumper launcher, and two sizes of plastic bumpers. Above the bumpers are a choke collar, leashes, and a long check cord with a snap; below, whistles and earplugs on a lanyard and a .22-caliber blank pistol.

Demonstrating the lesson is the goal, and using the *minimum admonishment* to effect the desired change in behavior and performance is the key. A few quick, stern licks are far more constructive than extended assault; dogs rarely appreciate the difference between a misdemeanor and a felony. An old dog adage allows, "The first three whacks are for the benefit of the dog, any more than that is for the benefit of the man." Your threatening stance—with arm raised—can result in flinching and hand-shyness. Any head blows are to be avoided.

Trainers using sticks should have a collar and leash, or a rope restraint, or a firm grasp of the student before administering punishment. (A few rare dogs will come in and voluntarily accept a licking.) Wielding a switch or stick at an unsecured subject simply inspires a game of dodging, and looking out for number one. Once a dog thinks "keep away" from the handler, the object of the intended lesson is lost; defensiveness interrupts the dog's initial concentration on work. Chasing a dog with a stick generally teaches him that he is a lot faster on foot than you are.

Some trainers use the following "sticks":

• *Buggywhip.* May sometimes reduce the impression of an overhand blow.

• *Riding crop.* Some models make a noisy pop as well as provide a sting.

• *Leather quirt.* May be folded unobtrusively in a pocket and introduced as a surprise. It stings, but does no skeletal damage.

• *Bat.* Hollow, light plastic model, the ultimate rolled-up newspaper. Noisy, but no physical damage.

• *Long poke pole* of bamboo, aluminum, and so on. Sometimes used in shore breaking to keep a dog in the water. If you decide to use this tool, be sure to have the end safely blunted; a handlebar grip from a bicycle will often suffice. A house broom is also a handy, safe tool for this chore.

• *Stock prod.* A long-handled electric prod with a plastic or fiber-glass stem is best. A stock prod may cause a defensive biting reflex. A short prod used at close range seriously raises the odds of getting yourself bitten. While the dog may not intend to nail you, he involuntarily bites the tool and may get you as well; this also may inadvertently teach the dog that deliberately biting you gets good results. Zapping a dog with a stock prod is a very powerful correctional means of force. After contact experience with it, some very tough dogs will quail and acquiesce at just the sight or sound of a prod. I believe it represents an intrinsic danger or threat to them, as do snakes. If you doubt this, try it on *yourself* occasionally, and make sure the batteries aren't run down.

— *Remotes* —

These are distance tools that reprimand the unsecured dog beyond the trainer's physical reach.

· *Slingshot and marble.* Limited by user's accuracy. Can chip a bone.

· *Air or spring BB gun.* Stings, and could blind.

· *Rat shot, in a .22 caliber pistol.* Stings, and can penetrate hide at very close range. Be sure weapon is a smooth bore, since rat shot can ball up in a rifled bore and kill a dog.

· *Shotgun.* An old-time tool for some field dog trainers. It preceded the electric collar as the ultimate remote. It is a very powerful tool and represents an easy way to blind, maim, or destroy your dog. (There is a working formula for shot size and "safe" yardage. I decline to print it.) Seek an expert or professional's advice *before* you make a mistake. Dogs may learn to hate the sight of a shotgun, which is a shame in itself and can reduce the animal's ability to perform well on shot birds alongside his boss in the field.

· *Electric collar.* The most controversial of remote tools, and a device with few masters. The shock collar is simultaneously attractive and repellent to many dog trainers. It is a very strong tool.

What's good about electric collars? Some veterinarians who train dogs have pointed out that the collar-trained dog is never physically damaged by its use. Shock punishment is therefore more humane. Hand-shyness in a dog can be avoided with this tool. Extremely tough dogs can be impressed by electricity when all else seems to fail. The speed of a correction is so quick that the lesson is more easily absorbed. Some dogs tend to try harder because of their respect for it and therefore require less actual punishment. A trainer can work alone without a great deal of physical assistance.

Using an electric collar, the physically disabled, the elderly, and the lazy can accomplish lessons they could teach in no other way. Correcting the dog across water and inaccessible islands and points is possible; this represents clean training—no wading or slopping through mud. Many collar aficionados see themselves as the sophisticates of force correction, and old-fashioned practitioners as primitive stoics whose training methods are akin to having your teeth pulled after waiving the rights to Novocain.

What's bad about electric collars? Although they may not leave physical damage, they can absolutely hollow out the brains of some sensitive, well-intending retrievers, harming them psychologically, sometimes permanently. Many poorly trained collar dogs are slow, piggy, and robotlike, devoid of natural zest for their work—quite unpleasant to watch or judge. Some of these dogs are burned out at a very early age. Laboratory rats in electrical mazes can learn to choose and perform. They have also been reduced to functionless, terrified paranoiacs and neurotics by indiscriminate, arbitrary, shock punishment. Some dogs become "collarwise" by learning to cultivate a double standard of performance, depending on whether the collar is on or off. Collars are expensive to buy and repair, and they are by no means a durable, reliable, or precise tool. Many serious collar trainers own at least three: one on the dog, one in the repair shop, and one en route to repair via the U.S. Mail. Their mechanical functions are sometimes random and capricious, reducing the trainer's skill in timing the punishment and increasing the risk of losing the lesson. Collars usually refuse to perform in brackish or salt water. On most models, the punishment that the collar emits cannot be varied. Collars are clumsy and can be accidentally activated by the handler, other radio signals, or a training companion's collar transmitter.

Perhaps the worst aspect of the electric collar is the heady spell that befalls many trainers who treat this tool as a panacea. It creates the Son of Zeus syndrome: thunderbolts are hurled for every affront that displeases the trainer's eye. Hotheads (like myself) and oddball perfectionists, especially after years of frustration, are poorly qualified for zapping out squirts of hell. The push-button mentality seems to leave little room for physically touching the dog, in praise or rebuke.

Spot use for specific problems, rather than total dependence on the collar, is the preference of several pros; however, many amateur trainers show little ability to limit this "cure" to a specific problem. Instead, they use it to address a multitude of problems. This tool works best to reinforce lessons the dog already understands. Dogmen who have completely trained one or more dogs conventionally, "the hard way," are the ones who seem to have the most success with electric collars. There is a saying that goes, "If I knew enough about dogs to use a collar perfectly, then I wouldn't have to use one." It takes no talent to mail-order such a potent device when you pick up your first forty-nine-day-old retriever pup.

For total familiarization with these tools and methods, an amateur may enroll himself and his dog in a complete instructional program of conditioning to this device with a proven collar pro. Some professionals couldn't train the large numbers of dogs they do without it, but this should have little bearing on the average amateur's intentions.

Electric collar training generally works best with a certain type of candidate dog and not with others. The exceptionally tough and resilient dog often needs a form of training that is one-dimensional and impersonal. This dog's reward is the absence of electrical punishment; achievement represents capitulation. Because some *experts* get excellent results with this tool, many onlookers envy their control and assume the difference is not in the expert but in the tool. They naïvely conclude that "zapping, nicking, or burning the bastard" is a shortcut to glory. If this were the only way to go, all the national winners would have been trained with electricity. Happily, they are not.

—— *The Trainer Is the Tool* ——

This is an appropriate motto for the rare retriever and trainer who can achieve the most results with the least reprimands. The one-in-a-million dog who trains so easily and advances so quickly is usually of the finest combination of breeding. He is a natural and a genius; he makes his owner appear smooth and expert. He is proud and can be easily flattered by praise. He worships your approval of his work and can be embarrassed by voice disapproval, scolding, and failure. His bravery is nonchalant and untutored. His pain threshold is so high that he fine-angles into floating chunks of ice or thorny cover undaunted. In fact, he can severely injure himself by carelessly disregarding his body and obliging your wishes. This dog has a memory like a microfilm library and has a gameness for new material. He wants to train every day, all day.

The trainer's head, hands, eyes, and voice are his chief tools for corrections. A pinch or twist of the ear is plenty to effect a change of this dog's mind. A shake by the coat (feet off the ground) is impressive to him in spite of his natural toughness and strength. Repetition, not thrashing, imprints his lesson material. He can accept a good thumping and never avoids it by reluctance to come in or by bolting, though this thumping is unnecessary to advancement and a waste of both parties' time and energy. However, if the trainer does become annoyed, sprinting out into the field to the dog can increase his "presence" and usually gives him time to make a correction plan and to dissipate the heat of his temper. (A collar, leash, or attached length of rope free of knots is sometimes handy for drawing the dog toward or out of a water or cover hazard.) This type of dog hates making mistakes and therefore despises being "set up" or trapped into error. Positive reinforcement is the ticket to his performance. The trainer of such a dog must be intuitive about how much, when, and where to advance. This dog's trainer cannot be guided by the training and force work successful with the typical good retriever, as there are few points of similarity with other trainers' dogs. I've had *one* dog like this; I sometimes wish they were all this way.

Two other tools are indispensable to good dog control: kennels and crates.

Kennels. A kenneled dog cannot be stolen, poisoned, run over; he cannot run livestock, hunt on his own, breed, or be torn up in a fight. A decent kennel run is approximately four feet wide by fourteen to eighteen feet long. It should be tall enough for you to stand up in easily, have a tunnel-proof floor, and include a lid or roof to protect bitches in season. Doghouses, shade, air conditioning, and other amenities are dependent on location and weather conditions. A proper kennel for your working dog is not a prison to languish in, but a staging area for hunting or serious training, and a place to sleep.

Giving a dog the run of a fenced backyard is a mistake. Yard dogs often establish this ground as a territory, squirt-mark the perimeters, and commission themselves to defend it. This is poor practice, as the dog then entertains himself by deciding who your enemies are, thus allowing himself a second occupation besides retrieving. A kennel run is too small to make a territory, but large enough to represent a "den." After a workout, your dog can feel secure, sleep, and digest each day's lesson without interference. Staking or tying up a dog on a chain is awkward and primitive, and can make him territorially mean. Bringing a dog into your house is your decision, though this can cause him to resent his kennel as a banishment.

Crates. Aluminum or wire traveling crates are convenient and orderly and, like your home kennel, they provide security and safety. Hunters and field trialers often travel long distances with their dogs, and hotels and motels are sometimes intolerant of dogs in rooms.

You should teach your dog that his crate is a great place. Feed your young dog his meals in his crate aboard your vehicle several times before his first ride, for acclimatization. He should learn to leave his kennel and "load up" in his crate on command. The same verbal command will serve to cue him to enter an auto, truckbed, light aircraft, hunting blind, or duck boat. The use of a crate directs your dog's attention to the work you want him to be interested in—training, hunting, or trialing. Your dog will associate you and his travel crate with everything he finds fun and exciting—expeditions, birds, guns, and retrieving. And he can't eat your game birds if you stop for lunch and a beer.

The crate should be comfortable, with enough room inside to allow the dog to stand, turn, and lie down. Waterproofed Masonite pegboard may be installed as flooring to spare him from lying in a puddle if he enters his crate with

An ideal kennel run is a clean, well-lighted place.

Aluminum (left) or wire (right) traveling crates provide a safe means of transporting your dog, whether by car, truck, or air.

a wet coat. Good ventilation in the crate and the vehicle is absolutely essential. The crate should be designed for air travel; you may want to ship a bitch in season, for example.

If you should swerve abruptly or have an accident in your car, a crated dog can move only ten or so inches to a supportive wall instead of being thrown several feet. I once flipped a smugly acrobatic bitch from the bed of my pickup at sixty miles per hour while evading a sauntering skunk. The incident cost her some wall-to-wall bruises and scared the hell out of both of us. Since then, my dog always travels in a crate. I subsequently bought a good aluminum crate, anchored it well, and we both learned to like it. I also ceased to worry about her sticking her head out the window or around the cab of the truck and taking a high-speed grasshopper in one of her precious eyes. A hasp installed on the crate door means that a dog can be left on the truck, securely padlocked.

If you use a station wagon, pickup, or van, be sure the slot between the car body and back bumper is covered with rubber, carpet, or silver tape so that your dog doesn't catch and rip off a toenail while loading or unloading.

Whistles. Unless you're an expert at whistling through your teeth, you may want to buy a plastic whistle. Two of the most popular models are the Roy Gonia Special and the Acme Thunderer; these are generally available at sporting goods stores.

A few points regarding force and pressure before discussing advanced aims and techniques:

One refers to a training approach that I call Magnum Force. Its three ingredients are unlimited training time on unlimited birds with unlimited punishment. A saturation trainer working a dog steadily, all day, seven days a week, with shot live birds (pheasants and ducks), making complicated retrieving demands, and using powerful force tools (collar, prod, shotgun) leaves no slack, latitude, or room for forgiveness, and no alternatives if the dog sours or slumps. This "never-back-off" approach is psychologically dangerous to dog and man. Some dogs that are constantly regarded as culprits and outlaws learn to accept their own counterfeit behavior as normal and oblige with more rotten, go-to-hell performances and sulking. This, of course, escalates the problem, bringing on a fresh onslaught of heavy artillery from his disgusted owner. Some professionals try to alternate their force tools and methods so that the dog is not jaded by the reprimands or by anticipating the punishment.

Giving a dog a period of restoration to recharge his ardor is not always a mistake, as many trainers believe. Kennel rest and recovery time should be conscientiously supplied to compensate for strains caused by difficult-to-grasp lessons and physical exertion. The number of training bumpers thrown to enhance marking accuracy versus the number of birds shot for excitement and emphasis should also be carefully balanced. The fluctuations between rewards, praise, and birds on one hand, and rebukes, punishment, and pressure on the other should be closely related to each dog and his *attitude*.

I've noticed that some of my dogs have had favorite fields or pieces of water that affect them with a contagious high. One of my "good medicine" places is where the Pacific Ocean drums a fine salt spray into the fog and winds. I've watched visiting friends' dogs consistently turn in extraordinary performances there. Be alert to your dog's preferred spots and use simplicity, birds, and this happy ground to pull him out of the dumps. If you *do* have to reprimand your dog there, he may not resent it as much or associate it with that location. Some trainers also believe that bringing their dogs into their homes after a rough day is reassuring and bond-strengthening.

SECONDARY FORCE

Secondary force is an interesting means of influencing your dog's level of field performance without the unpleasantness of direct punishment (primary force). Coming down hard for a minor infraction, such as barking in his kennel, can later result in your authority being enhanced in the field.

A friend of mine trained his dog, who barked incessantly, to respect his order for SILENCE! by aiming a lawn sprinkler into his dog's kennel. The hose was hooked up through the kitchen window to the sink faucet. When a noise violation occurred, the unattended command SILENCE! boomed out into the yard and a hissing spray doused the culprit. This verbal cue was recognized and respected, and the dog soon achieved quiet and dry sainthood.

My favorite bitch once refused to take a decent "over" hand signal. She was on a vast hillside trying to avoid some beef cattle that were blocking her course. (She always felt snotty and arrogant toward cattle.) I made her sit for fifteen minutes while the whole herd lumbered in and surrounded her as tightly as a wagon train. She sat—chagrined, ears down—as they all sniffed and nudged. My next command was met with welcome relief and was brilliantly executed. Apparently, it seemed less humiliating than being bunted by bovines.

Another excellent secondary force discipline for hunters and trialers is the LIE DOWN command. It is important for two reasons: it may serve you well in the duck blind and can as well be a point of force for the very headstrong Alpha male. Lying down is, to him, a large concession to you. The stronger the dog, the more he resents submitting. In order to further emphasize this discipline to certain Alpha males who begrudged my leadership, I have carefully and methodically pinned *down* the dog with my full body weight and breathed into an ear. This act of dominance, through canine symbolism, often results in a total surrender of resistance to you and your wishes. By accepting this posture, a dog often then acquiesces in other areas of trained behavior. I recall watching FC AFC Trumarc's Raider, an Alpha male if ever there was one, in the holding blinds during the National Open in Nevada. Jim Swan, his handler, exacted a LIE DOWN form of submission with demanding voice intimidation. Raider was

47

"Can" decoys.

respectful in his manners and spectacular in the field, and he almost won. It can be a hell of a job getting a dog to submit to this posture, but the subsequent cooperative results may be worth the struggle.

— *Attrition* —

This method of avoiding primary force is similar to insisting a child eat all his carrots before excusing him from the table. A handler should sometimes be willing to stand and repeat a lesson until he feels the dog has a full grasp of the concept, or the dog has smoothed out his reluctant or stubborn attitude. It may be as simple as letting an advanced retriever with a sloppy mental approach hunt his guts out for ten or more fruitless minutes on an uncomplicated mark and then repeat it. The only punishment is the physical penalty of being worn down by a long, hard, unassisted hunt on land or water.

None of these methods is automatically recommended. Rather, they demonstrate that you can invent your own means to make a lesson. Before doing so, however, make certain that what you have in mind is not dangerous. Ask training friends if they can foresee any serious side effects.

Don't *waste* force. Beware of running out of daylight while trying to induce or subdue your dog in a complicated test. Wrangling without a complete lesson is often worse than no lesson at all.

5

Derby Training: The First Phase

CANVASBACK

The map was clothes-pinned to the visor, my dainty bitch was securely crated in the truckbed, and all the road-lights probed flickering patches of fog. That tall four-by-four Ford would do a hundred if you waited long enough. I was suffering a leaking common cold, and only fear and velocity seemed to open my nose. Three tons of us snorted along through the false dawn—quite late to our first field trial (where-ever-the-hell it was). Late to our very first Derby!

"Finally! There it is!" Glimpsed over my shoulder, across a marsh, were sun striking car tops, white-shirted gunners, and busy movement. Brakes squeeze. The truck comes about like a Percheron and charges onto the dirt road.

A dandy redhead with an official-looking clipboard inspects her schedule and informs me that I *had* been number one dog to run.

"But don't worry." She smiles. "Watch a few dogs, and I'll work you into the lineup." Amid explosive sneezes, I secretly wish she'd rebuked me and sent me home with a medical discharge. A single hen pheasant is shot in flight deep in a field across a water ditch. Many of the dogs are in trouble trying to find it. I study it—a piece of cake. If only I could borrow one of the handsome dead birds from the mounting pile, I'd show my little darling what the hell we are hunting today. She has never laid eyes on one.

It is our turn. Tottering to the line, I'm rigid, lame with awe. The gunners about to shoot a bird for us now appear to be a thousand yards away. I feel rank with our exposed newness, our flakiness, our total unpreparedness. My tiny partner is intrigued with the smorgasbord of fresh scents and the spasms of movement in the gallery. She faces the populace, not the field; but in nervous anticipation I signal for our bird. The pheasant lofts steep and clean, then hangs on its arc for a splinter of time, before the gunners neatly sweep it down.

"Too bad," one of the judges says. "Your dog never saw the bird." Grasping at salvation, I ask if I could try to handle her, out there, to the bird she never saw. The judges seem very kind, and remark how well conditioned she looks, and ask about her breeding, then quietly close their books. We are dismissed. Now we can go home.

EARLY TRAINING

Your pup's first real exposure to the world should be on daily walks with you—and you *alone.* No other people or dogs, especially litter mates, should accompany you on these walks. They provide the earliest opportunity to form a lasting bond between you and your pup. In this routine you are not only his friend, provider, and interpreter but also his security in new terrain. He comes to depend on you, the handler, as he encounters new noises and odors, streets, fences, water, different textures of grass, and other animals.

Begin walking your pup when he is seven weeks old; at this age five minutes will be sufficient, but you may lengthen the outing gradually as he gains stamina and ambition. When he is very young, carry him into a gentle field, set him down, and encourage him to follow you in a wilderness fraught with risks of being left behind. Change direction when he starts to anticipate a routine or loses interest in you. Let him explore, but call to him and move off when he is sniffing or preoccupied. When he is inattentive drop down in high grass or step around a tree or a corner. Let him panic briefly at the loss of your protecting silhouette, then show yourself and reassure him.

This early stage is the period of widest freedoms. These walks will gradu-

Young pup and owner take a morning walk.

ally be converted into yard- and fieldwork later. Maintain continual *eye contact* throughout every tour. Stop, *look,* and wait during all airings; congratulate, then proceed. Never turn your back on him. You are training yourself at the same time in these matters. Watch and learn your dog's gait, his ear and tail positions: this should help you later to recognize his attitudes and will benefit you when you must depend on his concentration and nose in upland hunting.

Feed your dog yourself. Feeding time provides another opportunity for forming a close bond with a young dog. Sit with him and praise him while he eats. Allow him to associate the good tone of your voice with the pleasure of eating. Letting your dog grow accustomed to your voice now will pay off later: if you shout compliments to him in the field after exceptional work, it won't sound to him like an angry barrage.

Sleep intervals are important to pups after a walk or short retrieving lesson. Put the pup up in his kennel or crate long enough so he can sleep and assimilate what he has seen and learned. Most pros automatically provide dogs with this time to rest, because the large number of dogs to be trained severely limits the amount of time spent with each dog. It is also worth noting that many pros are not geared for puppies and are best challenged by older dogs, whose training has begun, and advanced work.

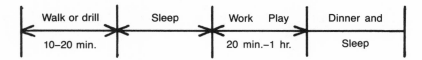

Diagram 1. Work and sleep.

A high-powered amateur, on the other hand, may want to train for a solid two days, simply because it's a weekend and he has counted on using the time. But if you push a pup too hard at an early age, without a chance to recover and sort out new material, he loses the value of the lesson. You waste time—and the dog. Amateurs with one or two dogs should restrict their training to clean, simple, short lessons, followed by intervals of rest. With a young pup (four months or older) I walk or drill out of doors early in the morning for ten minutes to an hour, kennel during the day, then have the pup mark on four to six retrieves in the evening. Others like to start in the house by tossing a knotted stocking down a dead-end hallway to encourage their pup to use his eyes, chase, and return to you.

— *Eye Contact* —

Eye language is one of the chief means of communication in many species. The numerous expressions: "laughing eyes," "steely eyes," "he wouldn't look me in the eye," and so on indicate its significance for us in conveying attitudes, moods, intentions. Some mammals find great significance and meaning in whether the eyes are averted or the gaze is direct. The eyes convey messages of peace, anxiety, or challenge to combat. Wolves carry out a large part of their social and pack business by eye contact. Our retrieving dogs are able and expected to assist us thoroughly with eye power as well as with nose work. I have developed a large part of my training around the use of the eyes—both my own and my dog's. Hunting or trial dogs that are most receptive to hand signals tend to look toward their bosses far more frequently than those that cooperate poorly.

Therefore, I suggest that your kennel be placed, if possible, where the dog can view the house and its goings-on. Make him more dependent on you by limiting, to some degree, what he sees. He should see that food, visitors, attention, and entertainment come exclusively from you. Try to reduce nearby visual attractions such as bird pens, road traffic, and so on.

One keen-eyed trainer friend of mine noticed differences in dog behavior during hot weather when the handlers wore dark glasses that obscured eye contact. The performance changes were subtle, but finally we agreed that the trainer who constantly wore sunglasses had conditioned his dog to assume that the glasses were his eyes.

Some evidence for the significance of eye contact can be found in an experiment I made on a nearby swimming creek. I ran a nice, young (high school age) dog on a fairly difficult channel blind 250 yards down the creek. The water wasn't fast or severely cold, but willows completely draped one bank, and high grass and hemlock concealed the other. My dog diligently lined the floating bumper. I watched him swim a third of the way back, then became distracted by a swooping White-tailed Kite hasseling a young Red-tailed Hawk over hunting rights. When I looked back toward my dog, he was gone—home. I brought him back and reran the blind, *looking* at him the entire time. He did perfectly. Later I repeated the same blind with three superior water dogs, two Field Champions, and an Amateur Champion. I asked their trainers to look away or turn their backs on the incoming dog, thus breaking eye contact. The results were always the same: broken eye contact, broken work.

Even though dogs see in black and white, a good retriever's eyesight is absolutely remarkable—far better than our own color vision. Veteran duck dogs often spot incoming birds long before their gunners, and good hunters learn to respect this ability. Some retrievers, like good basketball players, are gifted with uncanny peripheral vision. These are the "flash" markers that are able to pinpoint downed game that their handler swears his dog could not possibly have seen. Dogs seem to see exceptionally well in low light conditions, such as dawn and dusk. Besides being a hunting advantage, this trait suits well the amateur trainer who rushes home from work to squeeze in a few marks before nightfall. I believe a black dog is well aware of his camouflage at night. When my dogs are out in the pitch dark, I fool them into believing I can see them by giving omniscient, assertive voice commands. This is good practice for walking to your duck blind in a fog or dark, and can save your dog from being smacked by a car at night: he understands he can't get away with disobeying simply because it's dark.

Some marginal marking dogs may simply be the victims of poor vision or nearsightedness. I've trained a fine chocolate Lab that could promptly nail any mark under eighty yards, but a mark deeper than that was executed only slowly with graceful, myopic goodwill and the aid of a veteran's nose.

A proud working dog wants to see and be seen. Develop a language with eye contact and cultivate it.

— *First Discipline* —

As previously suggested, a good point at which to establish your authority and willingness to dish out punishment to your dog is in teaching a command for silence to prevent and eliminate barking in his run or on the truck. You may begin to discipline him any time after three months of age, but if you wait too long, he will be less impressionable and may regard barking as his sacred right.

Use QUIET! or STOP THE NOISE! or any other brief command. Connect words with action: issue voice commands *only* when you can back them up with your immediate presence. Hold the pup's muzzle shut or shake him by the scruff with all four feet off the ground, using your voice command. Never use an overhand head blow, and always attempt to look him straight in the eye. Persevere until your intent is understood perfectly and instantly. If the pup should start barking again, reinforce the command and punish him again, until his barking is simply no longer worth the consequences to him. He must get an absolute A-plus in the lesson, day and night.

Your no-noise command is extremely handy if your pup is vocal in the duck blind or indulges in loud yapping at birds on the line in training and trialing. Noisiness eventually becomes a major fault with him. Owning a quiet dog makes things easier on you, your neighbors, and fellow hunters, as well as wild birds. Similar measures and assertiveness are excellent for teaching your dog to KENNEL on command (to load into his travel crate, kennel run, or duck boat)—and *not* to chase cars, eat manure, dig holes, or chew things. The biggest benefit, however, is that *you* become the boss, a figure of power, without hindering his retrieving or stifling his love for birds.

I don't regard housebreaking as being in the same category; this should be accomplished as instructionally (no "rub his nose in it") and painlessly as possible, even if it means that the puppy does some maturing in his kennel before he's invited inside the house.

— *Obedience* —

My field champion had just spent twenty minutes digging a four-foot pit under a woodrat lodge to extract a crippled quail—a bird my hunting partner had given up for lost. Now he raved about *keenness* and *persistence* and announced that he wished his own pup would grow into just such a retriever. But then he qualified his remarks by adding, "I mean as a hunter, not as a trial dog." I repeated a litany I've used a hundred times: The basic principles of training for *hunting* and *trialing* are the same!

There are entire books devoted to the myriad methods and expectations of obedience training. I'm not going to plow much new ground here. Nevertheless, any dog intended to be a good field companion should initially be taught to move on a leash, sit, come when called (HERE or COME), and heel. Later he will learn to be steady to shot ("staunched"), to lie down (CHARGE), and to retrieve or hunt on command.

It's critical that basic obedience jobs and commands such as NO BARKING be kept separate from field retrieving; this allows you, as master, to boost your authority without stifling his "birdiness" or other natural abilities. He should be introduced to each task in sequence, and should not be graduated to further chores until he satisfies you with constant A-plus performance. Many well-bred field-trial stock pups seem amazingly cooperative about carrying things in their mouths and following you around; don't delude yourself into thinking you are one hell of a trainer because of this talent. Make sure your dog gets a good foundation in obedience in spite of his volunteer responses. One word of caution, however: everyone likes keen, hot, stylish puppies; your actions during this obedience teaching period should not be so heavy-handed that they spoil this zest. *It is easy to take the zip out of a youngster, and very difficult to replace it.*

Leash breaking. Furnish the pup with a light link choke collar for several days, until he forgets he has it on. Always put it on for his walks. It should be snug enough to go over his head and neck with room to insert two fingers. A loose chain collar can trap his lower jaw if he is alone and tries to chew it off. When he is at ease with the collar, snap a six-foot leash to both rings of the collar. Reactions will vary, depending on the dog's nature and age. Some buck at the end of the tether like a bronc coming out of a chute. Let them buck it out. Comfort them when they finish. Some larger and older dogs will want to drag you around like a sled dog. Set yourself carefully and firmly (or get some stout help) and bowl such a dog ass-over-tea-kettle a few times. After this show of strength, light short jerks should be sufficient. Other dogs think nothing of the leash. Allow your dog to drag his leash and become accustomed to it. Attach it routinely for walks and it will come to represent "good times" for him.

Sit. This is the critical command, the key to future learning and retrieving. Your aim is to impart the definition, but more important, the notion that sitting in itself is wonderful—that good things happen upon taking this position alertly. You don't want him to think it is restrictive, or that it *prevents* his having fun.

Some trainers use SIT and STAY as separate commands; I think a single command communicates your intentions best. Repeat the SIT command evenly; at the same time, tap the dog's hindquarters down with your hand or a light stick, while keeping his neck and forequarters vertically stable by lifting on your leash. You may gently depress his hind end with a light push of the hand, but a few light upward jerks on his collar are more functional. Choke collars are used to cause mild discomfort—not lynchings. You are seeking square, attentive posture. I regard hips askew, both legs out to one side, as unacceptable half-heartedness or insolence. Show him where his legs go. High praise and congratulations should accompany progress. After good sessions, the dog should be clapped in his kennel to absorb his lesson and dream about what a hell of a good dog he is.

Once the dog understands the command and the proper position, tell him to sit when you deliver his meals. Don't put his dish down until he does; then, feed and praise him. Hold up your index finger or point directly at him as you issue the verbal command, and fix him with your eyes. This will soon be his first learned hand signal. Eventually, he should learn to sit at this raised-finger sign without any audibles. All these applications will later be converted into the STOP-SIT at the long single blast from your training whistle.

At various times I have allowed my puppies, one at a time, to ride with me in the cab of my pickup. They want to look out the windows, check the instruments, and so on. I've directed them quietly to SIT as they stand on the seat. If they ignore the order I casually bang the brakes. They quickly learn that life is secure and smooth when they mind their boss. (They don't blame you for sailing them into the dashboard.) Later, on walks, when the pup is slightly more advanced and retrieving for you, give him a surprise SIT when he is off sniffing or hustling along several yards ahead of you. If he is exact and cooperative, pull a hidden bumper from your coat pocket and flip him an easy mark as a reward. Use your collar and leash until he is capable of obeying SIT consistently. Later, when the dog has learned to heel, the SIT command may be reinforced—especially if he remains capricious or stubborn about it. Walk him at heel in a straight line followed closely by a helper equipped with a stick. By prearrangement, the dog is struck firmly on the hind quarters at each verbal SIT or corresponding whistle toot. In this drill, the handler is friendly and passive beyond stopping and starting the walk. Sit your pup before crossing every gate, stone wall, bridge, and barbwire fence you encounter. Learning this routine etiquette will pay off greatly in upland gunning and can easily save his life around auto traffic. Shooting can be sorry enough when birds burst out as you are halfway through a fence with your gun open, but it is unforgivable for your dog to put up birds in the next field while you're still hung up in the wire.

A

B

C

The initial steps in teaching your pup to come. (A) The trainer gives her attentive pup the SIT cue, using voice, eye contact, and a raised finger. (B) She repeats the cue while backing away several yards, then breaks the SIT by (C) clapping and calls the pup to her with HERE or COME.

Come or "here." Attach a thirty-foot or longer nylon check cord to your pup. Firmly order him to sit, then back away slowly, facing him while holding him with your eyes, repeating "sit" at each retreating step. If he begins to follow you or to "creep" forward, pick him up and return him to the exact spot he has just left. Give him a light swat on the chest or rump if he persists. At three to five yards, call him to you with a firm but pleasant one-word command. If he hesitates or heads elsewhere, reel him in with the check cord and praise him. This should be done in a yard where there are few distractions. You might consider giving him a food reward when he comes to you perfectly. Repeat this drill frequently, varying the length of time he's held at SIT and increasing the distance between you as he succeeds. Then try the whole routine without the check cord. Use your raised finger SIT cue, eye contact, and voice; then drop your hands to knee level, clap, and call him. When he is a picture of virtue and can't wait to be called in to you (this may take weeks), disappear around the corner of a building or behind a tree (thus breaking eye contact) and call him. Keep him fresh and intrigued with this approach, but always be sure to enforce your intentions. (Older, spoiled, or outlaw dogs may require a great deal of pressure before they comply.) When your pup has advanced in this drill and is out and preoccupied on his walks, call a SIT *first,* to set his train of thought. After each successful SIT, hesitate, then call him in with much praise. The COME or HERE command will eventually be replaced with short, broken toots of the training whistle.

Heel. At the time you choose to teach the HEEL command you must decide on which side, left or right, you prefer to work your dog. This is most commonly determined by whether you shoot right- or left-handed. If you are right-handed, the dog should heel and deliver on your left, and vice versa.

　　HEEL is usually taught with a six-foot leash and a choke collar. Leash jerks steer the dog into a satisfactory walking position at your side. Praise him lightly while he occupies this approved "safe" zone. If he dallies on your right-hand side, move him to the "safe" position (snug off your left leg) with a light outside crack with a switch as you walk. He should not lag, lead, or pull you. After he has mastered this position completely, stop short and SIT him abruptly. Before you resume forward motion, say "Heel!" and then move out. Your aim is to achieve a militarylike marching drill.

　　When he has a patent grasp of stop and go—sit and heel—reverse your brisk walk with a quick **U**- or ninety-degree turn; sometimes turn away (right turn) from the dog as he heels at your left side with the command HEEL and a sharp jerk on the leash, or alternately make left turns by cutting your right

A

B

C

(A) Correct collar position. Use a light, link-choke collar and long leash in training your pup to heel. (B and C) Start forward evenly on HEEL, maintaining a steady position beside your left (or right) leg. Sudden crisp turns across his path (D) or away from him (E) force the pup to pay attention to you and your movements at all times.

D

E

A

B

Plant both feet evenly. (A) Step back with left foot while drawing the dog toward you and rearward. (B) Turn the dog with the leash, commanding HEEL, moving your left foot forward even with the right. (C) Jerk up on the collar, SIT. (D) Praise student.

C

D

knee across his path as you execute this change of direction. Vary the lengths and intervals between turns and move at a quick gait to keep him guessing which way you will head next. This forces the pup to concentrate on *you,* your direction, and his position. Employ light leash jerks, verbal commands, and encouragement throughout this drill. With enough practice and effort, he should be able to shadow you alertly while both of your hands are free and the training leash is draped over your shoulder or neck. When this lesson has been thoroughly learned, your student should be able to perform HEEL equally well *off* the leash. You may check his advancement by putting his food dish down and heeling him close by and past it several times. Reward his success with the meal.

Later, a crisp heeling drill can be used to "tune up" your dog and quickly capture his full attention before attacking more complicated and demanding tasks. The stop-sit and start-heel drill will also come into valuable play when you teach him to sit at the sound of your whistle and move with you, again, at the command HEEL. Finally, when he begins to mark multiple birds, it is the HEEL that will enable your dog to pivot and aim like a piece of artillery.

When your pup precisely executes SIT, HERE, and HEEL commands, it is possible to add another, a new cue that releases him for free time: to explore, relax, air himself, and have fun. The traditional command is HIE-ON, but any (such as OK) will do. I use GET-'EM-UP, an old exhortation lodged somewhere in me from deer hunts behind a pack of hounds long ago.

As your retriever finally reaches the point that he enters the field with you as a hunter himself, this serious command will come to mean go forward, make game, seek, use your nose. Further application of this cue, as he learns of your manner of hunting (upland) will be to "quarter" ahead of you, investigating matters within your gun range, and *not to follow* at heel unless directed there. When quartering a dog into a breeze (ideally in a sweeping, "windshield wiper" fashion), he should not come up from behind unless on a valid scent trail. If he does circle back, he will probably delude himself by whiffing whatever is carried in your game vest. Use your command to place him *before* your gun once more.

MARKING

Marking is the ability of a dog to observe the spot at which a flighted bird falls and to successfully retrieve it. This ability is the backbone of the retriever's work. The term originates in the expression "marking the fall," which was familiar in the English hunting tradition. A "single mark" refers to one downed bird; a "double" or "triple" indicates that two or three birds have fallen.

In training for hunting, dummies are usually substituted for birds. Today these are called *bumpers,* after the larger ones hung over the side of a yacht to protect the hull from bumping a pier. They are available at many sporting-goods stores in plastic or canvas form.

The Derby stake for young dogs is a field-trial contest limited to marking. Puppies six to twenty-four months of age are expected to come before two judges, exhibit *steadiness* (sit quietly unleashed, without starting the retrieve until commanded to do so), mark the fall of the shot bird, retrieve it, and deliver it to the handler.

I believe that marking is a natural ability, which may be enhanced through proper training. It is virtually impossible to instill this ability if the dog has no instinct for it. Some dogs are naturally "birdy"; others mark out of a desire to please you; and many simply enjoy carrying something in their mouth.

Your pup may show signs of wanting to mark as early as five weeks, but little is to be gained by starting before two and a half months. Even that is very young, and one should proceed slowly, since the pup's bones are not yet fully developed. When you start, use a low, pleasant surface, such as a lawn, with no hazards or surprises. Throw white bumpers—mouth-size, cylindrical vinyl or canvas dummies, or dead or clipped-wing white pigeons, onto this green "fast track." Hurrah your dog up into a small frenzy and throw them for him yourself until he gets the idea that he'll get another chance at a chase every time he brings the object back. If he is "birdy," take advantage of it. Some trainers turn pups loose in a full pigeon pen to build a manic birdiness. Using birds with clipped wings at the early training stage usually heightens the pursuits and the pups' pickup. Make sure you don't use large birds too soon, as a wing slap or a peck from a chicken or duck can easily dampen youthful enthusiasm. A veterinarian friend once directed his tough, powerhouse Field Champion, Wild Hearted Dinah, to rescue a sick wild swan for him. The big bird gave her a terrific wing-beating. Henceforth she refused to assist with all salvage work on "sick" swans.

If your dog wants to run off with thrown bumpers or birds, work him in an environment that is foreign to him and run away from him while calling to him. Or you may stand in front of his kennel door and throw single bumpers out in the yard. If he is possessive and wants to hoard the retrieved article, he'll have to turn it in to you as he comes toward his "bedroom." Similarly, he can do little water retrieves in a pond with only one entrance and exit point on the bank or through the surrounding vegetation, so you are sure to end up with

Marking a single flyer. The second dog (Lab) honors for the working dog (Golden).

the bird. The direct-return routine may be enhanced by throwing the bumper out from the tip of a point of land that thrusts into a lake. Most youngsters will swim back to the closest shore—where you congratulate him and receive the bumper as he exits from the water. You eventually want him to understand that all these bumpers, dummies, and birds are *your* personal property and he is allowed to use them purely out of your generosity. A long check cord and collar may be necessary to reel him in. If the dog happens to fasten hard and kill the bird he carries, don't jump on him and crush his enthusiasm. Simply pinch his upper lip against a canine tooth to remove the bird or bumper from his jaws.

Keep your working sessions short, particularly on warm days away from water. I've found that seven or eight minutes without the advantage of a cool-off swim or rest (in the heat) is about maximum for one burst and for positive achievement with my dogs. The learning level and interest threshold is highest when a dog is warmed up, yet fresh. A tired or out-of-shape pupil is likely to be sloppy and imprecise. Set an alarm clock on the hood of your truck if you have to. Stamina is not something automatic but a quality to be built up gradually.

Another important reason for not working a young dog too long for marks, especially in medium or rough cover, is that it can easily lead him into the habit of poor "pickup"—that is, standing over the bird before dawdling back with it. By the time these dogs finally locate the bird or bumper they are tired, exasperated, and bored. They try to catch a breath before the return trip or take a leak as they relax on their way in. For a well-started dog, a loose banty rooster flighted into medium-light cover can induce a jolt of interest and liven up his pickup as well. The rooster will squawk and start a foot race as the dog draws a bead on his target, and will also fly out of his mouth if he stops and plays around on the return. A natural, flamboyant pickup of a bird is a thing of beauty, but all dogs are not equally talented or skilled in the art.

For a substantial amount of physical conditioning for older dogs on back roads, I use a bicycle, with my dog heeling alongside. (I've taught the dogs to heel carefully to a horse or bicycle.) As another way of improving a lackadaisical pickup, I ride along at twenty miles per hour, heel the dog, and throw a bumper out ahead of us. I command him to fetch it, and, as we pass it, I pedal furiously, blowing a COME IN whistle and commanding HEEL.

Some trainers warn against marking a youngster uphill for fear of slowing him down. Contrarily, I think a real hot pup won't notice an uphill sprint; neither will he be aware of his rapid return, as gravity pours him swiftly back to you. The added exercise is also good for his legs and lungs.

The learning level and interest threshold are highest when a dog is warmed up, yet fresh.

Before starting any work session, thoroughly "air" the dog—let him empty his bladder and bowels. This is a true safety precaution, removing one more excuse for him to delay his hunt and muck up a speedy return. Also, be sure the ropes attached to the dummies are not so long that they trip him up and slow his return momentum.

There are forceful methods of speeding up a return, but the above suggestions should suffice with a keen student.

A great marker discriminates with a pair of laser-beam eyes, and records what he sees in a cameralike way. As you train and devise marks for your dog, remind yourself that you are encouraging him to rely on his eyes. Old dogmen know that if you show a dog how to use his eyes, he'll figure out what his nose is good for soon enough. I've shot birds and thrown marks for many National or Amateur National Champions, River Oaks Corky, Kannonball Kate, River Oaks Rascal, Ray's Rascal, Shadow of Otter Creek, San Joaquin Honcho, Wanapum Dart's Dandy—and the one attribute they all shared in the field was that they come out looking.

To be sure, some really hot pups may ricochet all over a good light-cover training field before they settle down to look or mark. This is an exuberant celebration of *running,* not seeking. Use this athletic joy and channel it into self-assurance and accuracy. I have found if you throw into even, light, or medium cover three separate, short (forty-foot), white-bird singles that the dog cannot possibly miss; he will get the idea that you and he are going *marking* today, not just hot-rodding all over the acreage. After that, let him rest to catch his breath, and *then* start his first substantial single mark of the day.

Remember, too, that as your dog marks, barking and squealing can be corrected with your QUIET command. Don't *send* at all until he understands the rule: The retrieve is the reward for silence.

Retrieving distances should be a main consideration during early marking. Most people tend to train pups on marks that are short, then longer, and finally quite long before they depart for home and kennel. I prefer to begin short, move to longer ones, then back to short distances. Similarly, I employ single marks first, sometimes mild doubles, then back to singles. If you work up to forty-yard marks on Monday, it isn't necessary to start at forty on Tuesday and get up to sixty, then go from sixty to eighty on Wednesday. Keep it comfortable for him at this stage; don't make a mystery out of marking. After your pup has been acclimated to gunfire (see pp. 103–104), it's a good idea to start and finish a marking session with a shot flyer single to keep his attitude and accuracy high.

6

Force-Fetch Training and Steadying Your Dog

BEACHED BUFFLEHEAD DRAKE

There comes a time in the course of a pup's development when he simply must learn certain rules if he is to have any future as a serious working retriever. The force-fetch period is one.

As the term implies, this involves the deliberate use of force on the dog. Though force and pressure may sometimes be required in other areas, depending on individual dogs and special circumstances, this is one instance where I feel force is justified as a routine training method. (Routine, that is, for the *working* retriever; if your dog is a city-bound companion or a decorative bench dog meant for show, the force-fetch phase would be a needless burden for both of you, and should be skipped.)

I'll readily admit that undertaking a project of deliberate pain for a promising young dog is unpleasant. Indeed, I tend to shy away from the whole matter of forcing such a pup with the same distaste I feel in facing a dentist's appointment—or, for that matter, in facing the prospect of writing about it here.

But it is necessary, especially to a hunter. Many retrievers, who otherwise work well, will suddenly *blink* (ignore or overlook) a bird if it is too shot up, or fluttering, or too cold and stiff, or the water is too cold, too wet, swift, or noisy, or if he feels his labor union forbids it.

If force-fetch is correctly taught, the trainer gains allegiance and added respect for all his voice commands. The dog's personality, verve, courage, and style are not diminished—though there may be brief, temporary lapses. Force-fetch, in fact, usually enhances the style of a dog's performance by instilling in him confidence in his work and dispelling any confusion of responsibility or any question as to who holds the ultimate authority.

Force-fetch work *won't* make a dog mean, but during the course of it, personality traits that had previously been only latent can be brought to the surface. At graduation time, you and your dog will both know a lot more and have a better feel for each other. You should know for certain if he's physically tough and mentally sensitive, or pleasing and bright, or stubborn, or stupid. And your dog in return will realize that you, the master, are prepared to back him down by pressure and perseverance.

Force-fetch helps dogs excel and feel solid on the memory birds in their double and multiple marks. The final benefit is the most important of all: if you have to punish your dog for any of a wide range of field sins—flushing birds too far ahead, refusing to enter water, giving up his hunt on a mark, bank-running, refusing to pick up a wet, soggy bird or a plastic bumper after retrieving shot birds, and *breaking* (leaving to retrieve before he's sent)—FETCH is the basic command to resume work. It means hunt, retrieve something, and GO. With the FETCH command, you are demanding that the dog hit the accelerator after a red light—that he *go* again after a correction, despite his discouragement.

I've rationalized in the past against "force methods" by recalling certain highly successful competitive dogs that had been spared them. One of my own favorites was deliberately exempted from the process because of his obvious and natural retrieving prowess—only to become retarded and sour later, directly due to his having missed this training. To restore his abilities, we had to go through a special and far more anguishing "crash" force program.

I'm convinced that force training is the primary foundation for a retriever's life work. And a worthwhile undertaking, even if you—like me—have to force yourself to force-train your dog.

FORCE TRAINING

Several conditions should be favorable before you even begin to force-train. The pup should be at least six months old and have his permanent teeth, so there will be no teething tenderness about his mouth and gums. He should be entirely healthy, with his ears clean and free of irritation or tenderness due to infection. He must have his obedience work down perfectly; must heel, sit, and come when he is called. Be certain beforehand that you have a happy, ambitious retriever who loves to go and bring back endless shot birds and bumpers, with joy and élan.

Once you've begun, do your teaching in the same place every time—and *never* in the field. Choose a garage, a yard space, even a single closed room where you can be alone and free from distraction and interference. Ideally, use short sessions in the same place at the same time, twice or more often a day.

Discontinue the pleasure of all field training and bird work during this force-training period; this will help prevent the dog's identifying any misfortunes with those activities. As a reward and a device to help pull him out of any possible depression or funk, resume the flow of bird work immediately after his graduation.

To avoid associating pain with bumpers, some trainers prefer to substitute a wooden dowel instead, or some other alien object. I dismiss this as unnecessary and use a bumper with the throwing rope removed.

Remember at all times that a hot temper and overzealousness are your enemies as well as your dog's. Try always to use a firm, calm tone of voice command.

Try, too, to make every lesson progressive, a clear step forward in accomplishment; aim to limit each lesson to five minutes. This frankly isn't always possible. You want to end up each lesson as the undisputed boss, and it may well take more than fifteen minutes to do so if your dog happens to be in an obstinate mood. Never quit until you've outlasted and mastered his obstinacy. Different animals require varying amounts of time to absorb this routine. Overall, three weeks is the average duration. Mark the calendar and carefully monitor your progress.

Your timing sense and ability to "read" your dog are most important during these sessions. If you slide through this fetch program without a hitch of resistance, you have probably failed to reach or deeply impress your dog. A certain battle of wills should be expected and even welcomed. Be generous with voice encouragement, and let the dog understand exactly what you want, session by session. Remember that everything can't be taught at once; this is a routine to be pieced together, one segment upon another.

Different breeds of retrievers will differ in the way they accept force. Goldens, for example, seem to resent pain more than others; in the opinion of many professionals, they can be the most stubborn if not the toughest to force-break.

At this juncture of training any dog—no matter what his breeding—may show himself to be a fear biter, however smooth and gentle the procedure. Some dogs react defensively and retaliate by biting. If this fear biting becomes chronic, it is better for the serious trainer to get rid of the dog and find a more suitable candidate. Almost every true fear biter will eventually prove too mentally delicate, too defensively selfish, for the rigors and pressures that lie ahead in hunting or field-trial work. And such a dog's weakness can be a direct physical danger to you and others. You want a dog whose desire to retrieve is greater than his resentment of discomfort.

Ideally, you should arrange to watch an expert amateur or professional go about the business of force training before proceeding yourself with your first little genius. If you are at all unsure, have a proven professional help your dog through this vital process, smoothly and correctly.

The accompanying photo and text sequence should give a clear idea of how to proceed through the force-fetch training regimen.

Fully expect your dog to balk at any time during force-fetch training. (When he does so, you will learn where his refusal point is; then you can anticipate the problem and work on it.) The pup may do perfect fetch work three times, then refuse to cooperate on the fourth, or give eight greats, then say "to hell with it" on the ninth. Try not to mistake an early willingness for training success. Eventually the dog should be 100 percent clear about his role—what is expected of him, what he is to do—and about his handler's commands. Be certain that every step is fully understood and digested before advancing. Stay sensitive and alert to his mental attitude and changes.

Remember that gun dogs, meant primarily to be hunting companions, may require a less demanding force-fetch program than field-trial candidates.

After graduation from the yardwork stage of fetch training, pour on the real birds and drill on the FETCH-COME-HEEL-SIT-HOLD-DROP sequence thoroughly in the field. The dog will revel and take pride in it; your birds will arrive promptly and be deposited in your hand.

A

C

B

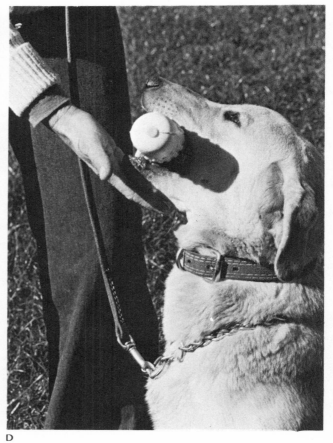

D

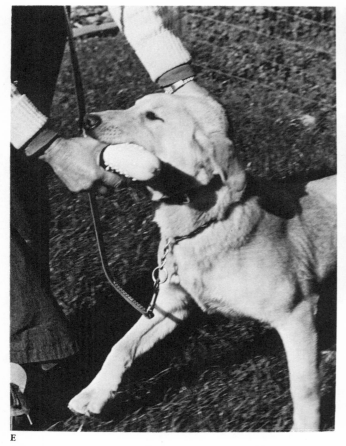

E

F

G

A. You will need a six-foot leash, a choke collar, and a heavy, snugly fitting work collar. Start off with a quick, attention-getting tune-up by going through the heeling drill.

B. The HOLD command. Grip the dog's muzzle and pinch his lip against his canine tooth to make him open his mouth. Then place the bumper in his mouth. A bumper with the rope removed is preferable.

C. Show him that you *want* the bumper in his mouth. Hold it there with your thumb around the bumper and your fingers under his jaw. The dog may balk during this "hold" stage and a disagreeable confrontation may occur, but you are in complete control; your other hand is at the back of his neck, gripping the collar. The release command is GIVE, OUT, or DROP, when you remove the bumper from his jaws.

D. He is holding the bumper and you are in a position to tap him firmly under the chin with each repeated command, or each time he tries to spit it out.

E. Walking with the "hold" intact. Have the dog walk, stop, sit, and then proceed.

F. He knows what you want and is pleased and proud to do it. He can now move with you and "sit" as he carries out the HOLD command. HOLD must be totally mastered before you proceed to the FETCH command. If he learns to obey the SIT and HOLD commands during the first two or three days of this procedure, he is making good progress. Do not rush him immediately to other steps.

G. Begin preparation for the FETCH command: with the dog at your left, slip the fingers of your left hand under his collar. Notice that the collar is wide, snug, and high up behind his ears, and is not apt to twist.

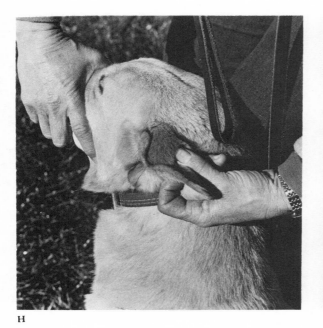
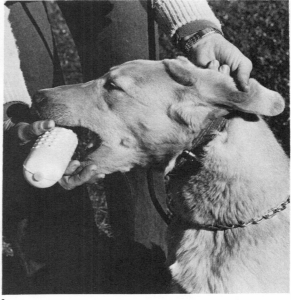

H   I

H. In this position you will be able to pinch the dog's "outside" or left ear, using the thumb and first two fingers of your left hand.

I. The key to the entire force-fetch discipline. Give the command FETCH and simultaneously pinch the ear continuously and hard. As the dog opens his mouth to protest or cry, place the bumper in the mouth and *instantly* relax the pinch pressure. This is the "it-feels-so-good-when-it-stops" principle. In the course of command and repetition, the dog will feel relieved and secure when he is holding a "fetched" bumper in his jaws.

J. Here, the bumper is held farther away from the dog's mouth. He will learn to *reach* for it on the ear-pinch FETCH command, and to hold it afterward with absolute dependability.

K. This requires the dog to reach slightly farther. If he drops the bumper or spits it out, shorten the distance until he functions smoothly again. Backtrack to the HOLD command, and have him maintain this position for a solid minute or two, as reinforcement.

L. This step is usually a big one in the force-fetch procedure. Hold the bumper at a slightly greater distance than before, with one end touching the ground. Even though your dog has been obediently reaching and snapping the bumper out of your hand, he may very well rebel at picking up the bumper from the ground. The solution is to go back and repeat the preceding steps, until his performance is satisfactory for FETCH, HOLD, and DROP.

M. Now the pup has almost mastered his force-fetch training. He is moving to fetch the bumper off the ground, at a distance.

N. Graduation. The pup will now work his way through a stack or pile of bumpers—far exceeding his previous limits of interest—because his boss is directing him to work. He is learning to learn.

TEACHING YOUR DOG TO BE STEADY

Soon after the force-fetch period of training, your dog will be ready to be "steadied," or "staunched"—that is, not to dash away and start to retrieve until he is *sent*. Steadiness is no less important in shooting birds in the field than it is in trials. One important reason for this is that the dog who holds his enthusiasm in check and awaits the handler's command to go has more time to mark subsequent birds if more than one is downed, and to carry out a double or triple retrieve.

Steadiness should be taught only *after* your dog has learned to fetch—to *go*. The "steady" training period should start when the dog is approximately eight to ten months old. Up until then, the pup has been allowed to "break" (leave to retrieve before being sent) or has been restrained from "running in" to the field for his marks by leash and collar or by being held at the shoulders. He has been released on his call name or other verbal cue. (A dog's call name, "Billy" or "Sam," is his *individual* release command to retrieve. "Fetch" is the *universal* command for the same response. By using the individual's name, one hunter may send his dog on a mark without releasing his partner's dog as well.) Be sure to choose a short, simple name that won't conflict with the similar sounds of other commands, for example, "Teal" and "heel," "Nora" and "no," or "Sidney" and "sit." Avoid any name that might conflict with the common numbers that a trial judge might call for your dog, for example, "Ken" and "ten," and which could result in inadvertently sending your dog prematurely.

I've discussed the necessity of your dog's performing well on the SIT or STAY command. Now is the time for an important application of it. Before a "steady" session, conduct a reminder session by asking your dog to sit promptly a number of times as you walk briskly with him on a leash.

Take the dog to a fresh location, firmly order him to SIT, and have a helper throw a short mark—a white bumper, for instance—on open ground. Any attempt by the dog to retrieve should be met with a stiff verbal reminder to SIT, and a leash jerk. The helper picks up the bumper and the approach is repeated. Once you begin these lessons, a break must *never* be tolerated again.

This drill is an exercise in pure concentration for your dog. When he can remember to *sit* long enough to watch the throw and the arc of the fall, send him quickly at first; then, gradually, begin to stretch the delay time after the throw hits the ground as he learns to *remember* SIT longer and to *listen* for his release.

A

B

C

D

E

This pup has advanced to the point that he performs all the steps in retrieving without leash and collar. The trainer uses voice, eye contact, and physical cues for (A) HERE, (B) HEEL, indicating proper side, (C) SIT, (D) HOLD, (E) DROP, right hand below jaw. Don't grab.

Some trainers believe sending a dog fast helps teach concentration; others prefer a long delay. I believe that younger pups should be sent fast, to keep them keen, but that eventually you should vary the interval. Let him drag the leash or check cord. If the dog hesitates to go, send him on FETCH.

As with force-fetch training, schedule short sessions, twice a day if possible, on easy singles. When the dog seems to have mastered this step, advance to easy doubles. These often precipitate a break toward the second mark. Remember that *any* movement toward a fall increases the chance of a break, and lifting or shifting the hindquarters just about guarantees it. This movement is known as *creeping*. Never reward the dog for creeping or breaking by sending him. Always return him to the spot and discipline him—verbally or physically or both—while the helper picks up the bird. Then try the exercise again.

When your dog seems to grasp the mechanics of SIT (stop), MARK the bird, FETCH, or GO when his name is called, shift directly to live birds on open ground—an unshackled banty rooster parading close by, for example, and then ducks thrown in open water. If the dog moves out before you send him, nail him. Your command must govern his wishes. If he does remain steady, reward him by sending him to get the bird. Add two 12-gauge shotgun pops to further heighten this test; he must be steady to birds and shot.

When he can remain steady for a noisy double, try simply passing the loop end of the leash through his collar, catching it with your forefinger and holding eight or ten inches of leash taut as he watches the mark being thrown. If he is steady, send him on his cue and simultaneously release your "trigger" finger.

Some trainers prefer to tie one end of a check cord to their truck, or a tree, the other end to the dog, leaving a few extra coils alongside him. (If you try this, include a bicycle tire inner tube in this tether as a shock absorber, to be sure the dog doesn't snap his neck.) If the dog breaks, he travels several yards at speed before he is suddenly upended (at the same time, you again command him to SIT or STAY). He must then try the test again. When he finally learns to sit still to mark, he may be sent by opening a quick-release catch on his leash; or the handler may stand on the check cord and shift his weight off it as he releases his dog—but this is a good way to end up on your tail. Some trainers employ both methods. Finally, you may want to keep a short six- or eight-inch rope with an end knot permanently dangling from the dog's collar as a ready handle for restraint and release; it will also help you in teaching him to pivot well on doubles.

Whatever the method employed, good, accurate practice brings clean results. Eventually the dog can be trusted to do all his retrieving work without leash or collar, controlled only by your voice or whistle.

WET COATS

At this stage in your dog's training you may want to add another command—*when* to shake the water from his coat. This will be especially helpful if you wear eyeglasses when shooting, or duck hunt from a pit blind.

As your dog delivers the bird after a water mark, simply give an exaggerated SIT command with your raised forefinger and verbally remind him to maintain a continuous SIT. As he hands you his bird (when the urge to shake is greatest), step in front and face him, still insisting he SIT. Change your raised hand into a traffic-cop stop gesture, then waggle it left and right at the wrist, issuing the new command of SHAKE or OK to release him from SIT. He will immediately do so instinctively, but button down this routine with discipline, timing, and the SHAKE cue after all water work, and your duck hunting will be much drier.

7

Derby Training: The Second Phase

CINNAMON TEAL HEN

Now that your pup has mastered the basic obedience commands and perhaps force-fetch, you may begin more advanced early training in which the trainer simulates actual Derby trial or simple hunting conditions. The dog becomes accustomed to hearing the sound of gunfire and to working with a thrower or gunner. Many trainers reciprocate this service for each other's retrievers. Professionals generally employ "bird boys" who either throw or shoot. Your dog will advance gradually from short single marks on flat terrain to more distant doubles and triples on rough ground and in water.

Many young dogs in their first retrieving efforts have difficulty gauging the distance to faraway marks. They run only to the vicinity of the gunner. To remedy this typical behavior, for most Derby-age dogs I recommend a forty-five-degree back throw (a throw farther away; see diag. 2). I usually provide this kind of mark up to the dogs' fourteenth month and avoid throwing a jumble of other marks at varying angles, that is, "square" or "flat" (meaning throws of ninety degrees), birds thrown somewhat toward the dog, which are called "in-birds," and straight throws "back" that prevent the dog from recognizing the arc of the birds' or bumpers' flight. The forty-five-degree back mark teaches him to think deep, run bravely, and carry past the bird thrower. This helps him pass by the misleading scent of the bird box (near the thrower), especially on cross-wind marks. This makes his guesses pay off and so builds confidence.

When retrieving a shackled duck—one whose legs and wings have been firmly tied—in open water, any angle throw is reasonable.

Vary the length of these forty-five-degree throws from average dead bird throws to Olympian sixty-yard tosses (Canadians used to hurl dead birds with a lacrosse stick for extra distance), with little reference to the thrower's position. If you should get "square" or "in" throws in a field-trial Derby, too bad; don't start spraying in-birds all over the countryside in your practice sessions. Wait until your dog is damned deadly, then advance to other designs. If, however, he develops a tendency to run *too* deep, the cover or field hazards are probably preventing a clean, *visible* payoff. Here is a simple cure that can help him to use his head and eyes (see diag. 2, right-hand section):

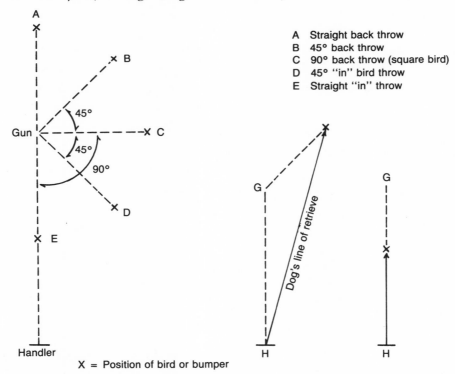

A   Straight back throw
B   45° back throw
C   90° back throw (square bird)
D   45° "in" bird throw
E   Straight "in" throw

X = Position of bird or bumper

Diagram 2. Marking angles. To vary a routine of 45° back marks, occasionally provide your dog with a straight "in" thrown bird (E).

When setting up puppy marks, always have the thrower or gunner placed visibly in the field *before* the dog comes to the *line* (the predesignated spot you wish to work from). Teach him that it is his job to quickly look, locate, and register these throwing positions. Throwers should always face the direction they intend to throw and continue to do so while the dog is working. Hold the pup under his front legs and across his chest, use the cue MARK! in pointing out the throwers; when he focuses on them, signal to have the mark thrown immediately. A thrower should holler HEY! HEY! to get the dog's full attention just before he lofts the bird. If your pup has been acclimated to gunfire (see pp. 103–104), pop with a .22 blank pistol or 12-gauge shotgun before the throw. Do not allow a pup to casually watch you set up a training test. Develop a familiar routine and cadence. Bring him to the line—locate the gunner—mark the bird—release him on his name—retrieve—then put him away in his crate, or repeat and correct him on the same test if he's imperfect. Encourage him to concentrate on the most difficult bird (known as the *key bird*) to be thrown. Make him memorize what he saw and be confident in it. Congratulate him when he does well.

Do not throw "mommas and poppas" or "fountains," that is, more than one bird from the same gun station, or two single retrieves on each side of a bird thrower. This encourages hunting the wrong side of the gun and looking back to the gunner for another bird after the first one is down. Some trainers like to shoot several live birds from the same gun position as singles with slightly different falls. I think this is a fine sharpening drill for *advanced* dogs.

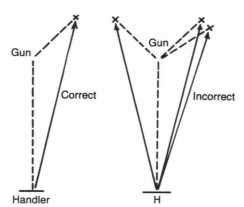

Diagram 3. Marking.

Here is a sound single-mark drill for youngsters: Have your helper throw a dummy or bird forty-five degrees back and retrieve it with your dog. As he is coming in to you with it, instruct the thrower to move to the exact spot of that fall; then, when the pup is set to go again, throw another forty-five-degree mark. This can be continued for a half dozen consecutive retrieves, and tends to discourage the dog from returning to "old falls," since each retrieve is onto fresh ground. It also makes him travel a bit farther with each throw, perhaps without realizing it.

ADDING ELEMENTS TO THE MARK

Change of cover. There are three basic kinds of change of cover or visual barriers, plus variations. They are diagrammed here:

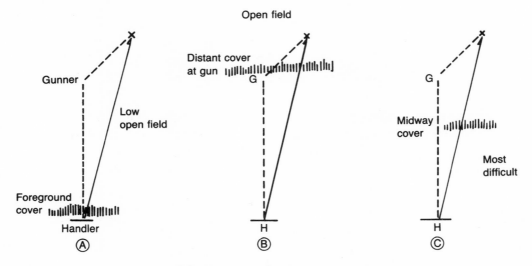

Diagram 4. Working with cover.

On a fairly fast surface, where a light bird or bumper should be visible, find a wall of tall grass or light brush and use it. In the course of your pup's training you or your helper should throw hundreds of marks to familiarize him with these three simple A-B-C cover hazards. Use a long check cord if you have to reel him in and send him again. He should perform these marks masterfully on land before addressing them in water.

If your dog avoids the cover problem, a growl of disapproval (like the protest made when you chomp down on No. 4 lead shot during a duck dinner) is more effective than simply saying no. Move closer to the mark and simplify and repeat the exercise until your dog cooperates and understands your expectations. Below are some advanced configurations, to be attempted *only* after your dog has mastered the above A-B-C.

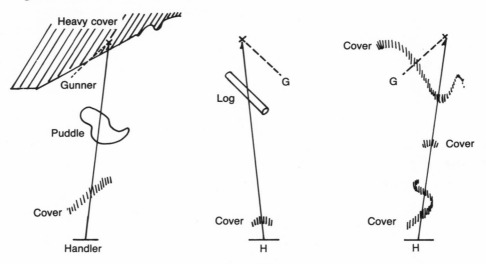

Diagram 5. Additional elements and the mark.

Adding elements to the mark. With marks in heavy cover, across ditches, on steep hillsides, and so on, I often point with my hand to show my dog the direction of the approved (straight) route to the bird. To demonstrate this concept further, I sometimes set up benches and lawn furniture in the backyard, then direct him straight over them in the correct manner, to a bumper.

The return of the retrieve should be as perfect as the outgoing line. Maintain eye contact. A good straight return is at least half of the value on a training retrieve (and some trainers believe it's 80 to 90 percent of the job). A "banana" or curving return line obliterates all the dog accomplished on the way to the bird. A clean, straight return line emphasizes and reinforces these virtues—demonstrating to both of you that he truly understands and is willing to go straight. At this point, you are fostering good habits that will serve you well with future, complicated multiple marks and blinds. An advanced dog, no matter how good a marker, returning on a crooked, sloppy line with his first bird of a triple or quadruple mark will most likely *cancel* in his memory the lines to the remaining downed birds in the field.

A louder variation of the normal COME whistle should be developed on your whistle. This extraordinary *threat* chirp is useful in reminding the student of your presence as he returns through difficult, *avoidable* cover or water. Go out and meet him; stop him at the point of swerve and show him the correct route by segments of the line. Repeat come-in routes until they are perfect, regardless of pinpoint marking or precise outgoing lines. Walk through the hazard yourself, then call him through in your footsteps. Use high praise and compliments as he succeeds.

It is important to watch not only your dog's route as he marks but also his style as he does so. Dogs that place their forelegs forward and their chins on the ground limit their true marking ability. Discourage this from becoming part of their "finished style" by not tolerating it in puppyhood, even though it appears to be caused by zealousness. Use a collar and leash and hold him erect as he marks. Don't release him to retrieve in this low sprinter position—it reduces his depth perception in tall grass and often obscures the mark completely.

Teaching by adding new elements to emphasize a concept should not lead you to push your dog too fast. I feel more comfortable with a pup that is marking well but is otherwise undertrained at seven months than with one that is overtrained, so long as his appetite for work is keen. Try not to *test* and push him beyond his limits. If you set up overly complicated marks, you may invite error. Avoid this if you wish the dog to carry out the drill perfectly. In some instances, however, you may deliberately set up a mark in which you know he will fail in order to show him the right way and correct him effectively. (For an example of this approach, see "corn cobbing," p. 146.)

Memory stretchers and multiples. One of the toughest deterrents to a good, solid mark is another mark. Keep in mind that an A-plus on a difficult single is worth more than a C-plus on an average double in training. At this stage, A-plus on a respectable training double (which includes one good "memory bird") is worth more than *any* triple. I don't train on triples at the Derby stage and find that many people who do are simply titillating themselves with pride over their new puppy, or fantasizing over what he'll be doing at one year if he can do a triple at five months. You rarely hear of these dogs again, because after such intense early training, they are so overburdened that they are rejected, and often sold to some unsuspecting hunter.

Many fine trainers, however, do believe in throwing a good dose of double marks to a young pup, three to six months old. At this age I recommend only enough multiples to determine whether your pup has a second-bird memory.

Start with one mark north and another in the south. Later, stand at the corner of a building or an unused road intersection and throw one bird along one side of the building, another bird along the other side. When the dog retrieves the first bird he *has* to return to you first, before heading for the second.

Use the most dramatic bird (a flyer) as the memory bird. When you are convinced your dog can remember the vicinity of a second mark, trust him and return to singles. If you insist on checking your dog out periodically with multiples, handler-throw five or more dummies spread wide, in open view, and have him pick them up in varying sequences. Repeat this exercise several times.

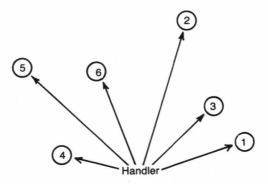

Diagram 6. A handler-thrown multiple mark.

Another good way to stretch the concentration of a confident young marking dog is to have the thrower "retire" or "disappear" on the key bird of a double. The equivalent occurs in hunting when another shooter reveals himself briefly as he stands and fires from a duck blind, then sits down again—thus retiring from view into the habitat. The thrower may disappear behind a tree or bush, for example, as the dog is retrieving the other mark. This encourages the dog to mark the fall specifically, since he can no longer depend on the presence of the thrower to find the key bird. Use trees, rocks, or bushes as natural reference points to help the dog maintain his bearings. Keep retired marks short when your pup is young and learning to recall the location of the second bird. A weak job is indicated when the dog tentatively remembers only where the thrower stood, and then eventually noses out the mark. The most difficult retired marks (to be avoided at this stage) are lengthy downwinders thrown in a vast sweep of unchanging pasture or cropland.

A fine training tool for quasi-retired marks and many other aspects of marking is the gas-powered bumper gun. This hand-held device pops a dummy varying distances, depending on the load, by the force of a .22 blank. Some models are capable of shooting several marks. This tool is also a good primer for early line running.

Another memory-stretching drill for your fine-marking dog involves delaying him briefly between the time the birds are down and the time he is allowed to retrieve them. Heel him in a 360-degree pivot after his birds are down, or take him off behind a truck for a second; return him to the spot where he watched the marks, then send him. This drill demands clarity and certainty in marking.

Here are some configurations that are natural memory stretchers. They help a dog look deep and look up (which he doesn't do naturally) and memorize the ground over which he must travel.

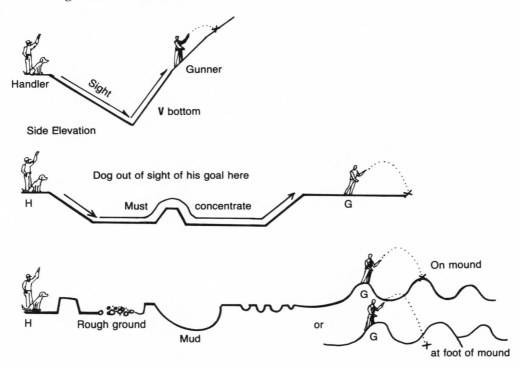

Diagram 7. Memory stretchers.

A good handler should recognize the challenges of tough terrain *before* he runs his dog. Think of your dog's view as he contends with rough going; like an expert dirt-bike rider, he is deciding, adjusting, and negotiating hazardous terrain at speeds of twenty to thirty miles per hour. Try to remember this as you stand there passively, hands in your pockets, ready to criticize him.

I like to mark in hills, as suggested in diagram 7. They can provide substantial training for every working retriever. Below is a diagram for *surprise water.* It's a favorite, and I use it whenever I can find it in a training field.

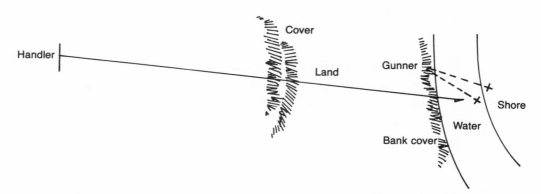

Diagram 8. Surprise water. The gunner throws the bird conspicuously into water or on the far shore.

Use plenty of white dummies and light-colored birds. Don't send the dog for any mark he hasn't seen fall. Bands of black electrician's tape on a bumper can help accent it against a poor background of trees or fog. Gray and red (less easily seen) dummies may be introduced as your dog advances. Supply an abundance of absolute downwind marks for the *eye* and the *heart,* not the nose.

Ultimately, you will find there are two basic ways to teach marking—the *hard* way and the *other* way. In the former, you ask your dog to perform doubles, triples, and so on "cold," as set up. Only when he fails do you show him the difficulties, mark by single mark, and how to deal with mistakes due to the terrain. This method pushes him unrehearsed and unassisted into the field by dint of his own determination, force, trained responsibility, or fear of failure. The burden of completion is on the dog. In the *other* way, you build marks; for example, you might set a triple, but run it first as singles. Only on the rerun do you ask the dog to perform the complete triple, possibly with such added difficulties as "retiring" the thrower or gunner. This method *pulls* the dog into the field by enticement—the promise of the easy, natural excitement of hot birds. The difficulties of such a test are demonstrated to him *before* he commits errors. If you use this approach, your dog is temporarily relieved of the burden of full responsibility.

As you approach more complicated tasks, remember, if you train more than one dog, to rotate the running order so each dog takes turns pioneering a job.

WATER

Although no serious water work should be attempted until your pup can manage simple land elements well, you should get him accustomed to water at an early age. Try to create the illusion that there is no elemental difference between land and water. Swim with him yourself or use hip boots or waders and walk in and out without pause; include walking considerable distances *in* water with your pup tagging along. Short-thrown ducks, unshackled, in a foot of water, or shackled ducks in deep water with an easy entry are great rewards for getting wet. (In the latter case, the duck's legs and wings are tied with strips of cloth or surveyor's tape, surgical tubing, or rubber strips cut from inner tubing in a manner that is firm, yet allows good circulation. One or two retrieves for a duck are usually plenty, even with a soft-mouthed dog—the bird is then released to dry out.) Because ducks are more gratifying to the retriever than bumpers, one professional training friend of mine uses ducks exclusively for all water marks.

With a very young dog, water retrieves of any distance should be in large puddles from approximately three to ten inches deep. This allows the pup to believe he is as fast in the water as he is on land, with no need to skirt or avoid it. Shorten the distance and rerun the retrieve if he does. Send the dog and receive the bird yourself in the middle of the water, thereby demonstrating your own amphibiousness.

No icy stuff! It is far too early to be checking a young dog's pain and tolerance thresholds with very cold water. Rather, I like to deliberately overheat the dog on land and then allow him to play in the water and cool off. Make the water his friend.

When dealing with *big water* it is good to remember that a lot of the behavior we eventually expect of our dogs is *unnatural* to them. They are not polar bears! My fourteen-year-old son and I took four very fine swimming Labradors out on an Indian-summer evening for a gang splash. We drove to a large lake in the hills and dove in. The water was warm, the winds had died, leaving the lake's surface like a looking glass. In our exuberance we decided to swim to the nearest point on the opposite shore, half a mile away, and encouraged the dogs to follow. Because of a lack of conditioning, I was the weakest member of the team. At roughly seven hundred yards I decided to give my still-frolicking son a speech on energy conservation and how I couldn't help much if any of us took a lungful of water. The dogs were bobbing and circling tightly around us; their swimming and breathing were very relaxed, but I noticed their eyes were anxious and worried, as if a primitive sense was signaling danger. I felt it too. In afterthought, I realized this reaction was due in part to the long distance. More important, though, it was unnatural for the dogs to swim without a *known destination.* If the work purpose is *clear,* dogs retrieving over great distances or in heavy weather from a boat, blind, or shore can overcome their doubts because a destination—a downed bird, whether marked or unseen—exists to reward them.

Never throw a mark into deep tules (bulrushes, or cattails). Throw into clear water in front of them or behind them. Never throw onto small islands, which would cause your dog to *land.* Throw the mark in front of or past an island, where the swim line directly to the bird is conspicuous and thus more inviting than landing. Similarly, I feel that it is poor practice at this stage to throw onto points of land. Throw only in front of, or past them. Even though you will encounter water marks on islands or points of land in Derbys, in major stakes, and in hunting, I don't think that preparing for them is worth the temptations and shoddy habits they spawn.

In water training, make a habit of blowing your COME IN whistle one to one and a half yards *before* your dog reaches the bird. This "preminds" him of the water route he came by and how he should return. It's also preventive medicine for bank-running.

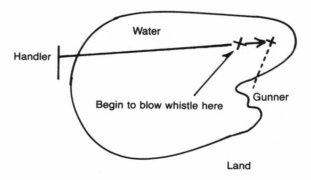

Diagram 9. Early water marking.

Your dog's swims should be short at first, with easy entry. Increase swim lengths as his confidence grows, adding islands, points, floating logs, tules, and floating cover. Supply plenty of ducks. Use two shots (see "gunfire," pp. 103–104) on these marks occasionally, in preparation for areas with echoes, which might confuse your dog. Back off from the water several yards to train your dog to make a *big* entry with a running start, and work closer to the water's edge for control of bank-running. Many pups have a zesty, vaulting, high entry into the water that is enjoyable to watch, while others prefer to hit the water low and hard with their chests. I think the latter style shows a dog who naturally trusts the water, but both these approaches are preferable to a mincing, splashless entry.

A decent water entry can be encouraged by sending hastily on a series of "quickie" marks, each thrown a distance of a few body lengths, just out of jumping range. These bumpers or birds should be tossed in deep water from a firm shore with an abrupt or undercut bank one or two feet high, and no beach. Your aim is to tantalize your pup into thinking he can jump onto the target in *one* leap, rather than in *two* stages—first entering and then swimming to it. Sending from a floating dock can help. *Excite* the dog in any way you can, with plenty of hurrahs and praise. One aquatically indifferent member of my menagerie turned into a maniacal torpedo after jealously watching his brother make a few frothy trips.

Years ago I coached a nine-month-old male retriever who seemed quite extraordinary—he had brains, uncanny vision, a willingness to please, and a memory like a pocket computer. He swam with casual, athletic strength, pulling himself easily along with huge webbed feet, unafraid—but at the same time unmotivated and unspectacular. I worried about this.

A friend invited me to join him for a duck shoot in the San Joaquin Valley. This was welcomed, as I knew him to be a hell of a wingshot who rarely wasted this talent "mining a dry hole." I asked if I might bring an inexperienced youngster with us, explaining how much I wished this pup would get the "big picture," and adding that I'd probably forget my shotgun and simply work the dog. "Bring him along if you like," he replied, "but for God's sake show up with your gun and chest-high waders."

His duck club—immense sheets of gleaming water, flooding over hundreds of acres of rice and safflower—set its decoys in a classic layout to attract sprig. The blinds are two concrete cylinders sunk so that their rims are just inches from the lap line of the waves. Between these cylinders a small board platform is slung with upright wires supporting a surreylike roof. Retrievers are expected to sit quietly on this shaky trapeze. Each set of blinds is surrounded by two thousand prominent "flash-sight" decoys made from chunks of auto tires splashed fore and aft with white paint and set on stakes. Wading out through blackness to the blinds our wakes jostle the hard moonlight. Still more decoys are towed behind us in gunnysacks. The pup swims contentedly, inspecting the

AFC Rip Snortin' Good Times enjoys a high water entry.

Rita hits the water low and hard.

A bold water entry is "stylish" to the field trialer and a boon to the hunter with game crippled or in swift currents.

totemlike staked tires. In the dark air above, real birds toot, honk, quack, and chirp.

Getting settled is hell. The pup tries to hop into the cement tube with me, splashing muck over my glasses. Half a dozen KENNELS and SITS fail to place him on the dog trapeze, so I physically deposit him there. He hates it. His tail hangs limply into the soup—he knows disgrace. My trigger-hand glove has floated away in the dark. As salmon dawn leaks in, I see the glove waving away among the goddamned tires. My hand freezes into a bludgeon.

Phhhhhhooooommmssshh. Teal, greenwings!

"Why didn't you take them?"

"I was watching the dog. Why didn't you?"

"It's bull sprig or nothing—Christ, look over your head."

Whaaasheeen geeen geeeng. "Sprig! Take them! Jeezus, nice shooting!" A bird pinwheels down, spraying pinks and blues as it bashes through the decoys.

"That's just what you ordered."

"Yep. FETCH!" The pup peers intently at the slick of bubbles, then looks at me. "FETCH!" He slips clumsily off his perch, paddling tentatively toward the ripples. The bird also *swims—away,* head and neck on the surface; then dives. Once the dog enters the forest of tire segments he's lost; question marks fill his eyes. I extricate myself from my cocoon and slosh toward them. "MARK!" The departing cripple is sluiced. "FETCH!" He churns in with his mouthful of shockingly beautiful bird; I have seen them and painted them many times, but I am filled with reverence once again. This one wears the immaculate tuxedo of the sprig drake. It glows.

Our blind gets hot and our gun barrels heat up. At our island, the pup on his trapeze begins to comprehend. Our whole world consists of stiff decoys, pounding volleys, tumbling prizes, and *water.* Nothing else exists.

By the thirteenth bird, spray flies; foaming with power, the pup cleaves the water like a porpoise. His bubbling return is just as brisk—he hurls himself onto his platform. Handing the birds down into my nest, he eyes me, then looks expectantly into the clear vault of the sky, filling with wheeling, sparkling riders, some sliding and tilting, some with wings set. Another glance—one that pleads: "Shoot, oh, shoot more!" We drop a last one for him. One more bull sprig. He explodes into the water for it.

Three months later this pup ran his first Derby, and *won*—there was plenty of water. At the end of that trial season he was the National Derby Champion. His name was Dr. Davey, Ph.D.

The author with 1977 National Derby Champion Dr. Davey, Ph.D.

— *Shore Breaking and Bank Training* —

No shore breaking or bank training should be done until your pup is thoroughly force-fetch trained (see pp. 68–71) and performs well on easy water entries. You can inadvertently teach an honest dog how to cheat around the water by starting too early and showing him land route options.

Always do shore work early in the day—*not with a tired, careless dog, or just before dark.* By starting early and fresh, you have time and energy on your side if you encounter difficulties and you will not have to abandon the site after half a lesson. You must teach and show—be prepared to get wet. Always have a clean, hard shore or bank, and deep, pleasant water, not running water, muddy beach or soft bottom. You want him to know that being *in* the water is good and being *out* is bad. Use bumpers often, so birds will not be identified with any training misfortunes. (Also, bumpers are easier to place accurately than birds.) Use ducks as soon as the lesson seems clear, as a sensible reward.

Shore work generally involves *angles* and *angling* into the water, often when it is faster for the dog to go by land. Angling should be taught first with a dry ditch, then a swimming ditch, then into large expanses of water.

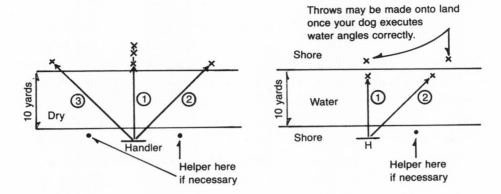

Diagram 10. Angling on land and water.

Diagram 10 is begun with all singles: (1) Self-throw several straight across; (2) then a forty-five-degree throw, lining the dog with hand down for direction and a fast incoming whistle; then repeat (1) and back to (2). Show him the difference between (1) and (2). When he understands that perfectly, then self-throw these as a double. When all is perfect, add (3) as a single; if not, retreat to (1) and (2) singles and repeat the whole drill often. Move on to the drills in diagram 11 (below) gradually, and only when your dog understands and performs the above angles perfectly.

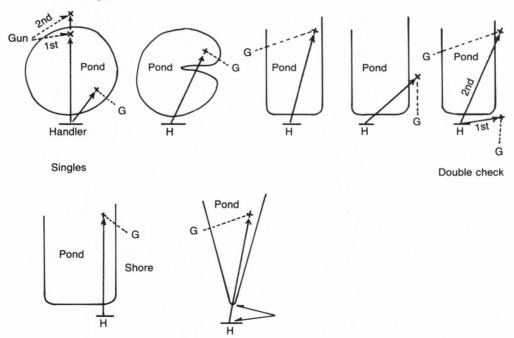

Diagram 11. Difficult shore angles. The difficulty of these exercises increases the farther the handler stands from the water.

Resist using the command NO on water work; NO is easily interpreted as "Don't go" and "Don't retrieve in the water." Depend instead on your growl to stop him, then rerun him. The object of all shore breaking is to teach the dog that water assures him of security and approval. Avoidance of water can be corrected in a number of ways. Some trainers use a helper equipped with a long poke pole, to intimidate the dog into the water and to keep him there by "walking" with him along the bank as he swims back on the return. You, the handler, therefore become the "goal" and represent safety. Other trainers pull the dog in from the opposite shore or from a boat, with a rope or ropes. Upon any water refusal, I prefer immediately to throw the dog in myself, by his coat. I must admit this is easier with a dainty bitch than with a boxcar-shaped male, and it sometimes strains both your back and your patience. But it is simple, direct, understandable force. All the above techniques are superior to calling the dog *back in,* thrashing him at the point of origin (on land), then attempting a comprehensive rerun. *Timing* in sending and correcting is critical to the lesson.

With rare, athletic exceptions, our dogs do not *angle* across or over elements *naturally*—ditches, banks, shorelines, side hills, or roads. Recognize that angles are disagreeable to him, but teach them carefully regardless, as he must take angles in stride to enter the water properly, and to run and swim a sure course. The dog limited to *right angles only* finds considerable difficulty and distraction in trying to "correct" his navigation and progress to a target area. The straight line to a mark remains the shortest and least complicated once he discovers how to deal with angles. If you think of your dog's inclinations while navigating these hazards as you would the safe operation of a four-wheel-drive Jeep—in which it is wise to make a square entry into creekbeds, not to sidehill too steeply for fear of rolling it, avoiding heavy brush at speed, trusting shallow water rather than driving into the center of the lake, and avoiding deep mud—you can sympathize with some of his discomforts. He doesn't want to angle any more than he has to; it isn't intelligent. The Jeep has four wheels at its corners and the dog has four legs.

All of the above steps and lessons should be thought of as increments of long, difficult retrieves, usually singles. I often refer to this system of counting increments or details as my "grocery list." I give each detail, such as change of elevation, poor viewing background, forbidding cover, type of water, distance, wind, angle, water temperature, and so on, a numerical value. For example: each change of cover or surface may be worth two or three points. A perfect "big league" retrieve is an assemblage of perfectly executed details, or a correctly added column of small numbers corresponding to these details. Think of

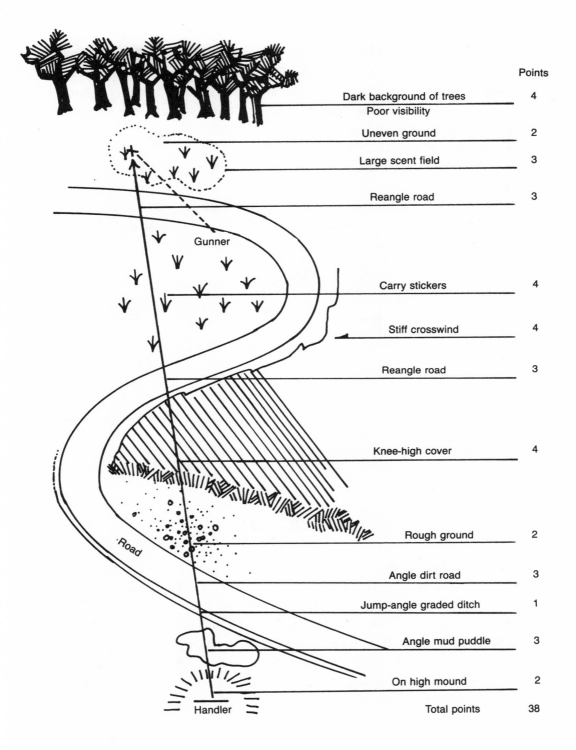

	Points
Dark background of trees	4
Poor visibility	
Uneven ground	2
Large scent field	3
Reangle road	3
Carry stickers	4
Stiff crosswind	4
Reangle road	3
Knee-high cover	4
Rough ground	2
Angle dirt road	3
Jump-angle graded ditch	1
Angle mud puddle	3
On high mound	2
Total points	38

Diagram 12. Increments in a difficult Derby single of 140 yards.

details and a numerical degree of difficulty when setting a training mark, or when judging it; this system will help prevent overly ambitious expectations. Train your pup frequently on details and aim for perfection, but only occasionally on the whole formidable retrieve—the total of the "grocery list." Very few amateurs, myself for one, with limited time and help could accomplish much if this approach weren't effective.

Furthermore, you should not set difficult tests routinely for your pup—even if he can do them. Choose one principle or concept and work on it repeatedly, moving and resetting the *same* principle throughout your training day, as opposed to a scatter-gun batch of conflicting ideas in the same day. To check your pup's retention and correctability, repeat lessons on alternate days.

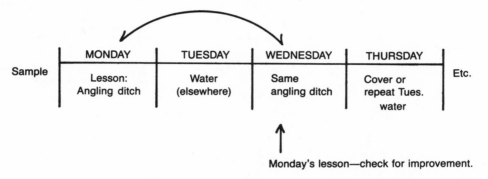

Diagram 13. Alternate day routines.

CHARTING

I'm not generally mathematically inclined, but I drew the following device (thanks to a suggestion from Roy Gonia, one of the most practical and inventive dogmen I've ever known), using a ruler on one-half-inch centers on a large sheet of paper. It could then be Xeroxed. I hung it on a conspicuous wall that I had to pass coming in from training. I think it's a necessary and valuable tool.

The benefits of charting your dog's progress are enormous if you are accurate and *honest* in your grading. Not only will you be able to keep track of the training process from day to day, but months and years later a chart (such as the one above) will provide you with a record of your dog's cycles of triumphs and failings. You will have an overall view of what methods work well, what exercises you overlooked, and the direction of your next session. Land and

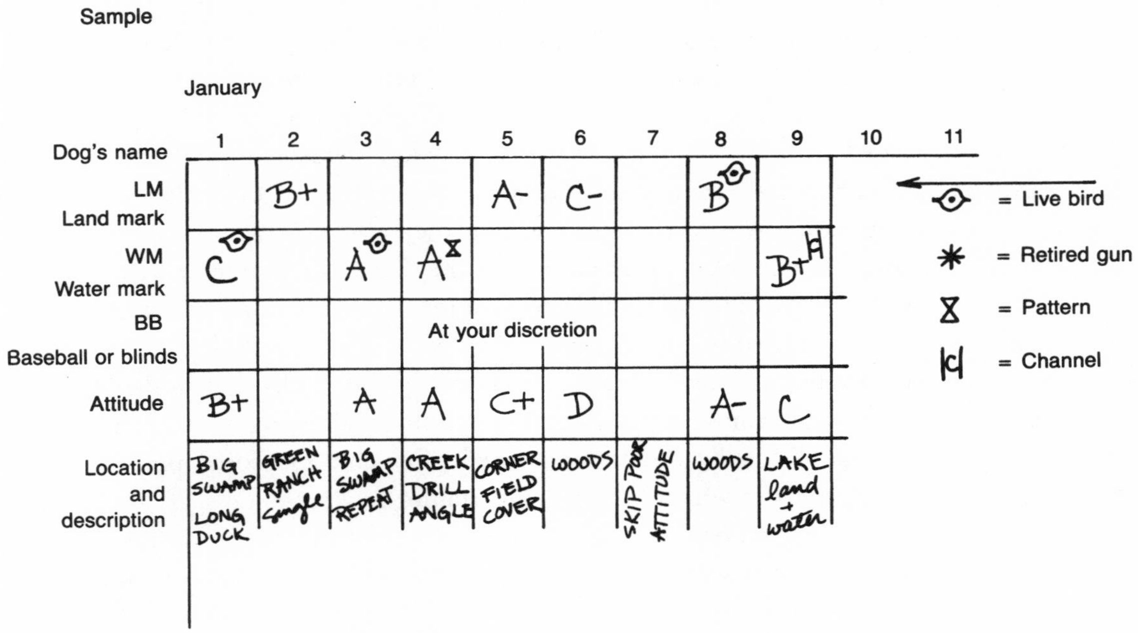

Sample

January

Dog's name	1	2	3	4	5	6	7	8	9	10	11
LM Land mark		B+			A-	C-		B⊙			
WM Water mark	C⊙		A⊙	Aˣ					B+ᴴ		
BB Baseball or blinds			At your discretion								
Attitude	B+		A	A	C+	D		A-	C		
Location and description	BIG SWAMP LONG DUCK	GREEN RANCH single	BIG SWAMP REPEAT	CREEK DRILL ANGLE	CORNER FIELD COVER	WOODS	SKIP POOR ATTITUDE	WOODS	LAKE land + water		

⊙ = Live bird
* = Retired gun
X = Pattern
H = Channel

Diagram 14. Training chart.

water "baseball" drills may be added later, when your dog begins more advanced work (see pp. 122–123). Many modern amateurs train on some facet every day, 365 days a year. This may not match *your* dog's ambitions. If not, devise a schedule that does.

OTHER EARLY TRAINING NOTES

Here are a number of assorted points that I've found important in training young retrievers.

• Leave a few decoys around the entrance of your dog's kennel. Add them to yardwork and training sometimes. But never let your dog help you pick them up from your pond after shooting. If you do, you may find that while hunting he retrieves a convenient decoy instead of the real thing—and possibly allows a crippled bird to escape.

• Gunfire and loud noises should be gradually introduced, first at long, then at decreasing distances. Slowly elevate sound levels—cap gun, .22-caliber blanks, and finally a 12-gauge shotgun. Feeding time is a good chance to introduce your dog to noise. Eventually, the pleasure of eating his dinner amid noise will be exchanged for the excitement of retrieving with accompanying gunfire. Noise and gun-shyness are a form of "spookiness." Some handlers don't want to be associated with any dog that exhibits "spooky" tendencies, but several experts believe that *some* spookiness indicates the presence of discretion and choice making on the part of the dog, and that the "fearless" dog may simply be a stupid dog. Any spooky apprehensions on the dog's part should be gradually reduced by familiarization and demonstrations that the frightening element will in fact not harm him.

• Once your pup is "steady," that is, sits quietly and marks shot birds, be sure to "honor" with him as much as possible (politely allowing another dog to retrieve the birds). "Picnic" trials (unlicensed, often club-sponsored, practice trials) are ideal events at which to begin this training.

• If field trialing interests you, get your own copy of the rules of retriever trials and any supplements from the American Kennel Club, 51 Madison Avenue, New York, NY 10010.

• Some very talented dogs don't travel well. Make sure you introduce your pup to his traveling kennel/vehicle gently. Feed him in the truck several times before his first *short* exposure to motion. Talk to him and reassure him on the maiden trip. Some dogs can't stand the sound of mud and snow tires at highway speed. Some trainers feel that a layer of foam rubber under a piece of Masonite in a dog's crate helps insulate him from the road. Drive smoothly on twisty roads, and make sure the dogs have plenty of cool air and water, as a fearful and queasy traveler will often hyperventilate, drool, and fall victim to dehydration. Midship is probably the best location in the vehicle, and atop the rear axle is probably the worst.

• It should be remembered that a fine Derby dog is often at the zenith of his marking life—before he's burdened by the worries and intricacies of advanced Open work. Pass shooting ducks over open water, from a boat or a blind, is probably the most easily understood and purest form of marking. (*Pass shooting* is shooting birds as they fly overhead rather than flushing them from cover.) Both gunner and dog alike may view approaching birds. Different species of ducks and geese exhibit different mannerisms, but a well-struck bird makes a dramatic, memorable fall and splash at forty to seventy yards. A poorly hit duck may sail a great deal farther, but is still an unobstructed mark, one with a virtual straight-line swim, without distracting scent, to pick it up.

By contrast, *jump shooting* ducks, pheasants, quail, grouse, snipe, and so on, in labyrinths of cover or across ditches and levees often results in scarcely marked or unmarked birds. If more than one bird is dropped, the problems increase. Perhaps the dog has marked one well and not others. Scenting and bird trails become factors in recovering game. Does the dog return to the previous fall and scent when released for a second or third bird? Cripples may scoot to the security of formidable cover. An advanced (veteran) dog may be capable of handling the most diverse game-gathering situations, but he must also depend on his handler. He can retrieve the birds he saw fall, and can also track runners. He must stop at his handler's whistle and accept hand signals toward birds that only the gunners know for certain are down—signals that may take him into and out of water, and through attractive bursts of bird scent.

• A solo trainer throwing his own marks all the time encourages his dog to "creep" forward. Go out into a field, tell your dog to SIT, then march out and throw singles or multiples while reminding him to SIT and MARK. Walk back to him and then send. This is a poor man's version of a retired gun, and it can be very effective.

• A dog with a wet coat is much likelier to drift off his course in a crosswind than a dry dog.

• Saturation trainers who go at it seven days a week all day and repeat everything twelve times automatically condition their dogs physically. Others with less time or smarter dogs may have to supplement their retrieving program with some kind of road work. A truck or car is dangerous and potentially lethal. A bicycle, motorcycle, and jogging are all fairly safe.

• Doubles are favorable to a Derby dog when they are "tight" enough to preclude a full-body pivot to watch both marks fall. Use a long-distance and short-distance double, not equidistant falls.

• Sometimes, for dogs over eight months of age, I build three or four long (up to 280 yards) established land sight blinds. (These are birds or bumpers that are clearly visible.) This preparation may serve well on a mark your pup hasn't seen down, or a retired gun. I also provide some brief "baseball handling" experience (see pp. 114–123) between eight and twelve months—I don't force it—and then halt it for several more months of Derby-type marking. I don't want a pup that can handle well and only occasionally mark, and I refuse to spend the time and grief involved in training a dog to handle if he can't mark damned well *first*.

• Head swinging is an exasperating habit, sometimes generated by too many trials when the shot flyer is habitually the last bird down and close by. The dog soon learns to disregard the "key" bird in anticipation of the flyer. In training, you can help correct head swinging by setting up full triples and running these marks as singles. Or hang a white coat on a likely bush and run your dog to a single mark past it. Try sending the dog when the throw is at the peak of the arc. In training on doubles, shoot the flyer first, or send the dog the instant he removes his head or his eyes from that bird. Other trainers use a long count or considerable delay between throws in marking multiples. You may also block the flyer source with your body, concealing it from your dog when you approach the line for marking.

• Making an attempt at winning the National Derby Championship (High Point Derby Dog) is costly to the natural advancement of the dog. The special schedule involved is desperately unforgiving. Also, there's a tendency to settle for a certain level of performance—and to strive only to maintain it rather than surpass it by teaching new skills.

GROUP TRAINING

If you are lucky enough to have a like-minded dog-training partner, try to maintain a careful young dog schedule together. If not, you may have to capture your children or hire neighborhood kids who are able to throw for you. If you should belong to a retriever training group, avoid using leftover portions of advanced training designs. Try not to compete. Apply a "grocery list" evaluation of the grounds and use your "chart" information for what *your dog* needs. Try to reciprocate the assistance and expenses in a group training session by rotating and sharing the tasks of throwing, shooting, wading, or providing grounds, and birds. I occasionally train with people whom I mistrust or dislike; this is great for self-discipline, but I don't make a habit of it.

QUALITIES OF A GREAT DOG

After completing the training lessons outlined in this chapter, you will know far better than at the outset what the strengths and weaknesses of your dog are. You may be particularly interested now in learning what some professional trainers look for in a dog, that is, what type, nature, and talent they prefer.

Jim Gonia likes to work with "a natural marker." "I think marking is a gift," says Gonia. "It involves more . . . than sharp eyesight. It entails a lot of brains; an ability to take a picture of the bird going down and keep it in mind.

Memory is involved, willingness to cut the cover and do all the other things just for the pure sake of getting the bird. The good ones seem to have more concentration than the dogs that don't find them."

Roy Gonia points out, however, that "a good marking dog is always very difficult to teach to handle because he's so set in his ways. He knows where he's going." Nevertheless, Gonia admits, "I'd rather have the marking dog because I think I've got more to work with. If I get him straightened out, I've got myself a great dog. Otherwise, all I've got is an ordinary dog."

Rex Carr agrees: "Natural markers are potentially the best; National Derby Champions fit this mold. Very few retrievers possess this marking potential. In field trials today there are many unnatural marks. These must be taught and stuffed into the dog's mind for reliable results. If a good marker is taught to do these marks and a natural marker is not . . . the good marker can out-mark the natural. Given the same opportunities, the natural marker will surpass all others."

In addition to valuing an ability to mark, Jim Gonia feels that a good dog "has to be birdy, trainable, and have the endurance and eyesight to get the birds. The dog has to be bright enough to grasp the different ideas that aren't natural—bright enough to understand how to be taught."

"Some dogs are soft and you've got to take it easier with them," says Roy Gonia. "I don't mind that; you've just got to be more careful, and as a rule, as they get older, they get much bolder and they'll take more correction as long as they know why. But you can't jump them as you would a tough one. [In general, though,] I like a good stylish, birdy dog. That's the foundation of all our great dogs. Most birdy dogs, when they find out what you want, like to please you."

8

Hunting and the Qualifying Stake

FLIGHTED GREAT BLUE HERON

When your dog passes from the Derby age, your next goal for him in the field-trial world will probably be successful competition in Qualifying stakes. These are trial contests open to all retrievers until their accomplishments send them on to a higher level of competition. Present American Kennel Club rules describe a Qualifying stake as one "for dogs which have never won first, second, third, or fourth place or a Judges' Award of Merit (JAM) in an Open All-Age or Limited All-Age stake, or won two first places in Qualifying stakes at licensed or member club trials."

Dogs in the Qualifying stake may be thought of as being in the high school level of training. While the Derby level is limited to marking, the Qualifying stake represents the first opportunity for your dog to display his ability in blind retrieves, both on land and in water. Competitors at this level include hot young prospects from Derby stakes, well-intentioned hearth and hunting dogs, and cunning old dowagers. Some dogs spend their trial lives here if they are unable to attain the levels of skill that makes them competitive in Open and Amateur stakes.

Many judges feel that Qualifying stakes are the most difficult contests to judge. They must select tests that balance the not-too-difficult with the not-too-simple, to sort out a gaggle of dogs of dissimilar age and varied levels of training.

The Qualifying stakes are shunned by some handlers with lofty ambitions for their promising youngsters, for two reasons. First, the usual demands of the Qualifying stake tend to retard the dogs: the distances run are too short and the marks too easy, tending to undo the sophisticated Open-type training in which these animals are engaged. Second, why bother with a stake where no championship points are awarded?

I believe Qualifying has its own merits, however. Fine young talent rarely stays long in this stake; such dogs do well and then graduate to more difficult work. The stake provides a good chance for a "shakedown cruise," and a measurement of your training progress. All the excitement and distraction of trialing is present: crowds, other dogs, hot bird scents, holding screens, and gunfire—and this is important, because many dogs behave and perform far differently in trials than they do in training. Some get self-conscious, overwhelmed by new sights, smells, and sounds; others become frantic and useless, unable to concentrate. Still other dogs bloom or "come up" at trials, showing courage and heroic efforts that rarely emerge in training. Sometimes the young act old, and the old get crazy.

Thus, Qualifying is a chance to learn your dog's aptitudes and limitations. It's comforting to find that your "only fair" training or hunting dog can, in a trialing atmosphere, suddenly become a dependable fire-breather. Further, the Qualifying stake and training for it represent opportunities for young dogs to execute blind retrieves on downed game birds they did not see fall, and take whistle/hand signals.

Whether pass shooting Band-tailed Pigeons as they weave through the high, draping limbs of Douglas fir, or scratching out doves over thick brown pincushions of bull thistles, or reflexively lacing phantom flights of Greenwings slicing through morning mists, your dog may never mark a fall. He knows damned well the shotgun fired, but what came down? Did you miss? The trust needed to retrieve an unseen fall, to make a "blind" retrieve, should be carefully instilled.

Some training exercises that have proven effective in preparing and advancing a Qualifying dog follow. Each of them can extend the abilities and polish the style of your retriever, both for trial stakes and for hunting.

Hunting on the salt flats.

MARKING THE SQUARE BIRD

I have suggested refraining from throwing "square," or ninety-degree, birds (see diag. 2) for your starting Derby dog—up to fourteen months. When you feel your dog's marking is confident and accurate in a wide variety of difficult forty-five-degree "back" throws, introduce the square bird.

In the same manner that you deliberately taught the Derby-age dog ditch angling (that is, ninety-degree–forty-five-degree–ninety-degree as shown in diag. 10), by contrast and repetition, now teach by contrasting square and "back" throws. Formally introduce the new square fall location in a special session. While the dog is fresh and cocky, have your thrower make a couple of forty-five-degree "back" throws for him. Move to new terrain—with no challenging ditches, water, and so on—and have your thrower toss him a square mark with a fresh dead bird fifty to sixty yards away in medium cover. When he overruns it into his normal payoff zone, let him hunt long and hard. Attrition resulting from a deep, fruitless hunt for a square throw can eventually be helpful, but if the dog is frivolous in his task, go out and collect him, shake him up lightly, then have him take another more careful look at the same throw. If he abandons the fall area of this "square" bird (sometimes called a "flat" bird in the Midwest), have your thrower help him by calling "Hey, hey" to the dog, and walking toward the correct spot of the fall. The helper may then pick up the bird by a wing tip (thus revealing it to the dog) and drop it in the identical spot. The dog may now return with the bird—and new wisdom. Repeat the identical throw in the same spot. Repeat until he begins to measure himself and this different position of fall.

Square-thrown birds and short falls take on significance in hunting and trialing, as retrievers are expected to mark multiple falls. Rarely do these falls occur at similar distances. In trials the yardage to each mark is varied to test the memory and perseverance of the dog. Typical patterns of fall are common in trials and wing shooting—in both cases they are difficult. In field-trial form these multiple marks can be: long fall first, short second, and long again last. In pass shooting this occurs with an incoming flock: a first bird is dropped at maximum tight choke range, a second as the flock passes close or over the shooter's blind, and a third distant bird is knocked down after the flock flares and is flying away. A second variation is short fall, medium fall, then a long one. Once the retriever has located the last bird down it is natural for him, owing to his success on his long run, to overrun the shorter birds. This same situation arises in the pass shoot as the flock of doves, teal or brant are even with or over the hunter's blind and the shooters drop the nearest one, the next one, and finally a long bird. The dog usually attempts to pick up the last bird he saw fall. If the shorter birds are across water or in humanly impenetrable cover, they may never be retrieved.

When your dog starts to get the hang of square birds, move the test to other ground and serve up more square throws. You may also consider introducing a verbal cue (see "Audible Cues," pp. 189–190) to help remind him that this is a different bird. I do not use light-colored, conspicuous birds. The recognition of the square bird is primarily done *in the dog's head* before he is sent to retrieve. When you see him deliberately check his speed, throw up his ears and start to scan with his eyes *before* he arrives at the square zone, you know he is beginning to understand the concept.

The next step in familiarization with square throws is to have your helper throw one square and handler-toss a bumper to the side. If you are satisfied with the recognition and hunt for the square one at a variety of distances, move to fresh ground and have your thrower toss and shoot a left-to-right live bird deep, about forty-five degrees back. If the dog's hunt is quick and accurate, have the same gunner throw a square dead bird to the same side at a ninety-degree angle. Can the dog now differentiate between the two locations of the birds? If not, review the above steps until he can. These deep (back-thrown) birds to square-bird singles from the same station are a demanding, difficult drill.

While upland hunting, if the dog's tendency is to overrun short marks (quail, for instance), stop him with a SIT whistle and then direct him toward the downed bird with a light COME HERE chirp and an arm signal. Or you may keep him at SIT and walk toward him; point to the bird and tell him to FETCH. *Show him* until he learns to associate the game and the drop zones, determined by the range of your and your partner's guns. One hundred and sixty yards is not an unreasonable mark on a long-gliding sprig with a broken wing tip, but that same distance for partridge, grouse, or pheasants is unlikely. In such cases the shooter himself should note and mark the general location of this bird. In cover that is tough to memorize or keep to my bearings in, I usually walk to the area where I think the bird fell and immediately drop my hat, or an empty shell; look for feathers, then call upon my dog's good nose.

In training, there is little point in making these square-bird throws any farther than a man can comfortably toss a dead pheasant, as they generally are dead in trials. Many trainers expect their dogs to *naturally* mark any fall, shallow or deep, whereas I believe that teaching the separate positions of falls *enhances* natural skill. Other trainers use square-bird throws to "cure" overrunning marks, but I feel this problem is corrected better simply by the use of obvious, light-colored birds or bumpers in light cover.

The next application of square birds should come in a double retrieve. Place your throwers widely at medium distance in the field, and have them throw the square bird first followed by the deep throw, but direct your dog to pick up the long first, then the square. I have found that exaggerating this principle with the help of a single field hazard is helpful. Find a wall of brush, a road, or a ditch and place your two bird throwers just in front of it. Have the square thrower toss his bird *in front of* the hazard and the deep thrower makes his fall into or across the same hazard. The dog must first deal with the ditch or brush and then *remember to ignore it* as he checks for his square bird. Plenty of mileage on this concept must be provided.

MORE ON PROBLEM MARKING

When a dog who normally marks well begins to falter in this skill, there are a few remedial steps available to you before utter exasperation sets in:

1. Choose a field with natural visual landmarks in it (a big tree, rock for-

mation, cliff, ditch, or even an auto). Arrange to have the mark or marks fall where the dog can measure and "key off" from these landmarks during his quest.

2. If a mark must be repeated, *move closer* toward the fall until you discover the troublesome segment of the line and rerun it from there. Only when you both recognize and have mastered the trouble spot do you move back to your original spot to repeat the mark from there.

3. A dog that mindlessly larks about and chronically overruns his marks may find that this habit is no longer a luxury if you have a key mark thrown just into the edge of several acres of heavy, unpleasant cover. Calmly observe, as he creates uncalled-for scrapes and discomforts for himself. Happily congratulate him when he gratefully finds it. Then repeat it.

4. Another technique for the dog that overruns his mark is to start with your longest single mark first (150 yards); your next mark should be at 100 yards, and your next at 50 yards. This is contrary to the normal puppy situation in which you throw increasingly distant marks to build his confidence. Here, you decrease the lengths of the marks in order to force him to concentrate on actual distance—not merely on accelerating.

5. Marking from atop a hill, mound, or levee can help a dog gauge the depth of marks accurately.

6. "Overrunners" will discover that another attrition design is costly: Throw marks in easy cover, but at distances of 250 to 300 yards (no obstacles). If the dog's hunt is long and silly at these exaggerated distances, he pays dearly in the lungs and effort department. Calmly, without reprimands, repeat the marks immediately; although winded, he may register their locations more closely. The same principle applies to deep-water marks: if he beaches himself on the shore, let him land and hunt long and fruitlessly. Repeat the marks and he will soon tire of unnecessarily circuitous hunts. If he is keen, he will realize he must stay in the water to score.

7. Choose your dog's favorite bird (live duck, banty, or pheasant). Have your partner go into a large field of knee-high cover (one with no landmarks and straight downwind) for thirty or forty yards. He will make an enticing throw (bird) into this sea of similar cover. You then throw a short (fifteen-foot), less attractive bumper off to your side. Fetch up the bumper *first;* the instant you send the dog for it, the helper "retires" by simply falling down flat in the grass. Upon completion, whether good or bad work, move forward into the field, passing over the scent and spot of the previous marks—and duplicate it. After a full dozen of these little magnetic retirements, a stale, struggling memory can revive.

HAND SIGNALS AND "BASEBALL"

This is the magical stage in retriever development work—the time when your dog can bridge the gap from useful to extraordinary in both hunting and trialing.

A traditional drill known as "baseball" should be learned before you seriously pursue *line running* (the ability to run an unswerving course) and *blind* retrieves (birds that fall unseen when hunting; the equivalent of the unseen fall in trials are dead birds that are hidden or "planted" in the field or water). Baseball can be introduced any time after your dog has learned force-fetch well. Build your dog on this drill, step by step, until he is absolutely certain of each requirement. Some dogs seem to relish baseball naturally; others yawn at the prospect and must be *pushed* through it in order to achieve its goals.

This brings us to two terms that are basic in dog handling: *back,* meaning farther away from the handler; and *over,* meaning in a lateral direction. The handler uses OVER and BACK as his verbal commands to send his dog in the desired direction. They also refer to the hand signals he uses for this purpose.

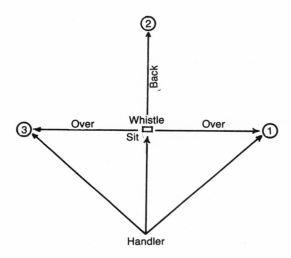

Diagram 15. Baseball drill.

To set up your baseball field, find a lot or flat area with no cover. Pace off a fairly accurate diamond configuration: home plate, first, second, and third

A

B

(A) Setting up. The trainer has the dog sit properly beside her, aimed in the direction he is to go before (B) sending him with a one-word command.

bases, with the pitcher's mound located symmetrically between. A school baseball diamond is ideal, if you have access to one.

With your dog at heel, place a pair of white bumpers on second base, then walk to home plate and cue him for the retrieve. (I use DEAD BIRD.) This is also the time you both begin to learn how to "set up" your two bodies with integrated team timing. Make sure he is sitting well and aimed exactly on a true line through his tail, spine, and nose. Always check this three-point alignment when "setting up," as a matter of routine, and reheel and reset him until he is correct.

Next, extend your arm and hand above and in front of his head, fingers pointed toward the line (the straight course he is to follow for the retrieve). Be sure his eyes look where the rest of him is pointed, before releasing him on the new command, BACK. If he doesn't understand, reset and send him on FETCH, then integrate the BACK command on repetitions.

After a few perfect runs at second base on BACK, sit him on the pitcher's mound as you walk out to second and drop a bumper while he watches. Then return to home plate while he sits squarely on the pitcher's mound, facing you. Raise an arm quickly and vertically to full extension and order BACK. He should anticipate your meaning, spin, and charge off to second base to retrieve the bumper for you.

Now, alternate between sending him from the heel-sit position on BACK, and sending from the pitcher's mound with the vertical hand-cast BACK. (Although generally called a hand cast, the signal involves movement of the entire arm.) You can drop a dozen bumpers on second base once he fully understands this work and is doing it reflexively.

In another session, place a bumper on first base and another on second. Start with the dog on the pitcher's mound; have him pick up the one on second base on BACK. Again, beginning with the dog on the pitcher's mound, direct him to pick up the bumper at first base on the command OVER, with your right arm extended horizontally and pointing in that direction. If perfect, replace the bumpers and repeat. Later, include a bumper at third base. Always emphasize the BACK first, and then give the OVER commands. Notice that the dog's natural tendency will be to favor the last bumper you've placed. (I don't throw these bumpers to the base positions during this orientation stage, although many other trainers do.) If the dog cannot concentrate on your hand signal, remove distracting bumpers from the other bases, leaving only those on the cast you want. If the dog goes for the wrong base, growl at him, reposition him on the pitcher's mound, and repeat the cast from closer quarters.

A Gallery of Paintings by Thomas Quinn

CHESAPEAKE FEMALE LOTTA

Thomas Aquinas
1978

SWIMMING CANADA GANDER

Thomas Quinn
1978

WALKING CANADA GANDER

RESTING SNIPE

GOLDEN MALE FC AFC RIGHT ON DYNAMITE JOHN

TIPPING SPRIG

PHOTOGRAPH OF
DR. DAVEY, PH.D., AT SPEED

HEN QUAIL IN GRASSES

APPLETREE QUAIL

BOBWHITES AND BROOM WEED

MALLARD HEN AND DUCKLINGS

LABRADOR FEMALE TEAL

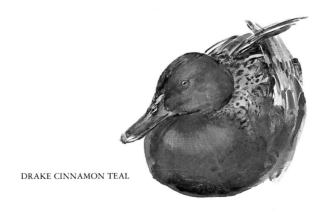

DRAKE CINNAMON TEAL

VIRGINIA RAIL

LABRADOR MALE FC AFC PALADIN VII

Some trainers use the commands RIGHT and LEFT for further refinement, or GEE and HAW, like mule skinners, as a substitute for OVER. Whatever you prefer and works for your dog is best.

At some point, check your casts in a full-length mirror, to make sure they read clearly and graphically. Keep your hands at chest level. When the dog progresses and is looking back alertly at me from the pitcher's mound, I like to shift my neck and shoulders or my body weight a little from side to side; if he is keen and tries to anticipate the upcoming cast, I give him the opposite one. This can train him to look at your *hands* and not try to outguess you.

When your dog clearly understands both OVER and BACK, you are ready for the key section of the baseball drill.

Sit your dog at home plate, walk out, and let him watch you drop a pile of bumpers at each base. You are teaching him that "bumpers are all over out there; you pick up the one *I* want, when I point to it." Send him on BACK for the center bird, then re-line him and send directly to first base to retrieve another bumper, followed by a similar shot at the third-base pile. Now carefully re-line for the second-base pile. Send him—and when he reaches the pitcher's mound, blow a long-blast SIT whistle. (He should be well developed enough for this "sit" from his previous work, outlined in chapter 5.) Most dogs turn and face you when they hear it. If your dog only looks toward you over his shoulder, give him a small COME IN chirp to turn and accurately place him on the pitcher's mound. Now, cast him to the bumper of your choice. Repeat the center-line trip to second base *without* the whistle-stop.

Besides the obvious control factor of being able to instantly SIT seventy or eighty pounds of retriever at your whim—say, before he is allowed to eat his dinner, or jump up on your mother-in-law's white dress, or dart under a moving dump truck—he should learn to SIT for *field* reasons. This STOP-SIT drill represents an alert prelude for more interesting signals from you: another whistle signal COME HERE, perhaps, or an arm/hand signal directing the way to a hidden dead or live bird.

My hunting partner calls over and reports he has just whacked a Chukar pretty hard, but the bird has glided across a sage-sprinkled valley with a swift creek cutting its floor. It finally collapsed dead on a shale slide three or four hundred yards away. Without moving off our hillside, my dog can pick up his bird and return with it for him—by employing a combination of whistle-sits and arm casts. For the bird hunter who has not been privileged to have a good retriever, this may seem an impossibility—or a miracle.

Whistle-sits should be sharply obeyed by the dog—no slow roll-out pro-

A

B

C

D

The classic baseball pattern (distances are shortened for demonstration purposes). (A) In this baseball drill, the dog sits squarely on the pitcher's mound awaiting a command from the trainer who stands at home plate. (B) The "back" cast sends the dog to second base. (C) The right "over" gesture signals the dog to retrieve bumpers on first base. (D) Left "over" sends him to third base.

A

C

D

B

The handling dog's viewpoint. (A) Whistle-sit—notice the dog faces the trainer in response to the whistle blast, (B) "back" cast, (C) left "over," (D) right "over."

Success.

tests! Some trainers believe that on initial whistle-stops, the dog should be on a long check cord and systematically knocked head over heels at the pitcher's mound at the whistle's toot—to "clean out his ears" and condition him for future, more remote STOP-SITS. I prefer to get a good SIT response out of pleasure—"Which way to the next payoff, boss?" rather than out of the pain—"Why are you stopping me from trying to retrieve for you?" But you may need to apply both approaches. One helpful, easy drill is to throw a bumper as far as you can—forty to fifty yards. Put your hand down to indicate the line and send him on BACK. Whistle-sit him half the distance to the bumper; as he sits facing you, throw another bumper or a clipped-wing pigeon out to the ninety-degree OVER position—then give him either the OVER or BACK cast, and then send him again for the one still remaining in the field. This encourages your dog to listen for a possible whistle, look at you to throw something extra, and stay receptive to changes of mind and direction.

Begin and end each baseball session by running all three lines. Mix in plenty of BACK casts. If the dog seems to have one weak directional cast, say third base, place a shackled banty or pigeon on that station to sweeten it compared to the other bases and their ordinary bumpers. If he overreacts to the bird, "force" him away from it with an opposite cast to first base. Put birds on all stations for cheer. If he tries to anticipate and run a line other than the one you choose, point your hand down the incorrect line and give a firm NO! to cancel it temporarily, then re-line to *your* choice of line. If he insists on choosing a different line, "tune him up"—check cords are handy for reeling him in and correcting the line of his spine in the right direction. Alternatively, you may move closer to the bird on the desired line to simplify the retrieve.

Try to keep the baseball exercise interesting to both of you. Most pros favor simple, fixed patterns. Some keep mowed swaths in the grass for correct travel lines. These basic baseball patterns should be explicit for "go," "stop," and directional "casts." Once your dog has assimilated the above material, I recommend using two baseball configurations: a small one with 35-yard casts, and a full-size, formal pattern with a 250-yard BACK line from home plate through second base, and OVERS of at least 75 yards. Set the center line in the prevailing downwind direction. I drive a short, orange-painted stake into the field at each permanent station to ensure *accurate,* not general, cast points. I start by using the small pattern as a refresher course, then rest briefly before moving to the big pattern. This saves both the dog's and my energy on rerunning the big yardage after a cast refusal.

For correcting a cast or whistle refusal, many trainers who don't use electric collars employ a fifteen-foot check rope. If the dog *won't* take that OVER cast, the handler runs out to him and shakes or yanks him in the desired direction while repeating the command, indicating with the right arm "east" or the left arm "west." Often a short COME IN whistle can change the mind of a willful dog or one trying to outguess and anticipate your intentions; this breaks his single-minded train of thought. Upon total failure, you have force-fetch and the small baseball diamond to fall back on.

Whistle-stops must be practiced to perfection, beginning with the dog at close range, then adding greater distances. You should punish your dog for a "slipped whistle," that is, if he responds slowly or ignores the whistle altogether. But be *certain* that he can actually hear you before you discipline him; running water and high wind can interfere with whistle response.

On the big baseball pattern, sloppy sits and OVER casts may be anticipated and corrected by following the dog up the center line yourself immediately after you have sent him; when you blow your SIT whistle, your surprise presence is effectively felt. This method of training by suddenly arriving near your dog is known as the "tennis-shoe school." *Maintaining presence* has solid training value. Calling the dog all the way in to you after a rule infraction, and then punishing him, is less effective for several reasons. He may learn that he'll always get a second chance with a problem. He may recognize that every time he comes in to you, you reciprocate with unpleasantness. Most important, he will probably not identify his punishment with his error because the two occur at different sites, and he has forgotten his mistake on his way in to you. A slipped whistle or cast should be accounted for *at that spot.* Going to the dog in the water, for example, lets him understand that it is a *water* error, not a shore sin. Your dog should learn that the water is *not* a sanctuary where he can forget all previous instruction. Show him that *you* are amphibious, too.

Only when your dog is willing and accomplished at baseball on a clear surface should you change locations, add hazards to the casts, and polish the results: OVER directly into strong wind, OVER into water or across roads, BACK up difficult cliffs, banks, ditches, and rockslides, or BACK casts through avoidable water or cover.

Baseball and other drillwork are often boring, grinding, and less than creative for both of you. But they should be practiced at varying intervals and be included on your work chart. (Add four more categories: LBB for land baseball and LB for land blind, and WBB and WB for equivalent water work.) Show your dog *how* on all drills, then demand *results.*

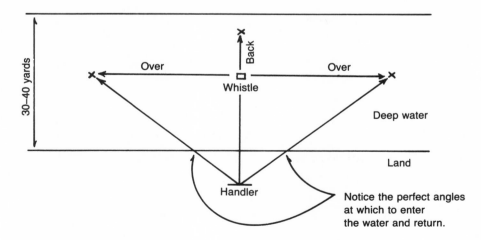

Diagram 16. Water baseball.

— *White Shirts and Hand Casts* —

In theory, the white handler coat should help your dog see you and your signals/casts easily at long distances by providing contrast with the background. Some handlers now believe in adding black gloves to heighten the contrasting image for the dog.

Be aware of the background. White is *not* a cure-all. If you are in white on a ridge with puffy clouds or fog behind you, for example, you are practically invisible to the dog. Wear a dark color in such circumstances. Be sure to extend your arms fully on casts. If your arm trails behind you on OVER, or is in shadow, or your arm flicks out too fast and too briefly, there is little chance for the dog to read your directions properly.

There are four primary casts for your dog at this stage of his development:

Right-hand "back"   Right "over"   Left "over"   "Come in"

Diagram 17. Directional hand casts with different backgrounds.

— *Additional Drills* —

Hand signals and "sit" whistles can be very useful in hunting pheasants. When you enter a field and work into a breeze with hot scents and running bird trails, toot your dog to a sit every time he begins to exceed comfortable gun range. Keep him at sit until you move up to him, then release him again with your cue to resume hunting. This continued practice will benefit you in at least four ways:

1. He won't run every damned pheasant to the end of creation.
2. The birds he *does* flush himself can be taken or passed according to your intent.

3. After the shot connects a few times, he may begin to understand the benefits of *quartering* before you within gun range.

4. The pheasants don't seem to mind your whistling in their field as much as your hollering.

Here's a dandy little drill that will help any young hunting dog before he goes into the field on opening day. Find a road or trail with a ditch and medium cover along its edge. Make sure a consistent wind is moving toward you and slightly to your right side. Plant six or eight "dizzied" pigeons (which have become disoriented by a windmill arm movement) thirty yards apart in this roadside cover. Mark each planted spot with a piece of surveyor's tape or a stick; then, with a shooting partner and your dog, walk the road again and let the dog "discover" the birds with his nose. Allow him to flush or catch the first few himself. Stop him on the whistle (and maybe a check cord) if he tries to chase the flighted bird across the field. Praise him, but call him back to find more game on this "discovery" trail. He should learn to leave the uneventful road to seek out and stir up action in the brush, but tweet him to a stop if he tries to ram ahead too far, too fast. Have your partner wing shoot the third or fourth bird if it is a *clean* opportunity to demonstrate to the pup how the whole team works—that is, "We go slow; we watch *you* use your nose and you buck the brush; we stay pretty close together; if you put up a bird, sometimes we shoot it and sometimes we *miss;* you retrieve it; sometimes you have to *sit* and wait for us—then we do it all again; and it's a hell of a lot of fun."

This chance for the dog to "honor" his nose (to act in response to the scent) is your opportunity to learn just what his body language projects when he is positively *making game,* clearly excited by the prospect of nosing out a bird. Some dogs express their birdiness by highly agitated tail action; others simply work superattentively in tight quartering quests. Probably the clearest signals for the upland hunter come when the veteran dog is fairly tired. Birdiness in a dog that has just exerted himself for two or three hours will usually mean he is genuinely *hot* on something, and not just wishful.

Making game or not, a hunter should never speed-chase after his hunting retriever, even though he wants to hurry and all signs say a flush is imminent. Stop the dog and move toward him. Pacing and restraining yourselves will usually yield more game by the end of a thorough hunt. Racing through a field or likely cover will cause you to shoot off balance and poorly, become winded, as well as prove to the dog that hunting is a speed contest. He is still a bit quicker than you are, but not as swift as a wild bird.

I want to shoot with both feet under me. I use a stop-go-stop rhythm when working a dog in cover for grouse, pheasant, or quail. This puts more pressure on a tight-holding bird, improves your hearing, and allows your dog the time to use his talents to the utmost.

When my dog is willing to muscle his way into promising brush and make game for me, I try to reciprocate by courteously waiting for him outside—until we both feel he's been thorough with it. I want to stay alertly planted in a position where my barrels can swing in the widest combination of directions. Your dog knows well enough if you abandon him in the wild grape or blackberry and walk on—and he'll remember this the next time. He also appreciates your ready gun when he sends some winged thing your way.

Hunting alone with a veteran bitch, I sometimes "sat" her at the end of a long, pheasant-riddled tule ditch. I carefully walked a C curve away from her and the deep ditch. When I reapproached the ditch a hundred yards away and posted myself there, I whistled a COME IN, indicating the corridor of tules with an arm signal. She knew damned well that pheasants were inside and responded. Caught in our vise, the birds rocketed as we joined each other—a practical impossibility for a dogless, solo hunter.

When I knock down a bird while my dog is deep in thick cover, and mismark it myself, I am forced to guess its whereabouts. I use a taught cue for my dogs to help me find it—before continuing our hunt. My cue, oddly enough, is FIND THE BIRD! In training for this, I drop an unseen bumper from my coat into medium cover, or during a slack period of a hunt, I do the same with a dead game bird. I point to the ground or cover three or four yards away from it and encourage my dog to work it out with his nose. If he moves away too far, I call him back and go through an excited patter of cuing and pointing until he discovers it. His reward is the find and high praise. I never use FETCH with a lost wild bird because I don't know where the hell it is myself. I don't use DEAD BIRD because that's his line-running cue, or whistles with OVERS and BACKS for the same reason. FIND THE BIRD simply means—we have one down; help me scour the area.

Once you have your dog taking nice sits, OVERS, and BACKS, never abuse or squander his new skill on cheap stunts, such as showing him off to your friends at cocktail parties, "over" to the party napkins, "back" to the vermouth. A great part of handling is convincing the dog that the boss *always* knows precisely where the bird is when handling commands are given. In the last light of one lovely summer evening, I asked my wife to help me with a long and diffi-

The air is dead and a light veil of rain twists, and unfolds quietly toward us. We are umbrellaed by a long canopy of broad buckeyes and pepper-woods when it whispers in. Scenting is prime for the bitch, and the leaves do not crackle. All the quail hush and hold, waiting for us and the rain.

We know. They know. We don't hurry. The lily-smooth safety snicks to *off* and the twenty is free to swing and speak. It is all about to start.

Before us, on the deep, leaf-carpeted floor, my eyes catch on the even symmetry of a barred, crossbow shape. I try to keep steel in my triggered concentration, but can't look away. In three silent strides, I kneel beside it. It is still warm. The large lemon-yellow eye is shocking and fierce in the gray, leaf-shaded light. A Cooper's hawk—female, immature, dashingly elegant and dead half an hour. She looks perfect. I feel along her keel and her breast sinks away in deep, emaciated concaves. Was she an incompetent huntress? Sick? Like a precious weapon she lies there, face-down and starved amidst her favorite banquet—quail. Yet even in death, it is she, not we, who holds the covey still, under leaf and branch, in air-raid terror.

cult mark. She tried throwing the bumper, but it was a low grass-skimmer and my dog didn't see it. I asked my wife to pick it up and try it again. She replied "I can't, it's across some water from me." My dog was a snappy freshman-class line runner and handler, so I figured, "I'll just let him take a stab at it as a blind." I sent him and he roared off. I didn't know where the bumper was and apparently my faithful bird thrower didn't either, because I hacked that dog around the marsh with OVERS and BACKS for twenty or thirty unproductive, blue-in-the-face whistles. In a rage I marched into the water, waded out to the vicinity of the mystery bumper, and had my wife handle *me* with more OVERS and BACKS. After four casts, I didn't think much of her authority, either. It was dark, the dog was still trying to help, and I was up to my knees in primordial ooze—so long, street shoes; adios, dinner in that nice restaurant up the road. The dog had totally lost the lesson. His confidence and my credibility were both seriously jeopardized.

Baseball and handling drills may be utilized long before your pup is out of the Derby, *if* he seems mature and has a thorough shot-bird marking foundation. I have seen a few trainers try to invert this procedure—to teach all han-

Upland hunting.

dling drills and forced patterns, line running, and blind retrieving *before* providing the dog with the confidence to mark birds. But the results have generally been disappointing. Stick to the program that experience has proven best—marking first—and when that has been mastered, move on to baseball and line running. Now let's look at the latter subject more closely.

9

Blinds and
Line Running

RUDDY DUCK CRUISING

The principal reason for teaching hunting and trial retrievers to run lines abstractly and handle over distances of land and water is to prepare them to recover game they didn't see fall. Ducks and geese that you see are hit but those that then sail a quarter of a mile into remote and inaccessible areas, and upland kills and cripples that fall in cover, could never be found without the help of a trained dog.

Line running is intrinsically the opposite of questing, that is, quartering to raise or scent game. In canine terms, line running would be akin to a wolf's pursuit by sight, as opposed to tracking the quarry's scent.

By teaching your dog to run directly at his marks during the Derby period, you have already begun the groundwork for good line running. If you have postponed any blind retrieves or lines until this marking material is solid, it may come as a shock to your dog—particularly if he's an excellent marker and an especially birdy dog—to find that there is more to learn than remembering where the birds fell. You may be forced to suspend *all* marking, regardless of his accomplishments, in order to concentrate on the *idea* of going for birds he didn't see fall.

By eliminating marks (which most dogs prefer to tricky blind retrieves) and employing a lean diet of lines, blinds, and handling work only, you'll get your dog to learn the new material, because he doesn't have anything else to do. The enjoyable marks can be reintroduced later when he shows a real grasp of lines and blind retrieves—usually in three to six weeks or longer.

If he doesn't resist the notion of blind retrieves and you haven't eliminated marks entirely, you may make considerable headway by creating the illusion that he has "forgotten" a mark somewhere and that you'll *help* him find it by lining him in that direction, perhaps assisting him with hand signals as he nears the bird.

This can sometimes be suggested by running a few double marks—one short and one long. Then move to a fresh, easy field, throw a short single—which he will pin—then attempt to run a blind where the long leg of a double would occur. This could be a north/south configuration, or north on the mark and east on the blind. One of my dogs used this system well with a short-flighted pigeon mark, followed by a medium-distance, 125-yard blind, forty-five degrees off the mark. His enthusiasm for the short retrieve of the shot bird seemed to enhance his acceptance of the blind retrieve.

The opposite approach sometimes works well on different dogs. Shoot the same short bird as above, but tell your dog NO!, heel him off of it, and run a short blind in another direction. Some receptive dogs hurry with the blind retrieve in order to get back to you quickly, so they can then go for the marked bird. This is the hunting premise, mentioned earlier, of going for the unseen, sailing cripple while leaving the sure, dead mark for later. In a field trial this is often called a "leave it" or "poison" bird test.

Another variation on the above two approaches is to place a live gunner out in the field. Show the dog the gunner and NO! him off that spot, then run him toward a blind. He may think the gunner has already shot a bird before he arrived and your lining him into the field is going to help him find it. Some trainers set out several wide-spaced blinds to improve the dog's chances of finding one quickly. If you can get him to pick up a blind in this fashion, instruct your gunner to shoot a bird for the dog in a *different* direction from that blind. When your pupil begins to understand that as soon as he completes a blind well, his reward will be a shot bird, he'll feel good about the procedure and will hustle on the return (a very stylish attribute in itself), in anticipation of his upcoming mark.

The axiom "Always plant the blinds deeper than the marks" is at this stage a very sound piece of advice. Repetition and patterns—repeated and memorized drills—are the keys to conveying to your dog the idea of taking lines to birds he doesn't see fall. Various forms of force training can open the door to control, but repetition involving real field conditions is what makes the dog functional. Pattern before you punish.

SIGHT BLINDS

Take your pup with you at heel and walk a straight line to the far, downwind end of a field. Drop a pile of bumpers at a conspicuous tree, gate, telephone pole, or rock and retrace your steps down the same line. Stop every fifteen yards and face the "blind," aiming your dog while cuing him with DEAD BIRD. At about forty yards, while all is still fresh in his mind, cue him and send him. Congratulate him on the first retrieve, then move another twenty-five yards down the exact line and send him again. Move farther and repeat. Two hundred and fifty to three hundred yards aren't impossible with a youngster. You are teaching him to run to an exact payoff *spot* without benefit of actually seeing a fall.

Use the *identical* line and planted spot two days later. Put out the bumpers without letting the dog watch, and attempt to run him from about forty or fifty yards out. If your star remembers the line, great! If not, walk him up and show him the target, then back off and *line* him as on the first day. This will eventually become an established, *permanent blind* for him.

Learning to recognize a series of these "permanent" blinds at different locations is his new task. Your first aim is to condition him to run or swim absolutely straight for a considerable distance along memorized lines. These "permanent" or quasi-blinds may not provide the mystery and challenge of a *cold blind*—that is, one that has never been seen or attempted by the student before—but they are the basis of the confidence to run hard and straight on cue for unseen, downed birds. Each of these pattern blinds may include one or more physical elements that require concentration for their correct navigation: a ditch, brush, water, and so on. Aligning, setting up, and aiming your dog for these permanent blinds is important practice. Your verbal cues for this job are a valuable part of the team rapport and credibility.

Another easy way to underscore line work is to walk your dog down a straight line in open flat land (I use the beach), and as you walk, plant white bumpers conspicuously every ten or fifteen yards. When you have arranged a precise line of six to ten clearly visible bumpers, cue him and send him—short, longer, longest. Some keen dogs actually worry about leaving a trail of valuable dummies behind and are anxious to gather them in for you. This drill is beneficial to the dog because he now must run over and past the spots where he previously picked up bumpers; in other cases he's been taught to pick up all the bumpers in one pile.

MARKED BLINDS

The marked blind is another useful exercise. Put a thrower out into the field and have your pup actually watch a bird or bumper thrown. Remove yourself and the dog behind a vehicle or screen while the thrower absents himself from the field. Return with your dog—after a period of from several minutes to several hours—and pick up the remaining bird with the commands DEAD BIRD and BACK. This is similar to the retired mark described on page 88; now, however, you are directing the dog to the bird, rather than letting him find it purely from memory. Use whistle-stops and hand signals if necessary. Try not to let him quest and hunt it out on his own.

A further variation is the *contrary terrain marked blind.* Place your helper on the far side of a forbidding field hazard—an angled ditch, downed log, or any other element that would naturally cause the dog to veer from a straight course. Have the helper shout to get your student's attention, then throw a bumper or bird high, straight up in the air so that it lands directly in front of him. Cue the dog with DEAD BIRD and send on BACK. This exercise conditions him to run straight for a target despite rough going at the start or in the middle of the trip.

You hope to teach your dog to *look straight and deep* into a field for a target or "picture" blind. You may start by putting an empty Clorox jug on a stake or a white paper plate on a bush above or behind a bumper or pile of bumpers. Natural objects, such as a tree, rock, fencepost, or pond, will eventually replace these as targets.

Some trainers prefer a technique called a "pop-up blind." A field is chosen with brush, trees or a rock, behind which the helper is hidden, downwind. The dog is then sent on a "cold blind"—he is cued and sent into a new, strange field with no enticing marks or aids. Presumably, he is advanced enough to carry part of the distance into the field on his own obliging goodwill. At the exact instant the dog begins to lose the faith and wander from his original line, the handler signals the hidden helper to shout, perhaps stand up, and flip a bumper to a preplanned spot ahead of the dog. (Sometimes the helper may stay silent and hidden and simply throw a bumper or bird on cue to the designated spot.) Too much of this, however, can create a dependence or distracting anticipation of the "pop-up" man.

Probably the most useful and reassuring means of starting your lining and blind work is to visit frequently your large permanent baseball pattern, running all three lines without whistle-stops or directional casts.

Another interesting idea for starting a dog into the field on a blind is one based on curiosity and rivalry. As a youngster, FC AFC Sunshine Rockabye Mickey, trained by Frank Lugo, was allowed to watch from the back of the truck as his older fellow retriever and rival, FC AFC Willie-Be-Good, ran his beautiful straight lines on training patterns. Once he had a good dose of spectator envy, Mickey was given a crack at the same lines. He thrived on it, and became the youngest dog to run and finish the 1974 National Amateur Stake.

One of the hardest adjustments for a good line-running dog is stopping on the whistle to be handled, and altering that first direction, even slightly. While some dogs are reassured by a whistle-stop and a signal BACK or OVER, certain virtuoso line runners, in fact, don't handle very well; they resent being interrupted once they're up to full speed. They have learned to pick out a target on the horizon, at which you have aimed your hand, and they're mentally prepared to *press on regardless* toward it, despite cover or obstacles. These dogs are so accurate and precise in their lines that they don't get much practice taking OVER hand signals.

Thus the better your dog learns to run a line, the more you should supplement his training with emphasized baseball, keeping his casts crisp. Don't accept mushy responses to hand signals—whether the OVER is into water, mud, the sun, or a stiff wind. Some of the trainers I respect most will forgo teaching the perfect line to firmly establish the solid cast. Train for perfection—stick to plain bread-and-butter ninety-degree OVERS and BACKS until your dog performs them accurately. At this sophomore stage, refrain from "angle back casts," especially when the dog is in swimming water (see pp. 165–166). It may help your dog visualize an "over" signal if you walk or run a few steps as you indicate the desired direction. Always attempt to handle your dog specifically and completely to the blind, rather than loosening up your control as he nears the desired area and allowing him to root it out independently with his nose.

Another handling problem that may arise as your dog learns to run hard down lines to blinds is "whistle-slipping." He may tell you and your whistle to, in effect, "shut up and watch me." This cocky new attitude isn't surprising; his force-fetch lessons have taught him to find something and hold it in his mouth by any and all means, and the early patterns are by now memorized to show where to go to get it. If this kind of whistle-slipping begins, I advance on the culprit, tennis-shoe style, when he's on his return trip—meeting him halfway, telling him to sit, slapping the bumper out of his mouth and recasting him empty-mouthed to a different bumper location. I don't like doing this too often; it can reduce his return speed. But it can help prevent him from thinking that all bets are off as long as he scores a quick bumper. I must add that I don't believe in handling the dog repeatedly through multiple OVERS and BACKS without finally rewarding him with a payoff for his effort.

You may find, in contrast to the above problems, that your dog is attentive to his whistle and directional cast commands, but his concentration on lines and lining diminishes easily—particularly in hot weather. What can you do about this? Start small, stay precise, carefully *build* your patterns with permanent lines to selected, memorized target spots. (I always try to keep a ten- to fifteen-yard buffer zone between a target and any dangerous or impassable objects—for example, barbwire or a cliff, or anywhere the dog is out of my sight.) Don't rush the elaborate advanced work. I find it satisfying to drive by an old training pattern that my dog has since outgrown. It's like kindergarten now—yet when we wrestled it earlier, it was a lunar probe.

I like to develop and expand twelve to fifteen permanent blinds gradually for my Qualifying-age dogs. Eventually, many more will be added. Each blind should involve one or more new elements—such as surprise water, tough foreground descent, a familiar landmark, wall of reeds, or difficult water entry. A tough Open-quality blind on land or in the water usually has demanding hazards in the foreground, in the middle, and at the end. After my dog has made a working tour of a dozen of these home blinds, I'm satisfied that he has experienced and succeeded in a sufficient number of different situations to try a "cold" blind on new turf.

Don't, however, then cruise the wilds, constantly seeking hairy cold blinds and running them, one after another. You will only shake your dog's confidence. One of the first things a good professional does, in fact, when traveling the trial circuit is establish workable, repeatable patterns to help strengthen his dogs. These blinds are similar in principle to their home patterns, and help remind the dogs of hard-won lessons.

Trainer Doug Orr of Washington says he never does cold blinds with young dogs. "I teach young dogs by letting them watch me tie the ducks up and go around the lakeshore with me when I put the ducks out. Later, when I take my dogs out of the truck, they *know* there are birds out there. I'm building enthusiasm and pictures. Cold blinds are OK for older dogs when you think they've been taught that picture." Jim Gonia, who lives in Washington, also likes to keep cold blinds to a minimum, placing greater emphasis on establishing twenty or so blinds in different areas that his dogs can perform well. Rex Carr of California, on the other hand, feels that "too many pattern blinds over a long period in the beginning without any cold blinds may complicate the transition to cold blinds. On days when you plan to do both kinds of blinds, favor cold blinds first, especially with young dogs."

Whichever training method you follow, pay careful attention to your dog's reactions and progress. As trainer J. J. Sweezey of Maryland says, "You get more out of maintaining confidence than you do out of pushing."

As your dog begins to comprehend his new handling work, I think it's necessary to begin eliminating any dependence you may have previously created by putting your hand down to assist him on marks. Use your hand *only* when lining him up for blind retrieves; release on his name for marks, but use BACK for blinds. This routine will help him separate his different responsibilities.

Eventually, you should also reduce the use of the conspicuous white bumpers, Clorox bottles, and other target devices, exchanging them for red, gray, and less plainly visible substitutes.

It is also advisable at this time to stop placing or floating large numbers of bumpers at the end of land and water patterns. As a beginner, a pup needs to know there are plenty of bumpers in the field, but when piles of them become commonplace to him, they merely encourage him to think that he'll get a second chance if he louses up. Amateur trainers have the advantage of being able to plant a single bird at each desired location and conveniently running it. Professionals with large groups of dogs to train—and a limited amount of time—must put out mountains of bumpers.

If by now your dog is strong on his formal baseball diamond work and has memorized a dozen blinds, you are equipped to reintroduce marks with his patterns—but cautiously. I think the center line of the large baseball diamond is ideal for this use. Run your dog on this long middle line to his familiar second-base blind. Put him in his crate while he catches his breath, and add a pair of bird throwers to the configuration. Place them near the lines to first and third, and instruct them to throw a simple, short double mark *away* from the line to second base. (Later, as the dog advances, you may *converge* these throws.) Bring your dog back out and give him the double. If he does it perfectly, carefully line him up for the long second-base blind and send him. If he tries to return to either mark, shout NO! and call him back, re-line him, and send him again. Don't *handle.* If he continues to be distracted by the marks, move up the center line by increments—until you are completely past the marks if need be—and send him again until he understands that his blind is still out there waiting. Then repeat the entire pattern.

The magnetic attraction of a mark, influencing a dog as he performs a blind, is called "pull" or "suction." Carrying past the marks successfully to a blind is referred to as the ability to "divert."

Once your dog digests the idea of short or medium marks followed by a long blind, visit each of your permanent blinds and pop a single or double mark to the sides, then run the memorized blind. Don't run the blind if he has much trouble on the marks. Save it for the next time when he does well. As he progresses with this work, try picking up the marks but delaying running past them to the blind for several hours. If he hangs up in the vicinity of the marks he has previously retrieved, retreat to the earlier method of running the blinds immediately after the marks.

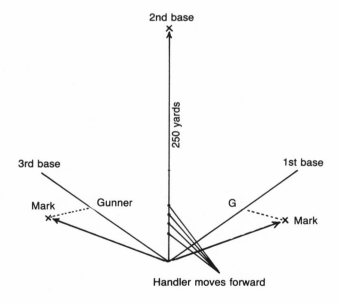

Diagram 18. Introducing marks to the pattern blind.

CHANNEL BLINDS

As with the Derby marks, try to refrain from water work until your dog has a good grasp of his blind retrieves on land. When you are convinced that he understands your commands, begin simple, direct lessons in water. Your dog should retain his earlier shore lessons (see pp. 91–102).

The cardinal drill for new water work is the *channel blind.* Find a straight, deep, narrow length of water. You are about to teach your dog that you definitely prefer his swimming to running the shoreline—especially on a water blind.

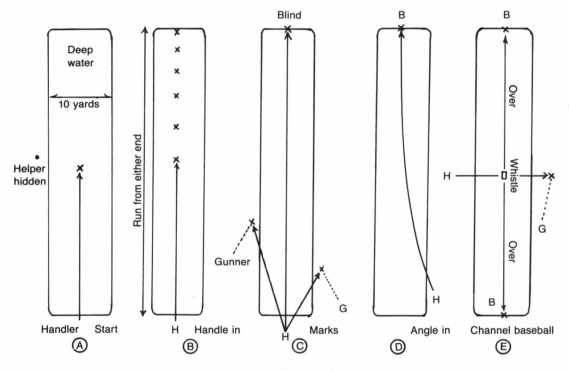

Diagram 19. Channel drills.

A. With your dog, start at the water's edge and toss a large white bumper forty yards down the channel. Make sure the bumper is precisely centered and not wind-blown to the shore. Send your dog on DEAD BIRD and BACK. If he swims on a true line to the bumper, encourage him to swim just as straight a return, without hauling out on the side banks. Repeat it again at fifty or sixty yards.

It will occur to most dogs, as the swim path is lengthened, that there *has*

The channel blind drill. In narrow corridors of water the dog should learn to swim in a true line rather than landing on shore and running along the bank.

to be a better, faster way to the damned bumper—such as climbing out and zipping along the bank and reentering. Your helpers may be stationed, even hidden, along each left and right bank to haze and intimidate the dog and thus "walk" him up and down the channel's middle. If the dog starts to climb out on shore, your helpers may order him back by voice, or poke him with a broom or blunt pole (see p. 39) or pick up the dog and throw him back into the water (see "Shore Breaking and Bank Training," pp. 98 and 100). You should remain at the start station, simply sending and receiving in a firm, friendly manner. As your dog discovers that the exact center of the lane of water is the wisest and safest space to occupy, the helpers' presence will act merely as a reminder. The blind should be built out and repeated until he has the power to swim at least 100 yards down this channel—from either end of it.

As your dog begins to gain confidence in this forced drill, remove the side help. He may have to be handled over and back if he tries bailing out on to land, but a series of such casts (known as "shoe-stringing" the banks) is not acceptable.

When you think your young friend genuinely recognizes the correct course, move away from the end of the water by five- and ten-yard increments, so he has a real choice of going by land or by water. He must be willing to vote for the water every time.

B. Face your sitting dog and try to handle him into the channel from 15 or 20 yards away, using a raised-arm BACK. If the center of this channel has already become his favorite place, find a narrower, longer body of water—200 to 250 yards—or one with a slight curve in it (see diag. 20).

On a bend of water, the handler, standing at H1, angles his dog into a channel blind retrieve (1). On completion, handler and dog move to the positions shown at H2. The dog must now swim past the previous blind (1) toward a second blind (2) to perform the retrieve successfully. The third and fourth positions show a repetition of the same principle.

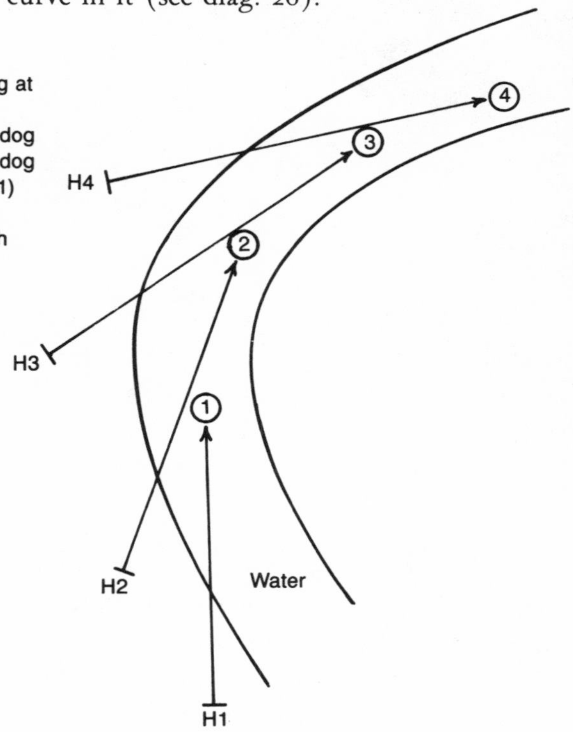

Diagram 20. Curved channel drill.

C. When he graduates from these exercises, drop land *marks* on the sides, so he *has* to get out and then back into the water in order to return correctly with them. *Then* run the channel blind up the center.

D. Next, try angling into the channel from a side angle, to convince both of you that he has the plan down pat.

E. Another reinforcement of this lesson is to use the channel in the manner of a baseball pattern. Approach the channel from one side and have your helper throw a single mark on land directly across the water from you. Send your dog. As he reaches the center of the channel, stop him with the whistle and arm-signal him OVER left or right to previously planted blinds at either end of the channel. After his correct completion of each directional cast, send him for the mark, and when this is retrieved, then throw the same mark, stop him in the water again, and cast him OVER toward the opposite end of the channel. Repeat the drill.

Why all this exaggerated water work? It is intended to prepare your dog for difficult patterns—paralleling shorelines, or long OVER casts into water (see pp. 172-173)—and to convince him that swimming the length of a lake is easy and logical; when hunting, and his boss loses a long duck in extremely cold water, there is no choice but to find it. This work also teaches the dog that water itself, not the shore, is the correct medium, and it helps eliminate the distractions of looking for convenient landing sites. The dog may finally learn to "channel" so well and so far that he'll have to be "taught" how to get out of the water again—not a bad predicament at this stage.

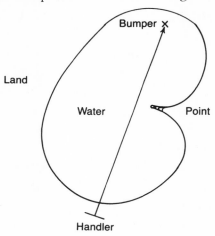

Diagram 21. Swimming past a point.

A good drill with which to follow excellent channel exercises is swimming *past* points of land. Select a site with deep water, firm banks, and a point fairly near to you. NO! the dog off if he tries to land, or have a helper haze him off as you did in the channel lesson. If he understands the "stay wet" message, move to similar blinds where the swim is longer and there's more time to tire out and study the attractive point as he swims toward it. Remember, as you plant or float these water blinds, that lessons are clarified for your dog if the bumper is in deep water and not on the shore edge. If land and beaching are part of your water blind, place the bumper well up on the land (at least ten yards).

SUNDOWN TRAINING AND THE TIME OF DAY

If the evening sun is just above the horizon, it's risky to set up complicated tests for your dog. You won't have time to repeat them, and he may not understand the lesson fully before all sunlight is gone.

Occasionally, though, I practice a surprise *time-of-day* drill, which flies in the face of most training rules I've tried to cultivate. I call it the "Moon-Came-Up Special."

Take your student and a change of dry clothes out to your warm-water channel at sundown. Work him repeatedly, the full length of the channel from either end to numerous waiting bumpers. At normal quitting time—dusk— he'll probably try to explain that his union doesn't allow him to work overtime, but proceed into the moonlight with those swimming laps as though you'd forgotten both your wristwatch and your senses. You may have to join him in the water yourself, but continue until he fully resigns himself to a *full night's work* and forgets the shoreline, the location of your car, and the luxury of his crate. Drastically altering your training schedule with such an exercise is useful, because smart dogs tend to learn their routines and program themselves for them and them alone. Amateur trainers with nine-to-five jobs are generally confined to predictable time slots for training. Due to scheduling, one of my dogs, for example, was prepared to do all his best work only at dawn or dusk; trial work at noon completely threw him off.

Trainers usually take their dogs from their cars or trucks and head immediately into the action of the lesson. Dogs understand this timing too, but in trial and hunting situations you are rarely afforded the luxury of instantly knocking down birds or heading directly to the line to run a test. If your dog is held up for fifteen or twenty minutes behind holding screens, he will frequently go flat before he even reaches the judges. Vary your *wait time* in training to guard against souring and boredom.

WEATHER

I have designed some special Qualifying blinds during the summer months. As several small stock ponds dry up completely, I develop some very contrary pattern lines that run handsomely through these empty ponds. During the fall rains they fill again and become extremely challenging Open blinds. In winter, they may even hold ice. Low and high tidal water, changing wind directions, and perennial stands of cover can vary the difficulties in these patterns for your dog.

The difference between swimming in and running in water is a complex subject. To some dogs *running water* brings out exuberance and slipped whistles, often due to splash noise; others slow down and worry or feel guilty about not being wet enough. The trial advantage goes to the slow animal—the "pig"—who makes only small ripples during his efforts. Eventually, you will have to teach your dog to *listen* in running water; but be sure to forgive him if you're doubtful of his ability to hear. Remember: a small, short-legged bitch can cruise quietly through water that creates noise problems with large, long-legged dogs.

Weather changes, such as the approach of foul weather, wind shifts, frost, and lowered water temperature, can change a Qualifying blind into a highly challenging test.

I recall a dog-destroyer of an ice blind at a National Open held in the mountains of Nevada. The sun had not yet risen, but the competing dogs were called forward. The first to run was NAFC FC CNFC River Oaks Corky. He plunged courageously through the frozen crusts and fought his way past slabs of creaking blue ice, as he carried his line to the bird without a hand signal or whistle. When the great dog presented his bird, his frosted coat resembled a silver porcupine. I looked at the same blind on a warm spring afternoon the following year—it was a piece of cake.

Watch the weather conditions before asking your dog to perform any drill. A number of National champions have been trained slowly and carefully in warm water, yet didn't buckle in cold-water contests in the fall or winter.

Some trainers I've known seek cold-water sites in order to force-train under these exaggerated conditions. If you are hell-bent on teaching your dog how cold and scary the world can be, remember that he is your partner, and that different dogs can have different tolerances to pain and cold. I wouldn't put my retrievers into breaking surf that I can't easily swim myself. Your dog has little to gain and much to lose by training in formidable conditions, unless these are conditions under which you routinely shoot. I've spoken at length about this with trainers from cold states like Alaska and Wisconsin. It is interesting to note that the best dogs invariably have the most careful winter trainers.

In addition to staying aware of environmental changes, be conscious of changes in your *dog* as well. If your male has just been bred, he may not give his full attention to his work. If he has had an exciting pheasant or duck hunt on Saturday, don't insist on abstract blind training on Sunday. Bitches coming in (or out of) season may be forgiven for a lack of the usual zip or ambition. Under such circumstances, try to use birds and reduce the complexities of your training.

MORE PATTERNS

As you work toward more complicated patterns, note the similarities of structure of those you are trying to teach now and those in the following chapter. Invent, borrow, cross-pollinate your own ideas as you need them and use a combination of *pressure* and *promise* of reward, whether on blinds or marks.

I like to develop a plain 130-yard blind through a foreground ditch. When the dog has this 100 percent pat, move over 30 yards and lay an identical parallel blind through the same ditch and run it cold. You'll probably have to fight him off his original blind, but once he's convinced that there are two distinct parallel lines in the same field leading to two separate blinds, he'll have advanced a big step.

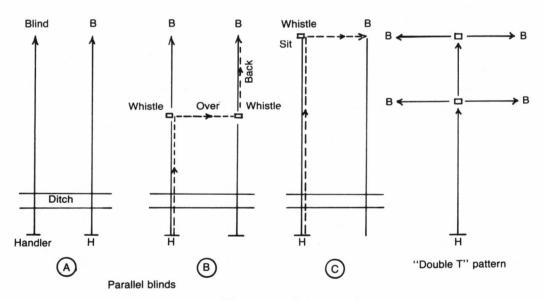

Diagram 22. Patterns.

(A) When both blinds are well accomplished, you can (B) stop him halfway down one line and transfer him on a straight OVER to the other line, then pick up that bird on a BACK. Or (C) plant only one of the blinds, but run the opposite line and stop the dog at the end and direct him with an OVER to the other terminal point. This exercise, as well as the "double T," is a variation on primary baseball.

Among some of the great line-running dogs I have known or judged are those that can inform the handler when they're *ready* to go and are "locked" on the sure line. However, even though the spine and nose are perfectly pointed, some dogs may continue to sweep the field for possible targets with minute shifts of their eyes. NFC AFC McGuffy would carefully scan, then *lock* at the cue of a light clucking of his handler's tongue—remarkable rapport. Other dogs can lock on a verbal cue, such as "No!, no!, no!" "Good!" or "That's it!" then be sent on BACK.

A commonly used drill, called a *wagon wheel,* was pioneered by professional Rex Carr. This is a series of lines radiating from a central point to an obvious ring of bumpers, thirty yards distant. You and your dog occupy the center hub with the "spokes" as lines to each bumper. You may throw them into place from the center or sit the dog in the center and walk the perimeter, dropping them equidistant from each other. Line and send your dog in the sequence you choose. Pivot carefully, set up, and aim specifically. NO! him off attempts to retrieve on a wrong line. Use big, conspicuous white bumpers.

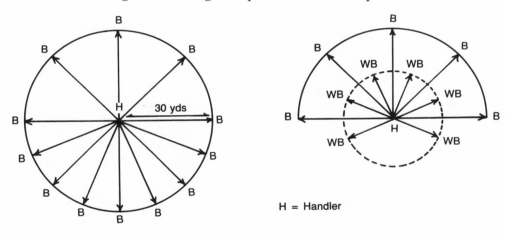

Diagram 23. Wagon-wheel drill using white (WB) and red (B) bumpers.

When this drill is solidly mastered, a very demanding variation can be substituted. Use the same configuration—but place less visible red or gray bumpers on an outer ring, forty yards from the central point, in the same arrangement as before. Now build an inner circle of white bumpers on alternate shorter lines from these reds and grays. Set up and aim the dog to retrieve *only* the deeper red bumpers. He must memorize your lining direction thoroughly in order to ignore the whites that he passes en route to the reds.

Most trainers practice their pattern work in quiet, unperplexing circumstances. Because of this, many young dogs that have just begun to grasp the concepts of handling are easily distracted by noise, voices, coughs, door slams, and so on. A resulting weakness in some formerly good marking dogs is the tendency to "pop," that is, to give up his hunt or stop running on a blind retrieve and look at his handler for help through a hand signal. A simple cure for noise-wariness is to make noise as you train. Play the truck or car radio loud as you do your drills. If you are training with a group, ask them to contribute small distractions.

During this period of teaching blinds and marks together you may find that the quality of your dog's marking becomes inefficient or frivolous, or that he begins to "switch" on marks, that is, he abandons his hunt for one bird and moves off to find another more easily remembered one during a multiple retrieve. A drill called *corn cobbing* or *dirt clodding* is useful as an "antiswitch," "antipop," and antifrivolity lesson.

Find a dirt clod field and put a helper out eighty yards or so, with a live or dead bird to throw. Place another helper at about the same distance, but at a ninety-degree angle from you and the first. Have your bird thrower toss his bird as a normal mark, then have the second thrower chuck a large dirt clod—which will smash on impact. Send your dog in normal fashion for this last "bird" down. Let him hunt fruitlessly for six to seven minutes. If he gives up the area, tell him to FETCH and hunt some more. If he "switches" toward the other memory mark, promptly punish him by dragging him over to the area where the clod landed. Your clod thrower, while you're doing this, should secretly flip a dead bird out to the spot where his clod fell. Your dog will be amazed to find, after his search and abandonment of the area, a real bird!

Repeat the same test with two real birds. The dog should feel relieved to find them both. But again, fake the fall if he can't learn to hunt an area thoroughly. This drill can also help a hunter find a downed bird that has run some distance, or hidden in a muskrat hole or crack in the mud. Corn cobbing is the identical drill, but executed with a tossed cob into a cornfield full of millions of them.

Happy bumpers are short, playful handler-thrown marks that allow the dog to race and *break*. They have a useful place in dog training, but care and discretion should always accompany their use. Individual dogs interpret happy bumpers quite differently. For some, these bumpers represent a reward after a job well done, and relief of pressure after a difficult lesson. With others, however, this fun time serves only to cancel a lesson you've both just worked like hell to master. A very tough lesson, followed by a few happy bumpers, and then *resumption* of the same tough stuff, is very stressful to some dogs and can result in a broken will.

After a long day in the field with AFC Rip Snortin' Good Times.

HUNTING VERSUS TRIALING

Many trialers feel their dogs are far too valuable to waste on casual, ordinary hunts. Would you take a richly engraved high-grade Parker or Holland and Holland shotgun out in a storm? they ask.

In contrast, I believe in hunting any trial dog I own. Many friends and rivals have hunted their dogs, too: Ray Goodrich with FC AFC Carmoney Brigadier and FC NAFC Ray's Rascal, John Anderson with FC AFC T. R. Tucker and FC AFC Wild Hearted Dinah, and Charlie Hill with NFC NAFC CNFC Wanapum Dart's Dandy, to name a few.

Remember, however, that if you are starting your pup with the goal of trialing in mind, it is sound practice to teach and structure his lessons toward that alone for two or three years before hunting him. The conversion of a young trial dog to a hunter is often far easier than that of hunter to trialer, though most of the basic work is identical. It's a very fine dog that can both hunt and trial well.

Hunting wild pheasants is especially corruptive to the intense discipline of trial training. On the other hand, I welcome the interference when a flock of teal or coot splashes through my training blind, laying their wakes under my dog's nose; I know this can teach him to ignore unscheduled distractions. Shooting coots, or other wild things, simply as "marks" for your dog is poor practice, since the presence and scent of these birds may distract him later when delicacies such as pintails or mallards are close at hand.

I love to watch the eyes of a veteran duck dog as he scans the sky for me. When a flight of coot or willets passes, he turns his head elsewhere; at a marsh hawk, heron, owl, or gull he yawns, but at a speeding wedge of canvasbacks he stiffens and fastens on them, and sometimes he quietly flattens himself to the ground.

— *Honoring* —

Your dog will probably be asked to *honor*—to sit quietly and alertly at the ready, while other retrievers work—during a Qualifying stake, or at some point during a hunt. Steadiness, control, and honoring are extremely valuable etiquette in your duck blind for incoming birds, down birds, or other working dogs. You must introduce a new cue or command to signal that you *don't want* these birds retrieved. I use NO BIRD! accompanied by some alteration in our familiar working procedure—such as folding my arms, facing in an unlikely position for sending him, or heeling and sitting the dog by my opposite leg, rather than the familiar one.

Commanding the dog to lie down (CHARGE) will sometimes help him to understand honoring, since the dog must respond with two movements in order to leave—get to his feet and then go—instead of simply firing off from the sit position. Even though some judges will not allow your dog to honor lying down in a trial, this command can be helpful in the cramped quarters of your duck blind or boat and in various other situations. It's also convenient temporarily to leave your dog in the "down" position while you investigate alone or visit with another hunter and his dogs. To teach your dog to lie down, collar and leash him, face him, and tell him to sit; then, with the leash suspended between your hand and his neck, step down gradually on the leash while commanding DOWN, CHARGE, or whatever word you choose as he is pulled down by your weight. A hand cue can also be included: extend your hand flat and parallel to the ground in a lowering gesture, as if laying it on a table. DOWN can also be shown leashless with a willing student by sitting him, then extending his forelegs and gently pressing his shoulders. Remember, though, that the big Alpha males resent and resist this position; to them it represents submission and surrender.

When your dog is finally capable of doing all the work in this chapter, you will have a solid hunting companion. Indeed, he will be a more accomplished and trustworthy dog than most hunters will ever be privileged to know. And the man who chooses to abstain from hunting altogether while his dog's trialing career is active—waiting until after retirement before rewarding him with outings and wild birds—will ultimately find himself blessed with a magnificent partner in the field.

FAVORITE DRILLS OF THE EXPERTS

Now that you have built up a repertoire of drills and patterns with your dog, you may wish to learn which areas some excellent trainers like to emphasize.

"To keep my dogs sweet and going well," says J. J. Sweezey, "I do a lot of singles, fairly short, not more than seventy-five yards—about 60 percent bumpers and 40 percent birds. I like to use a lot of shot ducks. I use these across water and into cover. I shoot birds myself off line and this seems to lift the dogs up. Also, I believe in petting and touching my dogs a lot, whether we're just exercising or working. I pat them on the shoulder when they have the bird in their mouth; let them be proud of it."

"A good rule to follow," advises Rex Carr, "is do multiples when a dog is marking well. Another good rule is to do multiples that your dog can do successfully. After three or four successful multiples there is no harm trying a nitty-gritty multiple regardless of outcome. If it's good, pursue multiples with added difficulty but if the dog fails, back off and go back to easier multiples, to build on success.

"Except in rare cases, you can't go wrong training on singles. Successful marking is most beneficial and productive. Successive marking failures can be detrimental and a serious mistake."

"My favorite drills," reports John Anderson of Winters, California, "include short pattern blinds with obstacles in the foreground. Simple things I can do in a large vegetable garden. I get a lot of good *control* results, and the dogs learn to cue to the hand as to where they are supposed to go."

Jim Gonia favors triple blind drills. "I have a variety of them," he says. "As the dog approaches the field or water I tell him 'dead bird' and he automatically knows there's one out there. He knows where all three of them are, but he has to relate to you to know which one he is going to get. You can hit him with a whistle and get an angle back cast. It's good practice for when the dog starts on a bad initial line; I've got to change his mind quickly, to build confidence in changing directions when he curls to one of the side blinds. Sometimes I let him almost get to it and then give a straight (ninety degree) 'over' to the other spot. I like it; it gives last-minute control. The dog likes it, too."

Sal Gelardi of Woodland, California, explains that "with young dogs and old ones, too, I like to do handler-thrown triples. I think it gives tremendous communication with the dog and gets him sharpened up, ready for a training session. I like to throw one in the middle short, then throw the hell out of the ones on the outside."

PROBLEMS AND PROCEDURES

Bolting. Bolting—sometimes called "selling out"—is when your dog panics and takes off in order to escape you and/or certain problems. Pressure is the chief cause; however, some areas of advanced work are quite bewildering and will cause a mental washout in a sensitive dog. Acceptance of the trainer's disapproval, pain thresholds, desire to please and to retrieve vary widely from one dog to another; in fact, a bolting dog may have litter mates that don't bolt even though their training was identical. When any dog begins to hold a "safe" distance between himself and his handler, or won't come in when called to readdress a field problem, or deliberately takes off for the next county, the lesson you have in mind for him is lost because he has split his attention and allegiance.

"Once they've started to bolt," says professional Roy Gonia, "some dogs will bolt the rest of their lives, even though they might otherwise be excellent dogs. Some of them just get demoralized and run. Sometimes a big, strange field will do it. Other times they take off because I make them do something and get on them too hard. I find them half a mile away, just having a good time."

Many expert trainers expect certain dogs to bolt and are careful to note for future work what triggered it. Calling the dog back to you in displeasure and then working him over will assuredly sow the seeds for it. It doesn't require a smart dog to figure that out. One aspect of bolting is certain: the more a dog bolts, successively and successfully, the quicker he is apt to leave again.

If a dog bolts to avoid a hazard or simple lesson, I believe in rerunning him on it after he has been recovered, so the bolt is not a direct reward or substitute for performance. A long check cord can safeguard against a recurrence of the problem.

Several experts believe they can "debolt" a dog. Some reinforce aspects of obedience and force work; others attempt to convince the dog he cannot escape. Effectiveness will depend on the trainer's skill and the nature of the dog. If you have a bolter, try not to lose your temper. Examine your training approach and be certain you provide gratification and reward in his work—and equip him with a collar that carries his name and your name, phone number, and address.

Popping. As mentioned previously, when a dog stops in the middle of running a line or hunting a bird to look back toward his handler for some form of assistance, he has "popped." Trainer Barbara Ornbaun of Suisun, California, feels that "most popping comes from some kind of confusion: (1) a lack of confidence in what a dog is doing or where he is going; (2) an honest fear of making a mistake—trying too hard to be careful to choose the most approved route; (3) resentfulness or unwillingness about where and through what he is being sent."

Corrective methods vary from one trainer to another. Roy Gonia advises, "Shorten up all work, marks, and blinds. Go back to easy work and [your dog will] get the confidence to go." Ed Minoggi finds that a dog usually pops in a new situation. "Run him over the old blinds every day a few times and then try to add a new one. The minute he pops on a blind, go out there and let him know that he's made a mistake. You can't compound it by accepting a single pop because you're going to get another right away."

Tom Sorenson, a fine Missouri professional, notices that "many dogs will pop at the same distance each time they are sent on a blind. If the trainer can recognize where this spot is, he can hide someone in the field and have him throw out a bird, on an agreed signal, just in front of the dog as he reaches that pop area. It can teach a dog to look ahead and keep moving forward, and give him confidence in a reward. Rather than rely on force, I like a dog to *want* to go for a bird."

My personal feeling is that to avoid popping, restrain yourself from using hand signals on a difficult set of multiple marks in training. Have the thrower help the dog, or let him hunt long and hard, or call him in and throw the birds again for him. Break the test into singles if absolutely necessary. Popping on blinds is often the result of running too many cold blinds, thereby eroding the dog's confidence in his direction and mission. I have watched legions of good marking dogs handled to marks they couldn't remember on their own, and not gain any experience from such whistle help. On the repeat of the same test they usually run the same erroneous route as before. What they *do* learn is to pop. Handling on a tough mark is a convenience only to the handler, an expedient for saving time or physical effort. A diligent dog is often surprised and offended when a serious hunt for a mark is interrupted by a whistle and hand signal.

One of the chief causes of insecurity in an advancing dog is not recognizing the difference between being sent for marks and blinds. He doesn't properly separate the two tasks. If you have handled your dog on two-thirds of a difficult triple mark and then attempt to run a double blind through these marks, it is very possible that he will come away from it thinking he has just successfully run a complicated single mark with a lot of gunfire and a quadruple blind. The result is mental spaghetti—eventually leading to popping and slipped whistles—no matter how beautifully the dog handled.

Bear in mind that your program of conditioning—to honor his nose for his marks and ignore scent on the blind—is further cause for doubt, confusion, and popping. Until the dog is bristling with confidence in both areas of marking and blinds, use an equation of easy marks and complicated blinds, or complicated marks and easy blinds, or just blinds. When my dog does not mark his birds well, however simple they are, I forgo running any blind in that area until another day. Decide which area you wish to emphasize, and bear *that* in mind as you see your dog through an exercise.

Hardmouth. This describes a dog that bites down overly hard on game as he retrieves it. I have worked with several dogs that were hardmouthed. One accomplished dog discovered the immense power in her jaws almost overnight (after being supplied with large bones to chew to clean her teeth) and abandoned her previous gentleness with birds; she began a smug campaign of killing, though not mutilating, almost every live bird she was sent for.

In exasperation, I discontinued all fieldwork and decided to teach force-fetch all over again. I bought a hundred cheap balloons that inflated to a bumperlike shape. I started in the yard with genuine bumpers (chomp) and gradually integrated the first balloon (chomp).... Bang! The explosion caused no fear, simply embarrassment for the disappearance. I reintroduced the old cue HOLD to help correct her jaw problem and continued the fetch lesson, alternating between bumpers and balloons. She began to learn new respect for the cargo and was soon able to retrieve a pile of balloons from rough ground. I then included a live bird on a rotating basis—bumper, balloon, live bird—with very satisfactory results, using the cue as a reminder, and much repetition. Fortunately, I was able to restore her lovely, soft mouth.

Another dog unwittingly damaged birds by dropping and gripping them again. He refused to retrieve balloons. He was cured by insisting that he retrieve uncomfortable objects such as wire brushes, heavy bricks, and a rubber glove filled with water. I also commanded him to sit and drop the birds at the point where he was most likely to rough them up—fifty or sixty yards from me. This so surprised him that when he was commanded to FETCH again he was relieved and conspicuously gentle with his bird for the rest of the journey.

In a similar situation, the owner of a fine-marking bitch solved the hard-mouth problem *in the duck blind.* As each shot duck fell into the decoys, her handler and his shooting partner simply delayed the retrieve by deliberately smoking a cigarette, or taking a coffee break, or exchanging conversation *before* releasing her to retrieve. Apparently her manic mouth was connected to the surge of adrenalin from watching the birds fall, and the delayed release provided time to level the "crazies," reestablish her gentle mouth, and still keep her wonderful style. However, retrieving with a delay is a luxury that cannot be offered to a trial dog.

Many trainers forgive and dismiss roughmouth behavior in training, noting that the game should have been shot dead and that its condition need only be "fit for the table." I find hard-used birds difficult to tolerate in my dogs and believe it can lead to sticking and freezing in a keen, possessive dog.

Stickiness. This is a dog's unwillingness or reluctance to release a bird to the handler. "Most dogs that are sticky experience *no real force-breaking* as a young dog," says Jim Gonia. "I force them to pick up [a bird] and I force them to let go of it when they are kids. If you have a sticky dog, he should be drilled at home and in training to let go of that bird anywhere."

Dogs should be carefully brought to sit and heel after they bring in *any* bird. *Don't grab.* If you are right-handed, take the bird methodically with the right hand below the dog's jaws while keeping full eye contact and holding an extended left index finger ten or so inches above his muzzle. If he hesitates on his release, deliver a routine *thunk* with the raised index finger across the bridge of his nose on a cue of DROP or OUT. Most dogs will quickly learn to drop the bird into your hand. The method of your distinct, well-timed commands is the key: (1) HEEL, (2) SIT, (3) HOLD, (4) DROP.

A ready, dependable companion.

A wet retriever shaking water from his coat will usually tighten his grip on the bird and damage or whiplash it. He may set it down on the bank before his delivery for a leisurely shake, thereby allowing a wounded bird to escape as a cripple. Condition your dog to shake *only* after delivery.

Freezing. This is a dog's absolute refusal to release the bird to the handler. Sometimes these dogs seem to be in an oblivious, catatonic state—fastened to the bird.

"A true freezing dog," Jim Gonia says, "actually goes into a trance at a trial—due to people, guns, and whatever turns them on. The trick is to break the trance. I prefer to use good eye contact rather than a word command. This transmits the implication, 'Guess what's going to happen to you if you don't let go?' Change the routine and thus break the spell. Make him uncomfortable; have him deliver the bird on the right or left side—opposite of normal. Sit him and walk around to his blind side to take the bird, for example; take the bird as you normally *wouldn't* with one or two hands. Vary commands from GIVE to OUT or LEAVE IT, so the dog thinks something different is about to happen. But there's no real cure for a true freezer. There are temporary cures, but he'll go back into it later."

If your dog has succeeded on the exercises discussed in this chapter, you should feel proud of him. He certainly will make a superb hunting dog, whether on land or in water, and a dependable companion for days afield. He will be a stiff competitor in Qualifying trials, but there are higher levels of achievement still. Exercises and drills for the advanced dog are taken up in the following chapter.

10

Training for Advanced Competition

MONTANA HUNGARIAN PARTRIDGE

The major stakes, Open and Amateur, provide an excellent opportunity to expand your dog's performance and increase your handling skills and experience. Dogs that have never been brilliant markers sometimes excel in advanced work. And many amateur trainers wish to go beyond the Qualifying stakes in dog performance.

At this stage of development, however, a handler should realize that his decision to proceed is a decision to go beyond most practical hunting needs. Nevertheless, it should not be assumed that the goal of developing a fine field-trial dog interferes with the dog's hunting ability. I've hunted over my dogs FC AFC Nakai Anny, 1977 National Derby Champion, Dr. Davey, Ph.D., his sister and brother, NFC AFC Risky Business Ruby and AFC Rip Snortin' Good Times. The letters *FC* (Field Champion) and *AFC* (Amateur Field Champion) before a dog's name, or nearby in his pedigree, are like the proofmarks on the barrels of a fine shotgun—symbols of excellence and dependability.

156

AFC Rip Snortin' Good Times delivers.

The levee was old, built of crumbling peat and dragline mud. Wheezing bamboo thickets and tight wildrose guarded its shoulders. A slough snaked alongside, its broad surface chiseled to white caps by a stiff wind. My three Labs frantically rammed their way through the cover and hot bird scent. Twenty-four hours earlier, I had stepped wearily off a jetliner in San Francisco. I still felt like hell. The National Open Championship had gone poorly for us. We hadn't won. But somewhere high above Kansas, the recovery process had begun. "Maybe I'll hunt tomorrow. Hunt pheasants. I'll take all the dogs; it ought to be a circus."

Most of the pheasants today were track stars; those that didn't run held close in the protective rose thorns. My two young males had already lacerated their noses and eyelids in their enthusiasm—Nakai, their seasoned mother, went about her hunt more carefully and thoroughly worried the holding birds. Two roosters burst skyward, their long tails twisting with each wingbeat. The Parker spoke once and a pheasant tumbled into the pickleweed; the second barrel tagged the next bird and he dipped toward the choppy waves, then managed to hold out his wings long enough to crash into the bamboo on the far shore. None of the dogs was in a position to mark him.

I called the dogs to me and sat them. Nakai had marked the first rooster and presented it to me. I selected Rip and sent him on a blind retrieve across the hundred-yard-wide channel and waited. Once there, he hauled out on the bank and entered the cane wall slightly upwind of the downed bird. I couldn't see him to give him further hand signals. I waited. No dog, no bird. Like an archer drawing a second arrow from his quiver, I lined up the old lady and launched her on a line slightly downwind of her son. She swam ambitiously across and entered the cover ten yards below Rip's exit point on the high bank. Again I waited. Nothing! Finally I called on Davey, sending him even farther downwind, hoping that he would wind the cripple as he passed even with it in the deep cane. He rapidly cut the waves and then drove through the wall. Alone with an empty quiver, I waited once more. Bubbles were still visible on the channel surface like three torpedo wakes. Still no dogs could be seen. At last I blew the COME IN whistle. Over and over. Three black faces appeared and began the swim back. Davey carried the lost rooster.

The National Open of the past week seemed very far away. All three were champions. They certainly couldn't have run such complex blinds if they weren't. Who needed an audience?

Much of the preparation for Open and Amateur stakes is a *refinement* and *elaboration* of earlier training—acute angles, greater distances and depths, and more demanding multiple marks. Yet despite the demanding, sophisticated appearance of contemporary trial tests, most should be taught compartmentally. If this were not so, most amateur trainers could not compete with professionals at all. As it is, the amateur ranks are growing, as are the abilities of amateurs to compete with *anybody*.

In preparing for advanced trials, amateurs enjoy certain training advantages: fewer dogs, more time, greater diversity of training locations, and an opportunity for team rapport.

Professionals enjoy different advantages. The good ones know a lot about dogs, training problems and cures, and the desirable qualities of each breed. They can go from dawn to dusk with a full squad of helpers and crates full of birds. When out on the circuit, they move methodically, almost militarily, traveling short distances from trial to trial, while most amateurs run relatively few trials in a long-haul, quick-skirmish manner. Effective pros are common-sense dog people whose egos do not depend for survival on the dazzling performance of one particular dog. An obvious disadvantage of training large numbers of dogs is the risk of a "truck dog" mentality in trainer and dog alike: typically, a mechanical, impersonal dog thus professionally trained has high bird interest, lacks team rapport, yet performs relatively well with less affection or praise.

As you proceed, keep in mind that there is no one irrefutable formula for training retrievers. There are dozens of valid methods; some may be superior to others, but there is certainly no single best way to train, because the dogs themselves are too varied and inconstant. The difficulty is choosing methods that match up with your own particular retriever, and these methods, of course, become more complex as you advance.

You had better *really* enjoy the game, or the dogs, if you plan to enter the major stakes. The outcome of a trial may hang capriciously on a puff of wind, a poor bird throw, a well-shot flyer, raw talent, a distracted judge, or a slant of sunlight.

FINE ANGLING

Many old-time pros felt that if they could teach their dogs the two angles described in chapter 7 (square ninety degrees or forty-five degrees), they could safely negotiate most field problems. Most contemporary dogs must go a step further in fine angling and lining to be competitive.

A

B

(A) A pup learns to run straight and vault obstacles in the yard, and (B) expands his skill in the field.

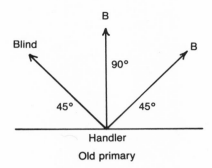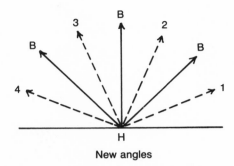

Diagram 24. Fine angles in relation to old primary angles.

The wagon wheel drill can help you here, or use your established baseball pattern and place four additional blinds between the three primary lines. NO! your dog off his three memorized old blinds and shoot him into unfamiliar gaps. This should eventually be applied to angled shore entries into water, across roads, and off high ground and banks.

Presumably your dog can now focus deeply and recognize certain responsible avenues of travel through field hazards on *picture blinds* (see p. 133). A new task will be learning to deal with foreground elements. These can be a wall of reeds or brush, an earth ledge, a conical mound, or a beaver dam offering no "picture" image. The natural tendency for well-intentioned dogs is to flare *around* this element. Once they do, they almost *never* recover their initial sense of line and direction (with the exception of a rare genius).

Teach your dog to take *blocked foregrounds* by running over or through them. Design a series of isolated lessons to demonstrate your expectations. You can start by jumping him over a bench in your backyard. Work him on a pile of bumpers with easy ways to skirt the hazard. Convince him there's a "right way" to do this retrieving chore: straight over the hurdle and straight back over it on the return. Next, build a foreground pile of brush in a field on a short, cold blind—again with plenty of easy ways to skirt it. Construct it in a slight **C**-shape and run him toward it, starting fifteen feet away at the concave side. Once he enters the **C**, its confining shape will lead him to jump over. If he veers to one side, holler NO!, call him back to rerun, or move closer (diag. 25).

The idea is to help him recognize these elements and his duty to address them straight on. When he figures this out, he'll be proud of his ability; threats or whistle and cast corrections to the blind will no longer be needed. In most cases, if the competitive dog can split the foreground elements, he is well on his way to perfectly *lining* most blinds. As he becomes more certain and ac-

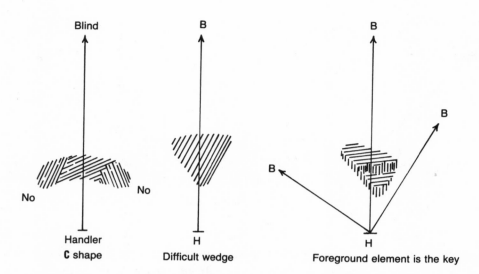

Diagram 25. Foreground hazard blinds.

complished in recognizing the foreground elements that you point out to him with your hand, you may add other blinds, double or triple. One blind may cut alongside this close hazard, but the key blind should be directly over or through it.

To isolate this foreground task for one of my dogs who was slow to learn it, I made a burlap screen from several feed sacks and suspended it on a piece of rope between two driven pickets. It hung low enough to be jumped but too high to see over. The dog could also run through it if he hadn't a mind to jump. After a brief introduction to jumping, I set it up on the home base of my large, well-known baseball pattern. This portable tool became quite effective, for it forced the dog to concentrate on the exact direction of my hand. It also required that he *hold* that mental picture and line after the BACK command and the barrier jump. After this lesson was absorbed, I used this portable screen as a middle-ground hazard on other permanent lines and blinds.

MULTIPLE BLINDS

Many trial judges today require dogs to run double and sometimes triple land and water blinds. A good way to introduce your dog to multiple blinds is to revisit sites of long, permanent single blinds. Your dog should recognize each as he is setting up to run. Carefully NO! him off the "old favorite" and re-line him toward a new, cold blind that is angled one-third as far away from you as the old blind. It helps to use your "wagon wheel" as a primer for this. If he successfully completes the short blind, praise him and send him for the long one. If he did poorly on the new short blind, skip the long blind until another session. If possible, use a rock formation, a tree, or brush to help the dog separate the two lines.

This procedure helps the dog to realize more than one blind is out there and guards him against too much pride in a short diversion. He must expect a rigorous blind to follow the first. This drill should then be expanded to three and four blinds in a given field, short and long (three hundred yards), patterned and cold. One effective way of teaching your dog to expect to run three hundred yards and still listen to a whistle, is to include some four- and five-hundred-yard distances in your patterns. As your dog begins to digest this multiple-blind concept, he may confidently anticipate more work and actually loosen up, picking up speed on other blinds after he has delivered his first bird.

When my dogs return with the last bird of a multiple mark, I always make them sit, deliver, and prepare to go again, as if there were another bird out there somewhere. Thus, if they *do* have to face a blind or blinds after completing their marks, they are not apt to be confused or disheartened. I think this habit prevents a dog from letting down mentally after a good job. Many other handlers seem to disagree, however, allowing their dogs plenty of time to unwind and jive around before "setting up" for additional blinds.

SETTING UP

The time lapse between cuing a dog for a blind and sending him is very important for good teamwork. Some handlers deliberately send fast in training, in order to *prevent* the dog from getting any picture of the blind's location; they desire, instead, maximum opportunity for whistle and cast practice. Others prefer a long, meticulous setup period. Some trainers claim they can slowly mesmerize their dog to run *anywhere,* through anything, after a careful setting-up routine.

I don't believe in lengthy setting up before marks, in general. A longer procedure can therefore be useful in helping a dog to recognize the difference between being charged to run a line responsibly and simply released to find a mark. Copious setting up is sometimes called "developing the blind frame of mind" or making the dog "sweat." This sometimes helps remove premature guesses or casual attitudes in approaching a difficult blind, especially a water blind. I have occasionally used a sweat system of *double lining* on demanding cold water blinds. I will set up, cue, and align the dog to my full satisfaction; the instant the dog is sure he is going to be "kicked off" for the blind, I heel him off the line, then completely reset him. By this time, the honest dog should be completely resigned to do the job for you, in spite of some unpleasant aspect of it—gooey mud, freezing waters, thistles.

In both training and trials, I prefer to take my time setting up for a blind to achieve some sweat, a good line and picture—foreground included. This creates the rapport on which both of you will learn to depend. You can "push" or influence him slightly away from you as he leaves, and away from or toward some field hazard, by "standing up" on the dog, that is, standing with your near leg alongside his head, neck, or shoulder. If you "stand back" of the dog, with the near leg in the vicinity of his haunch or tail, you may "pull" the dog slightly toward you as he is sent. These nuances in handling must be cultivated slowly and thoroughly during your training hours to be part of your team's language code.

THE DRY GUN, FLYAWAY, AND OTHER PREPARATORY DRILLS WITH PERMANENT BLINDS

While visiting your big, familiar pattern blinds, include a few licks that will help prepare your dog for unsettling surprises at trials. One example is the *dry gun,* an equivalent of a missed bird in a hunting situation. Station a white-coated gunner half the distance to, and off to the side of, one of your permanent blinds. Bring your dog routinely and formally to the line as if for a mark. Signal the gunner to shoot an imaginary bird in a direction away from your pattern blind. Keen dogs may want a bird so badly they can't resist exploring the area of a normal fall. NO! the dog off the "dry pop" and cue him for a permanent blind that is angled away from the nonexistent "mark." Call him back, tune him up, and send him again if he insists on being sucked into this trap. He should finally recognize his pattern blind line and ignore the dry gun.

When you employ dry guns—firing with no thrown bird or flyer—remember that a delayed third shot several seconds after the first barrage will strongly enhance the dog's illusion of a fall. Refrain from any shooting into empty water for a dry-gun effect. Sluicing a downed duck is extremely exciting to most avid duck dogs. If you feel it necessary to include such a sluiced bird in the water, instruct your gunner to aim to actually kill it, because the dog will make a separate mark out of any misplaced, adjacent geysers of water and mistakenly turn a water double into a phony triple by swimming to where he saw the pellets chop the water.

Another prevention of disaster in trials that falls into the same category as a dry gun is a *flyaway,* or missed bird. Use the same approach as above, but this time have the gunner actually throw a live bird, shoot at it, and deliberately miss it. Allow your dog to watch it fly to the horizon, circle, or land, but then NO! him off that direction and run the pattern blind. You may find that using homing pigeons is great for this because you can use these same obliging birds later, but a flyaway pheasant is the strongest test.

Even when your dog is accomplished with single land patterns that have been methodically built into solid, demanding double and triple blinds, you can wring still more from these permanent blinds. When the wind changes 180 degrees, run the patterns in reverse direction. Or shift your point of origin twenty to forty yards to either side of the familiar, established line. Your dog will still feel sure of the correct direction of the blind, but you may gather several difficult field hazards in the process. He will still attempt to run straight at his old target spot, negotiating the added traps along the way without undue concern.

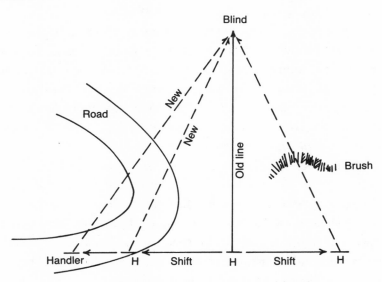

Diagram 26. New lines to old blinds.

Yet another way to use your old patterns is a serious "tear down," mind-changer drill. This should be done only when your dog is supremely confident of himself and his previous work. Send him down a long, familiar pattern line and sit-stop him where he is accustomed to finding a bird or bumper. He will find no bird scent or bumper this time, however, because you have planted it thirty yards off to the right or left or deep of the accustomed target. Attempt to handle him away from this conditioned payoff spot with an "over" or "back" cast. In disbelief, he will usually refuse to give up his preplanned idea of success and try to hunt it out on his own. You must "tennis-shoe" out there and help him "change his mind." This drill is intended to assist him on long trial blinds that hold a trap or hazard at the very end, such as a high stand of cover that impairs your view and control. Beautiful long-distance sits and casts are possible only when the dog believes *you,* and not his hunches or his nose.

Another drill that assures a change of mind, and discipline for dog and handler alike, involves planting two long, cold blinds on a **V** pattern. Carefully launch your dog at one of them. Stop him halfway there and handle him as crisply as possible to the alternate blind. Pick up the remaining blind yourself.

If the dog lacks confidence in his cold blinds, do a variation on the above by planting four to six blinds at the same distance on centers about forty yards apart. This may be done in a plain field or a large body of water. Send your dog toward this "safety net" of planted birds. If he should succeed in "lining" one of them without a whistle, great; if not, handle him toward the one he's closest to. As before, pick up the remaining blinds yourself.

Many advanced dogs have been hazed or intimidated into doing some unpleasant task, such as channel blinds, by assistants. As a result, those dogs may develop an aversion to running lines *too* close to gunners, at their field stations or on the way to marks or blinds. Because many modern judges insist that *true lines* be run within inches of the heels or toes of gunners or other elements such as a stack of live bird crates, it is advisable to remedy this problem. An exercise commonly called the *chair drill* can be helpful.

Again, go to your best-known pattern blind. Bring along two chairs and place them equidistant on either side of the pattern blind route, one-third to one-half the distance to the blind. You may hang a couple of white shirts over the chairbacks to flap in the wind. Run your dog easily through the wide gap to his blind, then put him away and move the chairs slightly closer together. Due to familiarity, he should not flare or swerve, but continue the line between them. If he *does* flare, call NO!, move closer up the line, and rerun him until he can accept these distractions. On reruns, continue to squeeze these worrisome chairs closer until he is threading the eye of a needle. On a different day, have people sit in the chairs and repeat the squeeze as before. Your "sitters" should not move or distract the dog as he skins past them. Finally, stagger the furniture positions and run the pattern. Try it later on a cold blind.

Most dogs seem to be right- or left-"handed." You should be aware of your dog's natural turning direction on a stop whistle, whether on land or in water, and the direction he takes as he turns *away* from you on a "back" cast. If he is swimming parallel to a shoreline when you whistle, his natural turning direction may inadvertently cause him to land; if he's on land, it may cause him to move closer to, or into, a trap.

Many advanced handlers believe in training their dogs to take *right* or *left* "back" casts, the direction of turn indicated by raising the right or left hand, respectively. Other trainers don't bother with such casts—they simply learn the dog's natural bent and adjust accordingly.

Directional turns can be taught with the dog on a long check cord and two obvious piles of bumpers. Start with the dog sitting squarely facing you and the bumpers at the ten o'clock and two o'clock positions, about ten yards behind him. If you want a left turn and a left bumper, take a side step left and smoothly and simultaneously raise your left arm from the left "over" to the left "back" position as you command BACK! (Do the reverse for right turns.) If he turns right when you have ordered a left pivot on the "back," growl at him and arrest his movement with the check cord. Reset him in the original position and try again for that desired left turn. He should concentrate on your hands. When he is turning easily with your left raised arm, show him the right arm cast to the other side. Later, mix the left and right arm casts. Resistance may appear when you are working him against his natural, comfortable way of turning. When he has a good grasp of this exercise, move the two piles of bumpers closer and closer together until they are a single pile at twelve o'clock and he is turning for them properly from either right or left.

Genuine forty-five-degree-angle "back" casts, as opposed to ninety-degree "over" and straight "backs," are taught after these right and left turns are pat lessons. Build an obvious small pattern similar to your small baseball diamond, as shown in diagram 27.

Position the dog as in the above turning drill, and turn and cast him toward the forty-five-degree right or left pile with a clear forty-five degree arm cast—that is, with your arm positioned at two or ten o'clock, between that of a straight "over" and a straight "back" cast (see diag. 17, "Directional hand casts," p. 124). When he is well versed and smooth on this wide **V** pattern, include a pile at the true "back" position set slightly deeper. After this is clear to him, add the true ninety-degree "over" casts, then mix the casts according to

In this turning drill, the dog learns to turn to the left or right in coordination with the trainer's left or right arm signal.

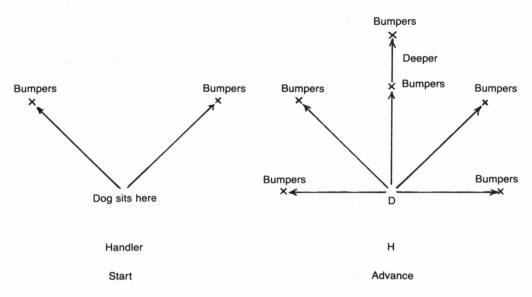

Diagram 27. Angle casts.

your will and his weakness. This drill can be built on the main line of an existing pattern with the forty-five-degree cast off that known center line, and the cast distances increased.

A word of warning regarding the above two drills: Up to this point you have diligently taught *only* clean "overs" and "backs"; when this new material, including angle "backs," is added to your dog's repertoire, he may become incapable of a respectable, true "over" for a long time.

One handy training boost for continued clean "over" casts is to set your dog in front of a wide, dense band of trees or brush, or under a long, steep bluff, where it's unlikely that *any* "back" or angle "back" cast would be given, and simply practice long "over" casts. A water version of this exercise is generally known as the *tule drill.* Find a large channel with tules along the edges; before bringing out your dog, plant floating birds or bumpers 150 to 200 yards apart. Then, with your dog present, throw a single bumper as far as you can— 40 to 60 yards across the water onto the opposite land. This throw should be made between the two floating blinds. Allow your dog to sit and watch this single throw, then send him for it to retrieve as a single mark. Throw this same bumper again and send him, but this time whistle-stop him just before he lands and penetrates the opposite wall of tules. Give him a strong, clean "over" cast toward one of the floating blinds. Walk your side of the creek with the dog and issue more whistles and "overs" each time he doubts your demand and tries to

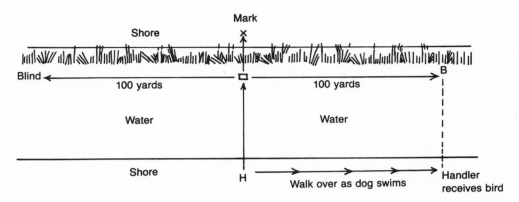

Diagram 28. Tule drill.

land or to enter the tules. When he finally scores, call him in and accept the bird, but retrace your steps to the original marking spot and ask him to pick up the mark on the opposite shore. Throw it again and repeat the big, right "over." Repeat, and work the opposite left "over." (See diag. 28.)

MORE ON BIG "OVERS"

If your dog concentrates so much on his line running that he thinks mostly "back" when he has been cast "over," the following procedure should help.

Return to one of your long, well-known patterns. Instead of sending your dog from your side toward the blind as usual, take him out and *sit* him along the axis of the route he knows very well; remove yourself squarely to the *side* of that line and cast him "over" toward the blind.

If he is in the habit of performing 15- or 20-yard "overs," he may stumble along at first. Move laterally with him and repeat the cast until he recognizes the cast direction as his old blind payoff spot, and understands your meaning. You want a clean, swift 150- to 200-yard "over" cast; repeat the procedure on other long pattern blinds. It may be executed from the middle of this blind with an "over" in each direction at the ends, or the handler can work from either side for long left or right "over" casts (diag. 29, A or B). To ensure your dog's return on the same line, walk to the spot where he was sitting when cast to receive the bird. Using live birds may enhance his desire to perform on these difficult casts.

The same big "over" principle can be applied to water blinds by sending your dog square into the water and giving long "overs" in his familiar channel

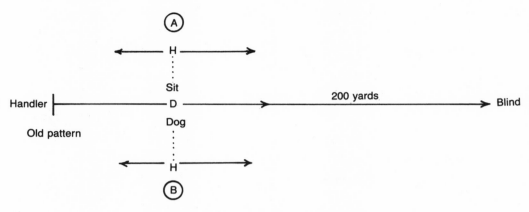

Diagram 29. Big "overs."

setting. This particular drill is extremely useful in recovery therapy for a skeletally disabled or injured dog. Give a soft command that tells him to *enter the water gently*—to walk into it and swim—rather than race into it with a flourish. When he has launched himself without aggravating his injury, give him the OVER command for this lengthy, therapeutic swim.

Subsequent casting drills should include casting into water. A version of baseball may be employed with one of the "overs" straight into the drink. (See diag. 30 for variations of this exercise.) Use floating white bumpers twenty yards into deep water at first, then replace them with gray bumpers or dead birds and lengthen the swim distance as he assimilates the material. Make the distance of the land approach short and then long. Repeat the casting-into-water drill sufficiently to cancel any hesitation at the disturbing sight of water, after he pivots into this "over" cast.

In water tests, floating blinds—dead pheasants or ducks—are often held in exact position by the use of a rat trap with its floating wooden base anchored to the bottom by a line and weight. The bird's wing tip is held in the trap. Some dogs have been known to spook around this piece of gear. Some experience with rat traps may be helpful *before* a critical trial situation. I've suggested previously that your dog be exposed to decoys around his kennel and yardwork. If you've never shot over decoys with him, it would benefit him to work into and through a large set of floating decoys and goose silhouettes, as well as decoys on land. After an arduous swim, a single floating decoy has a magnetic effect— even on some veteran duck dogs.

Other important, new exposures for your dog on multiple water retrieves are *boats* and marked falls that originate from boats. Marks that fall in deep

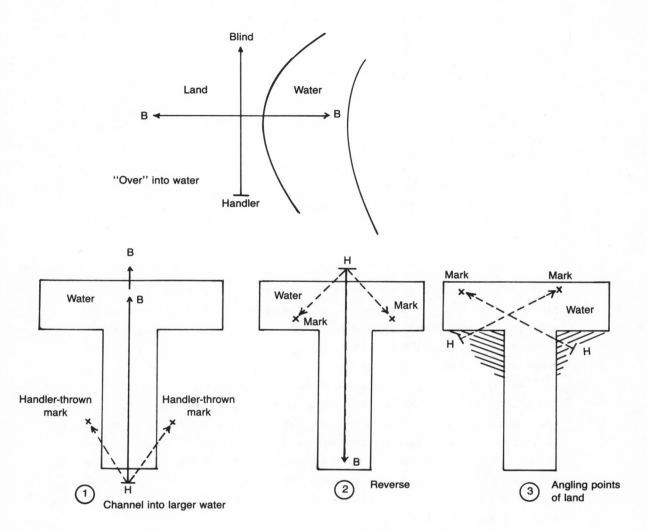

Diagram 30. "Over" into water and other shore drills.

water and cover (lily pads, water hyacinth, and so on) with little reference to land are valuable because they cause the dog to swim and search. When he begins to understand deep-water marking, include one bird in a water triple across the pond or lake and a hundred yards (possibly retired) up on land. If this deep-water-to-land mark is bracketed by one duck mark in deep water and another on the shoreline, it makes a very difficult concept indeed (diag. 31).

Having already taught your dog to swim *past* points of land on his way to water blinds through earlier channel work (see pp. 138–141), you should now train him to swim parallel to a shoreline without landing. It is unnatural for a dog to channel at all, but parallel shore swims are especially confounding for

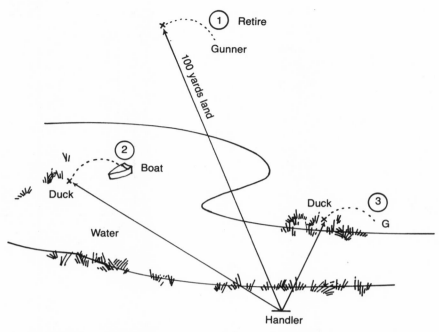

Diagram 31. Mixed-concept marking, incorporating land and water.

him—your well-intending young water dog may tend to "head out to sea" in order to please you.

Teach this new lesson by setting out a number of water blinds that parallel straight earth or concrete dams, and have your dog swim three or four yards off the dam. The overall distance of the blinds may be increased by increments. A corresponding land drill involves asking him to run pattern blinds that parallel three or four yards off a long, straight fence line while ignoring all other possible blind locations throughout the field. He must "picture" what you wish before he is sent. Ultimately, your dog should be able to understand whether you wish him to swim "out to sea" or hug a shoreline—or similarly, run into the center of a large field or run parallel to a fence or road. When he knows how to do both well, you can then NO! him off one "picture" and suggest or command the alternative (diag. 32).

As the dog masters his paralleling water work and conscientiously avoids shores, you will have to modify this accomplishment for yet another result. The very strength you have built into him—his ability to stay in the water—may become a trial liability during certain popular test configurations. You must now teach him *when* to get out of the water and yet retain his former "wet dog" virtues (see diag. 33).

Find a pond, lake, or tidal situation where there is an obvious point of

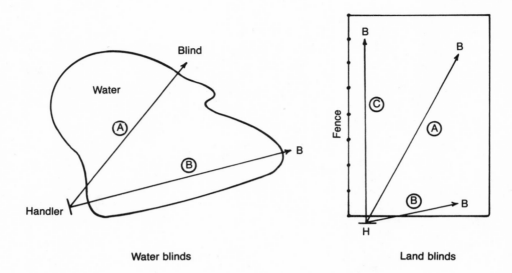

Water blinds   Land blinds

Diagram 32. Blinds for swimming parallel to the shoreline.

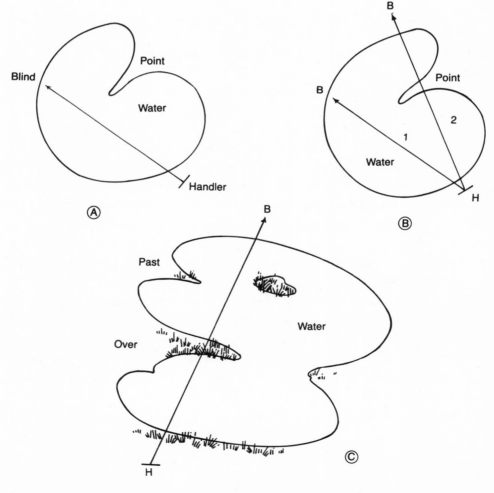

Diagram 33. Blinds located past and across a point.

land or a bar thrusting into the water; establish a water blind just past it and make your dog comfortable with this blind (A). On a follow-up training day, run him on the same blind (B1) and then attempt to line him *across* the point to a new blind (B2) that definitely involves landing on shore. NO! him off (B1) before you line him for (B2). When you succeed in this blind, run them both combined in a line (C). On other training days at this site or similar configurations, run only the *across* portion, or the blind he seems to have the least skill in executing. Eventually, when these across-the-point blinds become patterns, you may "salt" the points with bird scent to teach him to carry a line not only over land but through scent, as he proceeds into more water.

The idea you are trying to impress upon your dog is this: If land is in the path of your swim line, take it, but *always* be prepared to reenter the water (diag. 34).

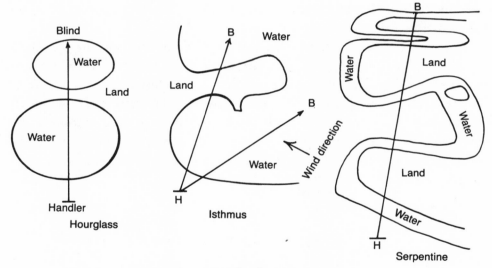

Diagram 34. Water-land-water concepts.

Some trainers, while they prefer their dogs to *carry* (cross) all points of land in the first half of a water blind, permit them to skirt the distant points or islands in the latter half.

— *Splitting a Pond* —

When you are able to put your hand down and watch your dog run on a line for eighty yards, plunge into water that could be easily avoided by a shoulder shrug or a slight bend of line, swim twenty yards, haul out, and run another hundred yards, then you've got an edge! If the angle of water entry is difficult, that's even better, because the dog not only has to hold his line but *will* himself into the water to keep from shearing off or missing it entirely. This singular configuration is far more dramatic to the dog than a long run at a broad body of water simply to get wet. Such small ponds should be obvious from the line—not surprise water.

Work of this nature is rarely demanded to this degree in a field trial, but if your dog is mentally prepared to take *any* water in his path, it can save you three or four whistles and provide a leg up on your competition.

—— *Running Water Stops* ——

If your dog is not heeding your whistles as he runs through water, it *may* be because he doesn't hear you. Keep in mind that the faster your dog, the louder the noise he will create in water.

In order to determine whether your dog's slipped whistles are actually deliberate and a cause for discipline, position a helper, also equipped with a whistle, near the dog's line of travel. Sound both your whistles in a loud, hard, unmistakable blast and watch your dog's behavior. If he deliberately ignores this signal, the trainer may justly discipline him. Remember, too cautious a dog, one that is slow and worried in running water, may self-consciously pop. The balance between control and style is a fine one; a small margin separates the slipped whistle and the pop.

DEALING WITH SCENT

Presumably your young dog is now able to pass downwind of bird crates on his way to a mark without disorientation due to scent. Now he must address a more difficult aspect of nose messages—running blinds through scent.

This task represents a dichotomy in dog work. Running a line to a bird through mattresses of fresh feathers, dander, and scat without a dog's lowering his speed or nose in enchantment is a feat expected by most major-stake judges. On the other hand, the same judges regard not honoring his nose when marking as a colossal fault: "No Evidence of Nose."

A primary drill for teaching a dog to run blinds through scent involves bypassing or negating *old falls.* Use the large baseball pattern your dog knows by heart. Run the center line of the pattern once with a dead or shackled bird at the end of the line. Put him up with praise and plant the bird again while he catches his breath. Bring him back to the same line and pick up a bumper mark thrown conspicuously on this line one-fourth or one-third the distance to the blind. Then carefully line him and send him "back" along that same line for the distant chicken, duck, or pigeon he had earlier.

If he hangs up and hunts at the mark, move up closer to the mark and resend him firmly with the cue DEAD BIRD or whatever you have chosen to use. If this is not sufficient to clear the mark, shake him up before resending him. He should appreciate the difference between a blind and a mark with the memory of the bird over bumper. Repeat the entire process to embed this single principle.

Within two days, return to this pattern and rerun the center bird blind. If he passes with perfection add the right and left lines and run the assemblage with birds on the deep blinds. Then add foreground bumper marks. Rerun all the blinds only if the marks have been done well. (See "Popping," pp. 151–152.)

Diagram 35 indicates what your dog is attempting to achieve. The blinds are considerably deeper than the marks or hot-scent areas in order to allow the dog to feel comfortable and proud of himself after he clears the spot of the mark and scent and trucks confidently on toward the blind on the same line.

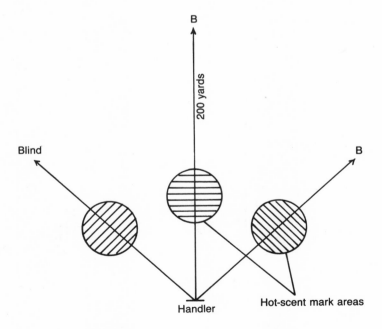

Diagram 35. Running blinds through "old falls."

If your dog has succeeded to your total satisfaction in running through these marks to the blinds, then it is time to convert the foreground mark to a shot flyer. Use the center line first, as before: you can add the outside lines later. When this material is fully digested, your dog should be able to retrieve any or all of the three blinds, as you choose, through plenty of scent. (Some trainers feel that picking up a plastic bumper on a long blind through hot bird scent is too small a reward for their dogs and usually try to make the blind a payoff bird. They feel that disappointment in the plastic will be reflected in style.)

The logical extension of this drill is eventually to visit every known blind pattern that you have developed (at least two dozen). This should include swimming over and through areas where he has picked up live or shot ducks. Throw an in-line flyer and then run this previously memorized blind. Nosing around the mark's scent usually results sooner or later in a radio reprimand by collar trainers, and some form of thrashing by tennis-shoe trainers. You must demonstrate and communicate the difference in jobs to the dog.

A good time to work on ignoring scent is in a good stiff crosswind. Think of wind-borne scent as smoke. Hang a gunnysack of chickens or pheasants in a tree, high enough off the ground so any retrieve is impossible. Use a crate full of ducks on the ground if no tree is available. Prepare in advance for discipline here. Then run a cold blind past this corridor of blowing scent. Variations are shown in diagram 36 below.

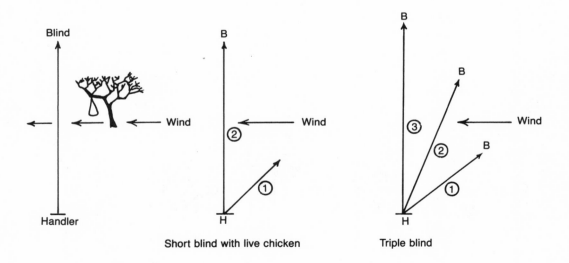

Diagram 36. Dealing with scent.

In trials dogs will assuredly be required by judges to run blinds through old falls. Furthermore, many trial clubs still run bitches *after* all the males have finished, thereby placing a burden of extra, possibly confusing, scent on the ladies. Drag-back scent and pockets of bird smell accumulate at the marks and on the way to the blind. While bitches are derogatorily called "trackers," running last is no benefit unless the bitch is trained to deal with plenty of scent.

Since working dogs returning from blinds or marks through water often stop, shake, or drop a dripping bird, or drag it through a stand of cattails, the next dog to perform must negotiate a minefield of disruptive odor. A cast off a "poisoned" or "salted" (scented) island into freezing water after a long swim is a very difficult request. Many judges believe it is their responsibility to have water test locations deliberately salted—possibly by eviscerating a dead bird—before the first dog runs in order to equalize the hazards and pitfalls for the entire field of dogs. The only way to prepare for this in advance training is to duplicate the situation. Run a known or cold blind for familiarization, then copiously smear the middle ground with hot scent and rerun it; this will show him what you want. Run it again if you have yet to see perfection, and be prepared to swim, wade, or run; perhaps an inconspicuously positioned helper can enforce the lesson. Return two days later and see if your lesson has stuck.

Bird boy trails. Blinds are usually planted in trials one at a time from the rear or a convenient side area. If a dog runs deeper than the planted bird, he is in immediate peril of encountering the bird planter's scent. Such bird boy trails can be a real trap. I therefore believe in handling all the way to the bird, including the last five or ten feet! Practice a come-in whistle at great distance, and a collection of close-coupled casts and whistle-stops, when your dog is in a scented spot. An accomplished, keen dog sitting attentively three hundred yards away with a pheasant between his front feet, waiting for your permission to pick it up, is a handsome sight.

An additional observation on scent:

Early one thickly fogged morning, before the start of a field trial, I went out with two training friends, Bob Woodrow and Gene Corona, to brush up on our young dogs' marking and to run off a little steam. One of the few places we could legitimately work our dogs was the area a gun club had traditionally used for live pigeon shoots; in fact, they had held a large shoot there the day before. The three of us, each with his dog at heel, formed a triangle fifty to eighty yards apart and "mailed" a red bumper from handler to handler by sequential retrieves. In amazement, we watched our dogs run through thousands of dead birds that had accumulated from the preceding day and the shoots of weeks before. Our action had been unintentional at first, but we continued to run them as they unerringly scrambled through foot-deep layers of feathers to pick up that piece of vinyl. Not a dog was confused by this bizarre warm-up. These dogs were: FC AFC Woody's Black Baby, FC AFC Willie-Be-Good, and my bitch FC AFC Nakai Anny, who won the Open and finished her field championship that weekend.

ADVANCED MARKING

No matter how advanced the training becomes, I don't believe there is ever a totally finished dog—even Seeing Eye dogs are recalled periodically for a factory tune-up. At this point in training, then, take stock of your dog's progress and identify his weaknesses. With the aid of your charts, draw up a list of doubtful performance areas. While working at them may not seem immediately rewarding to either of you, this appraisal will prove vital as you attempt increasingly demanding marks—some of which are intentionally devised for confusion and failure. Maintain a good balance between simple and complex tasks—you don't want a bored and jaded dog, or one that is lost and afraid. *Attitude* is extremely important as you address new material.

One factor in maintaining an interested and curious dog is establishing a good balance between marks and blinds. John Anderson of California practices a fifty-fifty ratio. "I do a marking test with every training session," he says, "even if it's throwing bumpers from my side—just to keep them thinking sharp." J. J. Sweezy uses 60 percent marks and 40 percent blinds, interspersing the blinds with the marks and using birds on blinds quite often.

According to Rex Carr, "The number of blinds versus marks depends on the individual. Anytime a dog takes off on a blind when sent for a mark, seek a better balance by stressing marks and easing up on blinds. It is most difficult to win a National with a dog that lines out as though on a blind when sent for a key mark. If you stress blinds too much it might help to qualify and even win a lot of licensed trials and pile up the points, but it is apt to wipe you out in a National." He adds that it is important to eliminate boredom from drills—if your dog performs well on a particular exercise, move on to other training.

A triple or quad at the advanced level includes three or four bona fide marks, with genuine birds, and throwers, laid out with a careful design of the falls. The "tight" or close proximity of multiple marked birds is probably the most effective pattern for eliminating dogs, and the one most widely used by today's judges. Trainers have responded by training their dogs to mark tightly, in preparation for marking tests that may be squeezed tighter still. (Variations are shown in diag. 37.)

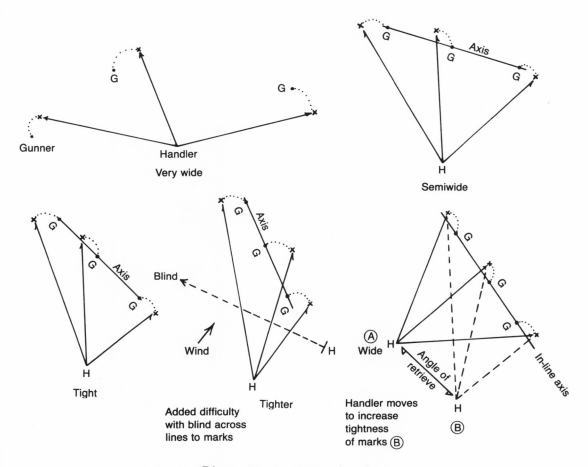

Diagram 37. Proximity of marks.

One conceptual approach to setting a triple as a trainer or a judge is to employ a virtual axis between the gun stations. The "angle of tightness" may be controlled by adjusting the throwers' positions and the direction of the throws, or the position from which the dog marks these falls.

The "three in line" principle is rarely more devastating than when these marks are thrown as *three across* water (diag. 38).

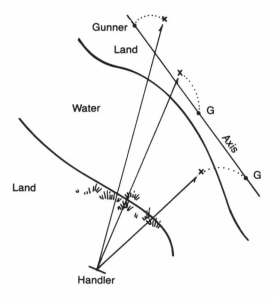

Diagram 38. Three-in-line across water.

Of course, the key bird or trouble bird in any set of marks is the one your dog consistently louses up—regardless of other dogs' performance on the same test. I have found that exaggeration of that particular bird through the following methods generally helps a dog on a tough mark.

1. Obvious gun: Enlist a full set of guns and throwers (2) in white coats, as opposed to a single, camouflaged thrower.

2. Noise: Use a full 12-gauge multiple-report, rather than a helper's shout.

3. Birds: Use the dog's favorite bird (duck, pheasant, chicken) as a shot flyer, instead of a bumper.

If your dog has trouble remembering a long, retired, center dead bird on land across a pond that has been bracketed by a short quacking duck in the water and a nearby shot pheasant, deliberately try to reverse the emphasis of this test (before beating him up and force-running it fifty or one hundred times). Place the emphasis on the key bird until he begins to feel and understand the mechanics and shape of the test—before running it again the previous, hard way. Place a full set of guns in white, with loud or live guns shooting a flighted bird in the key bird spot without a retirement. In place of the bracketing marks and with minimum fanfare, use bumpers or similarly uninteresting soggy, dead birds. If he still becomes confused, reduce the triple into a double and/or *widen* the test. Try to learn which bird, in the numbered sequence of falls, your dog seems to mark best or worst. Shift the exaggeration to any trouble bird.

A further method of applying extra emphasis is illustrated by the following story. A friend of mine was preparing for a National and found his sharp-marking dog suddenly unable to complete *any* ordinary retired multiple mark. The dog had become cocky, inconsistent, and blasé. We took the concerned handler and his dog to a huge, unfamiliar field with medium and even cover, and not a single marking reference point. I placed a lone bird thrower an impossible 300 yards away; with loud gunfire, this thrower flighted the dog's favorite bird, then retired. Twenty yards to one side another gunner threw a short, casual bumper with a mild yell. The dog aced the short bumper, then addressed himself to the preposterous key bird. He hunted short then wide, covered 70 percent of the field area, and finally, desperately, tried to use his empty head. But all the answers came out wrong. At last the dog was called in, tongue-lashed, cooled off in water, and given a chance to recover his breath. The identical test was then repeated with C+ results—and repeated again for an A+. The dog was now trying to make damned sure he memorized that key mark. The acid test came a half hour later when we set the identical test (same wind, cover, configuration) in a neighboring field but reduced the distance to the retired flyer to a mere 180 yards. He pinned it.

I find most dogs that are sloppy on retired birds try to mark where the gun stood instead of where the bird fell. As a variation on the above, throw a series of ten or fifteen quick retired marks over a short distance, letting your dog hunt for the key bird after first picking up a short bumper. This can convince him to take a critical look at that key bird.

Blinds and marks that are run under the arc of a flighted bird sometimes have a "windshield wiper effect"—erasing the dog's memory of deeper birds. Be sure your dog has been exposed to this situation before he encounters it in a trial.

Also prepare your dog for a flighted and shot duck or pheasant in the water as he swims in the last thirty or so yards with a dead bird mark. He may be tempted to spit out the dead bird and "switch" to the hot new bird—which is cause for trial elimination. This added interference, called a "bulldog," is also likely to cloud your dog's memory of any remaining marks. A handler shooting a flyer over the water for his dog, as he swims in from a long water blind, provides good "bulldog" training as well as restoring his dog's ambition, speed, and attitude. Generally, if an additional bird is shot *after* the dog returns to the handler with an initial retrieve in a multiple mark, it is called a "delayed bird."

When the lines to marks become so tight that they finally begin to overlap each other, the configuration is known as an *over and under*. This over-and-under marking was widely employed in early trialing for the guaranteed elimination of many dogs; today, however, it is regarded as a trick test—one that deliberately deceives normal canine instincts, abilities, and perception. I believe that tough terrain and water are the best ingredients of any demanding test. Here, the courage, heart, and memory of the dog—not just strict adherence to training—can be measured and appreciated.

SELECTION AND VARIATIONS ON THE RETRIEVING ORDER OF MULTIPLE MARKS

Many trainers insist there is no natural order in how a dog chooses to pick up a multiple retrieve, and that any strong preference is a result of earlier training; others disagree. However, most good marking youngsters seem to want to pick up the outside marks of a triple first, no matter in what sequence the marks were thrown. This tendency can create a real memory problem if, for example, the center bird of a triple—the last bird to be retrieved and hence the most difficult—is thrown *first* or even second. If this center mark is thrown at one-third the yardage of the two flanking outside marks, most dogs will overrun it by about two-thirds its actual distance. I believe our dogs tend to measure their trip distances by a metering system of strides and a consciousness of elapsed time. Having reached the two outside marks in a certain number of strides and within a certain amount of time, the dog anticipates a similar distance to the third mark. He often overruns it, then, despite his eyes and nose.

If the short bird is thrown square, whether in the center or not, and the other marks are angled forty-five degrees back, the difficulty is exaggerated. The interplay and relationship between differing angled throws and depths has become increasingly important and interesting to contemporary trial judges in triples and quads. Variations on this concept were introduced through the judging style of John McAssey, and are generally known as McAssey Specials. Although this test has fascinated handlers and trainers, most dogs simply cannot complete it to any degree of satisfaction. It too has been tagged as a "trick" test, but is often used.

Imagine that you are marking your dog through a common water ditch; a short, square, dead hen is thrown directly downwind as the center bird; this gunner may then retire. This mark is followed by second and third outside birds—converging, flighted roosters that are shot at forty-five degrees and at substantial distance (diag. 39). You now face a classic advanced marking test.

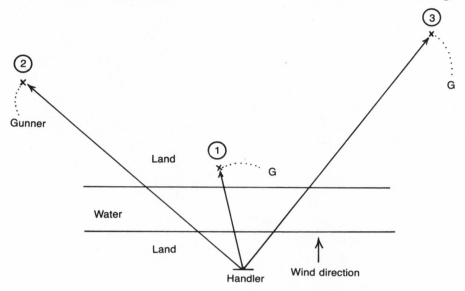

Diagram 39. McAssey Special. The mark at (1), possibly a retired mark, lies directly downwind from the handler (H).

This test is used in many club trials as well as the Nationals. It appeals to many judges because of the high degree of variation in performance by different dogs and because it can be set in a flat, unchallenging field (such as alfalfa), which may be the only available working terrain.

The horrors and hazards of "over and under" and the McAssey Special have led to a school of dog trainers who have observed that the short, dead bird in a multiple is so easily forgotten or overrun that in many cases it decides the winner of a field trial. Their solution to this critical problem is to *select*—that is, to require the dog to pick up this short, difficult, unattractive bird first, while it is freshest in the dog's memory. This formula, pioneered by Billy Wunderlich and Rex Carr, is a good answer, but certainly not the only one.

Good selecting dogs can often lose what they gain in accurately locating short key birds by bungling their marks on the deep and irregular shot flyers. I have discussed the merits of selection at great length with energized dog folk in and out of the field. National trials have been convincingly won by great dogs who have mastered this facility and by great dogs who have never been burdened with it.

Incoming game.

Training for *selection,* then, is teaching your dog to pick up multiple marks *in a specific order*—usually closest first, farthest last. Whether or not you undertake it depends on the strengths of your dog, your persistence as a trainer, and your own preference—the experts themselves are divided over its validity.

A perfectly executed selection on a demanding triple can be as elegant as a well-choreographed dance. The mastery of control exemplified by good selection has led some trainers to become hard-core proponents of it—zealots, in fact, brimming with stronger rationalizations for their behavior. Once their decision to train in this manner has been made, they religiously seek to exploit their skill, for better or worse—often with less than brilliant results.

I believe that, for a dogman, the thrill of watching one's animal pick up birds unerringly should be equally great, whether the sequence be determined by the handler or his dog. I cannot find fault with retrieves that are made swiftly and accurately, regardless of sequence. A fine marking dog should always be treasured.

—— *Training for Selection* ——

Selection is not only believed by some to be an "edge" in difficult marking during National competition but helpful in training very willful, independent dogs who lack handler respect and control. This technique is also handy for controlling the interest of some older dogs that have become bored with watching a dead bird throw. The selection, however, is not always necessarily applied to trials. Selection has a particularly useful application in hunting. If you have shot two birds from the same flock, for example, and one is dead, the other wounded, you might lose the cripple if the dog went after the dead one first. Selection gives you the control to send him after the bird of your choice, in this case, the cripple first, the other second.

Selection dogs are not always or necessarily electric-collar trained, but most trainers agree that this tool saves time.

Ideally, the mechanics of selection begin with starting a youngster thinking "short" very early in life. This involves plenty of explanation and showing.

1. Set a wide double using two dead birds (no flyer) employing a long-leg and a short-leg configuration in a pleasant field with no cover.

2. Instruct the long thrower to make his toss first, followed by the short-bird throw second. Pick up these marks in the usual sequence; that is, last bird down, the short one, retrieved first, then the long, memory bird (diag. 40A).

3. Repeat the same double in reverse throwing order so your dog picks up the short bird last, after retrieving the long bird (diag. 40B).

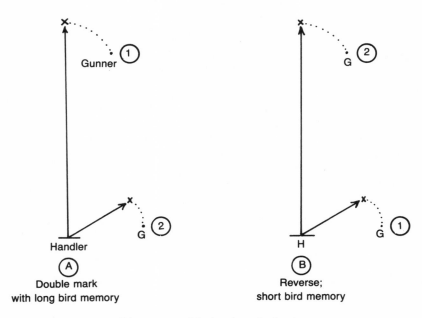

Diagram 40. Mechanics of selection.

4. When the dog understands both the above sequences thoroughly, advance to a fresh piece of ground and shoot a short flyer, followed by a long, dead bird in a similar double mark. "Select" the short, attractive flyer *before* getting the long, last bird down. This process is still in the *explanation* phase. If the dog doesn't catch on, have the gunner help show him where the short bird is before he commits himself to the long one. Or redo it. Or handle the dog to the short mark. Or NO! the dog off the long and point toward the short one. No heavy correction should be dished out yet. Use large, white, clipped-wing birds for controlled falls.

5. Work the dog on a repetitive double routine of a short-throw clip-wing first, followed by a long bumper. Select the clipper. Reverse this to short bumper first, and long clipper second. Select the short bumper for the first retrieve.

6. Go to difficult terrain, cover, or wind conditions, where because the short, dead bird or bumper is the more difficult of the two to locate, the dog is tempted to leave the area of the short mark and go after the long, dramatic flyer. Now is the time for correction and reinforcement of previous habits and lessons. The toughest part of teaching selection is the handler's ability to differentiate between an honest mistake and a flagrant violation of the training intentions. Close *reading* of your dog is vital in training and enhances team rapport on the line.

7. Full skill in selection is built from the above basic conditioning into triple marks where the shortest bird is the first (primary) retrieve and the second shortest mark will be picked up next (secondary) and the longest bird, whether it is a flyer or not, is last. The tightness of the angles between these marks is gradually increased.*

The proper selection training period represents an extra year of work. Many ambitious trainers tend to rush the show-and-tell period, with problematic results: the dog begins popping on marks, or coming back without a bird, and the trainer must recast. Never "dirt clod" the short bird to exaggerate and test the dog's willingness to switch areas of a hunt.

At least two myths have hounded selection: first, that it requires a very tough dog to endure the immense electrical corrections to keep him from going to the preferred flyers; second, that this training is very expensive, owing to the number of shot birds used in the process. Many successful practitioners disagree with both points: a dog with aptitude for selection need not be tough—some trainers actually prefer a sensitive, impressionable dog—but he must have good marking ability. Second, rather than shot pheasants or ducks, they recommend clipped-wing pigeons.

Generally speaking, most would-be selection trainers harm more dogs than they enhance, because the humans, not the dogs, are the weak link in the task.

AUDIBLE CUES

I have recommended early, separate lessons for assisting a young marker to recognize square-thrown memory birds (see pp. 111–112). Good marking dogs can be taught to cope with this "selection-type bird" by seeing it, training on it repeatedly, and being cued for it audibly. Voice cues are useful and interesting in a variety of instances to communicate to the dog a specific manner of doing a tough job. In marking, the popular cue word for the short key bird is EASY. It can be used in pointing out this particular bird to your dog as he views the gunners before his birds are shot, and again just before he is sent to pick up that key bird in whatever retrieving order. (Presumably he has already retrieved one or both of the long birds.)

John Anderson explains, "I started cuing when trying to teach the 'easy'

* The above portion of "Training for Selection" was prepared with the assistance of professional Dana Brown of California.

bird in order to put the brakes on the dog before I sent him for a short bird. Then I started on the things that were difficult to teach, such as 'way back, water' to help recognize the retired gun as across water and a good distance back on land. There's a tendency for dogs to hunt short. I cue twice, once when he first looks at the gun, and again when he is sent. Next, was the 'cover' cue, which means go through what's in front of you rather than around it. With a little bit of reinforcement it worked extremely well. The verbal command 'water' is another basic cue used primarily for water blinds; it gets that dog thinking 'Get in the water.' "

Although many experts do not employ a separate audible cue to distinguish between various marks, they do change the tone and volume of voice when releasing their dogs—loud on deep birds, soft on short. Obviously, it isn't what words you say to a dog that influences a response; Scottish herd dogs and German guard dogs have been cued variously for centuries. Whatever the trainer decides to use—from patting his leg or snapping his fingers to whispers or shouts—his choice must be linked judiciously to the dog's training.

In contrast to the above, the *silent* cast—no verbal "over" or "back"—can be very useful in assisting a directional cast or softly indicating a nearby bird. Many trainers feel that silents are their strongest casts. They have built the "silent" into a dire threat symbol from training pressure and claim they use it only in demanding circumstances.

THE TRAINING WEEK

Earlier, I mentioned shaping a training day to your dog's particular needs. If you and your dog are engaged in trial combat on successive weekends, whether out on the circuit or commuting to the fray, you should consider building an overall pattern or work curve for the intervening weekdays to hold your dog's competitive edge.

This curve should escalate in degrees of difficulty at the middle of the week and descend just before the trial to produce an energetic dog, optimistic and prepared for difficult work.

Sunday. If your trial does not continue through Sunday, you can both take a day's rest. (At least one of you is probably exhausted.)

Monday. Rest or light work with birds, to avoid the boredom of dumb bumpers after the trial's hot-shot pheasants and ducks.

Water blind at National Amateur, Portland, Oregon.

Tuesday. Work on some poorly understood aspect; anticipate tough upcoming trial demands and prepare accordingly.

Wednesday. Perhaps some familiar drills—handling or blinds.

Thursday. Ease off to build confidence, using marks, with shot birds to tidy up line manners. Then travel to the next trial.

Finally, when your dog is Qualified and you are preparing for a National, with enough time—often months—to bring the dog to the peak of his ability, adapt the idea of a work curve to this longer time period. Vary the degree of difficulty in his lessons, your own severity of pressure and force, and the number of shot birds, so as to arrive at the trial with a confident, controlled, ambitious animal.

"When I train for Nationals," says Tom Sorenson of Missouri, "I like to go back to simple basics. I throw away all the tricky stuff. I put three or four guns out and have the dogs pick up the marks as singles in the order they would pick up a multiple in the trial. For blinds I run them on plenty of repeats on patterns. I don't use drills that will bore them."

If your good dog seems totally down, when you've tried birds, tried tough work, easy work, force, and you don't appear to get anywhere, consider this advice given me by Dutch Butcher, trainer of FC AFC Dutch's Black Midnight, for my bitch who had run into flat spots while training for a National. "Trust her," he said. "She knows how to do it all. Forget more helpers or more terrain. Take a box of pigeons, a shotgun, yourself, and your dog out into a wide open field. Sit her at your side, throw a bird and bring it down, then reach in the box and get another, and shoot it, then grab another out and flight it and shoot it, too!"

"What about configuration?" I asked.

"Just pick 'em up wherever they fall."

"Then what?"

"Go home—and do it again the next day," he advised.

It was the best dog medicine I had ever received in a small parcel. My bitch's attitude positively bloomed. We went on to be National finalists. Years later a friend of mine was in the same pre-National fix. I repeated Dutch's recipe, and it worked again.

Dogs mature and advance differently and also burn out at different ages. Many sheepmen and cattlemen reckon that stock dogs' brains go after age nine. The English don't expect their trial dogs to be competitive after age five. These dogs develop a generally uncooperative attitude known as *running cunning*. Many American trainers believe that a dog has four good years and that they may come anytime between one and ten years of age. Other serious dogmen seem reluctant to acknowledge this aging and believe a very fine animal's prime can be extended competitively far longer than this—if the trainer can recognize the symptoms of "cunningness" on the dog's part and take steps to offset it.

Dogs may temporarily "sour" or "go into the dumps," yet are not necessarily ready for retirement. After serious injury or illness or a period of overtraining, for example, an older accomplished dog may slide into a sluggish, reluctant state. Indeed, you may wonder if he'll ever haul the freight for you again. Throw away your schedule and expectations and put him up for two or three months. Then, reconstruct him fully, from the bottom up—starting with short Derby singles and eventually proceeding to his blinds work. Take him through every step you'd assume would be trivial to a former high achiever. This double-trained, twice-forged dog can become more proficient than ever.

Late in December and damned cold, I drove through a blurred, crusty dusk on ice thick as Coke bottle glass. Station wagons milled in the snowy gloom. I joined with beautiful people in a last-ditch lunge at Christmas shopping. Obediently, I entered chic, tinseled shops for shearing, and felt relief when a holly-decked saleswoman congratulated me on having selected respectable gifts for my family.

Outside, edging along the parking lot, the dark banks of the snooty Saugatuck River are smeared with scalloping strings of garish lights held up by regiments of tiny dead Douglas firs. At the car door I flip the bright packages into the back seat. An ancient sound slits the taut river air—wing music! Hundreds of Black Duck and Mallard are using the festooned lines of light for glide paths to safe landings. Caught there under holiday trappings, I stand listening—and envy their directness and simplicity.

GAME PLANS

Know your competition and know your own dog.

I have lost a number of trials by trying to "John Wayne" every test—gambling for the *only* perfect job in the field—be the only one who didn't handle on a mark, or have the only dog that lined the water blind. Often this wasn't necessary. If I had been up-to-date and precise in my evaluation of the competitors, I could have played safe, stayed alive, and survived to win the trial. A handler must read and evaluate his competition and the difficulties of the next test before any dogs run it and be honestly aware of his own dog's strengths and weaknesses. Is the dog so strong in the water that he can gamble on land? What did the dog show in training last week? Is he such a stout marker that he might squeak by with flaky blinds? Is the dog qualified for the upcoming National? Current AKC requirements are one win (five points) and two other points. And if not, what does he need to get—a win or a single point? Play it accordingly. Most professionals do this skillfully.

Know in advance what the terrain, cover, and water will be like in the scheduled trials, and help your dog prepare for it by training on similar ground if possible. The temperature and altitude of the trial site are good to know, too. If you are going to a cold location, you might train a little harder and longer, since dogs may freshen in the cool weather. Old-timers claim a field of dogs will tend to overrun their marks in thin air at high altitude. If the trial is to occur in hot weather, limit training in the preceding week to ensure adequate energy reserves for the weekend.

Many amateurs and pros who campaign heavily keep records on the preferences and idiosyncrasies of the major trial judges. "She doesn't count whistles, but you better keep your dog on line." "He loves tight mechanical tests and tends to place the slow pigs." "He'll throw you out if you handle on a mark." Some competitors can almost predict certain test configurations, as certain judges have become patently set in their manners of testing.

I can remember being flattered after I finished judging my second major stake. At a dinner party, a professional dogman caught my eye and saluted me with his drink.

"Boy, I got a page started on *you*."

"How do you know those tests weren't the work of my co-judge?" I asked.

"Because I got a whole book on him—and none of those tests were in it," he replied with a wink.

As I enumerate the contingencies of advanced work, I realize they may appear overwhelming to a beginning trainer, no matter how committed. A diligent trainer at this level can learn far more from his dog and his competition than he can from any book—if he has the eye, the patience, and the time.

Good amateurs are eventually dependent on at least one good training partner or group. Much of the pattern work can be done alone, but without enough field time and access to good land, water, and able help, the training of the dog may be far better left to a good professional. In fact, I am sure a few of my favorite professionals could improve my own dogs' competitive capabilities and probably thrash me with them. My dogs would certainly benefit from their expertise and daily attention, and a greater number of shot birds with a full crew of help, too.

But what my dogs would gain, I would lose. They are my dogs; we do what we can as a team. Our triumphs, failures, exasperations, and delights are our own. I doubt that I would feel so closely involved with them if I did not train them myself.

THE QUESTION OF COURTESY

Like fly casting, bow hunting, and snipe shooting, accomplished dog control is not for everyone and, apparently, not everyone is capable of controlling dogs.

In recent years, this country has experienced a dramatic dog population explosion comparable to the baby booms of other decades. Much of this is due to middle-class affluence and social motivation: dogs are easily recognized symbols of status. They function as companions, protectors, baby-sitters, surrogate children, and offer vicarious identification with the rare and exotic. There exists an enormous poodle population in Alaska and a similar lust for sled dogs in Manhattan.

People who associate themselves with dogs seldom burden themselves with the responsibility of obedience training, even though the work is simple and involves but four commands: SIT, HEEL, COME, and where to AIR. Dog owners who care about their neighbors are uncommon. Because of this, there are far more slob dogs than good dogs, and the dogless portion of the public fails to recognize any difference between the two.

Although dogs may be vaccinated and licensed, I am not aware of any licensing mechanism that requires a prospective dog owner to pass an examination for qualification to own, operate, or maintain a canine—be it a King Charles Spaniel or an attack-trained Doberman. Motorists, doctors, aviators, and lawyers must demonstrate some skill and judgment by passing exams. Perhaps dog owners should be licensed as well.

All too many owners of mismatched, untrained working or sporting dogs suddenly "realize" that their dogs need to be "in the country" in order to "run free." (Frankly, I can't think of a single domestic canine that needs to do so.) These troublesome dogs only arouse hostility against *all* dogs, including our retrievers. Slob dogs can be noisy, filthy nuisances. They can host disease and parasites, endanger the health of man, children, and livestock, and destroy wildlife. They can cause farmers and ranchers to bait their fields with poison, shoot any dog on their land, and close their gates. Each time a property owner or a government agency closes land that could be used for dog training, hunting, or trial grounds, the opportunity for excellence in field dogs is diminished. It seems grossly unfair that the best-trained, best-cared-for dogs are penalized, while wildlife and livestock continue to be antagonized by outlaw dogs. Many disgruntled people, even dog-hating poultrymen and stockmen, could be readily convinced that there *are* worthy dogs left in the world were they to see a fine retriever and handler team working together.

FIELD-TRIAL ETIQUETTE AND PRACTICE

Field trialing represents a formal substitute for bird hunting. In the face of diminishing wild places—huntable, fishable land and habitat—all possible care and courtesy must be extended to the land and the landowner. Many present-day dog trialers, like clay bird shooters, have never hunted; indeed, as pieces of wild habitat fall to "development," and other lands are closed to dogs and hunters, the day may be approaching when field trialing is all the "hunting" we have left.

• Trial birds—pen-raised pheasants and ducks—deserve considerate handling and treatment: adequate shade, crating, food, and water. Ducks should be carefully shackled just prior to use and then quickly released. Wet ducks should be protected from cold wind.

• Human litter is the baleful signature of civilization. A broken bottle can cripple a hard-running dog or a barefoot child. Glass is slow to degrade; its worst haunt is underwater or in deep, soft mud where it lurks for years, ready to slash a pad or tendon. Retriever trainers are the only group I have ever seen on hands and knees, picking up sackfuls of bright beer bottle splinters from a favorite shore or field.

• Trial gunners seldom run competitive dogs, yet they usually know good dog work. Gunners volunteer to travel long miles to work in sweltering heat and freezing rain, from daybreak to dusk, to help test our dogs. A sharp set of gunners can make or break a test. The courtesy of complete, reasonable instructions and thanks by the judges is small compensation for their skill and service. Rarely are they accorded the glamorous status of their counterparts in England.

Judging. A veteran judge once explained to me, "Every judge has an ax to grind, every damned one of them. In fact," he confided slowly, "I'm the only one I can think of who can do it right."

Each judge brings his or her own bias and hope to each assignment. Furthermore, the expectations and emphasis in trials are changing faster than many of the trial judges. If judges were prepared to pour the hours of study and practice into their judging that they find for the study and practice of training (for most do both), the differential between understanding dogs and testing them would be narrower.

Regional judging workshops and club-sponsored judging clinics have been helpful to many trialers in appreciating the difficulties in setting up a balanced trial program that results in a satisfying winner.

Traditionally, there has been an apprenticeship period for young judges. The prospective candidate is matched up with a capable, veteran, eight-point judge. (Each major stake requires eight collective judging points between the two judges. An eight-point judge has worked at least eight major stakes, accumulating one point per trial, and can support a new judging partner with no points.) The apprentice is expected to learn and absorb the mechanical aspects: problems of site changes, gallery placement and parking, the logistics of time, birds, number of entries, and available help, as well as the exciting business of flyers, bird placement, and creative uses of terrain and water in changing daylight and weather conditions. Apprenticeship for a dedicated judge should be served in picnic and fun trials, then his skill should be practiced and honed in judging minor stakes. Would-be judges who shun this learning period and leap directly into the major stakes are like green dogs attempting to run an Open stake without the benefit of sufficient training. The apprenticeship system should, I believe, be maintained.

Some rather lackluster dog handlers have made intuitive, solid judges, and a few great dog trainers have proved dismal at judging. Most good judges try to design tests that cause the cream of the dogs to rise to the top. Yet, there exist a few wary judges who feel the quality of their particular trials is reflected in which dogs win and place. Although this is often true, such judges may arrange a convenient roster of quality by placing only previously titled popular champions. This timid attitude is a shame, as competitive dogs reach peaks of performance at different times in their training, the trial season, and their lives. If an unknown or young dog does well on the work required of him, he should be rewarded.

I'm concerned that in recent years the large entries of competing dogs and the high quality of training in retrievers have resulted in a burden on judges. They often seem forced to design tight, complicated, mechanical tests that result in slow and colorless winners. Old-timers say that a trial winner should be "the dog you would most like to take home," implying a stylish, pleasing, accurate athlete who possesses courage and heart. This view is supported fully by the AKC Field Trial Rules and Standard Procedures for Retrievers, and various updated supplement materials. However, the judge who is ready to penalize a dog for lack of style or desire to retrieve is increasingly less common. As newcomers fresh from the Derby and Qualifying stakes observe this in the major stakes, they may come to accept the slow, mechanical dog as having the quality required to win and may adjust their training goals accordingly.

The style of judging can directly influence the directions the breeding of working dogs will take. There are relatively few retriever family lines that thrive through natural ability and trainability under the demands of modern testing. In spite of the popularity and growing numbers of competitive dogs, judging itself has narrowed the range of breeding stock. Before any widening of the breeding base can be accomplished, we must broaden what is considered acceptable in terms of judged performance.*

We are far from the early trials when all birds were shot flyers and judges kept an eye peeled for the well-staunched, soft-mouthed dog that could mark. Today's grueling judging assignment is often interpretative and subjective—much more so than that of an umpire peering into a strike zone. It's often said that after four days of enduring driving rain, eating dust, or feeding mosquitoes, the only friend a judge has left is the man whose dog won his trial.

* The author is an eight-point Field Trial judge and has moderated and judged in AKC clinics on the subject of trial judging.

11

Health

SLEEPING CINNAMON TEAL

I was still euphoric as I flipped single bumpers a short distance into our home creek. My two-year-old bitch had just won the first Open Stake field trial we entered. The water was deep and warm as she practiced cutting angles through a thin green wall of tules. Her water entry was low, swift, and maniacal, and she seemed to gather more cannonball torque with every trip. Again I threw the bright orange bumper into the slough and once more she punched through the wall, but this time yipped and made a grotesque somersault. She surfaced, glanced back at me, then slowly swam to the bumper and dutifully returned it. I bent to receive it and noticed the odd color of the puddle that formed from her dripping coat: it became more crimson with each draining second. I groped beneath her, feeling along her brisket, ribs, and abdomen. My fingers pushed into a huge warm tear as she sat, statue-still and silent. I told myself the wound had to be superficial as I carefully rolled her over for a better look. A six-inch gash revealed working organs, entrails and wood splinters like a fine ticking watch with the backplate removed. She had been impaled on an unseen snag and was hemorrhaging freely.

I carried her in my arms, trying to hold the gash shut with one hand as I made for my distant truck and the nearest vet. The two regulars were both out doctoring cattle on local ranches, but I found a callow youngster mucking out stalls. He seemed primed for medical action. While he examined the awesome debris-filled wound, I asked sharply if he was capable of closing a hole that size, adding that I needed skillful doctoring on this animal, not student practice. He nodded: "I've just graduated from the university. You've got ten minutes to get to another vet's office or to decide to trust me. I can't guarantee anything except that she'll be dead in twenty minutes."

His bedside manner impressed me. "Just sedate her lightly," I said. He worked quickly yet meticulously, flushing, snipping, stitching. I assisted. Later the older vets returned; they peered at his handiwork and withdrew without comment. He worked on and she hung on. I was grateful for his care and skill; he saved my favorite dog's life.

She was FC AFC Nakai Anny, and years later, as previously mentioned, she presented me with a litter that became the highest-scoring bunch of Derby pups in retriever history. But the night they were whelped, a very different young vet from the same university lost a considerable portion of that litter through negligence and incompetence.

Retrievers seem so robust, athletic, and gamely heroic, it's easy to think of them as indestructible. They're not. I once saw a field champion at a National, conditioned to his physical peak, hop down twenty-four inches from his handler's truck and break his bladder. Within minutes he was surrounded by veterinarians. Within hours he was dead. Our dogs have their own weaknesses and strengths, and being familiar with them is an important responsibility.

This chapter is intended to give you and your dogs the benefit of lessons I've had to learn bit by bit, and often the hard way.

I've had the advice and aid of a superb veterinarian, Ed Maguire, D.V.M., who has trained field trial champions and hunts his own dogs hard and often in the Sutter Buttes of northern California. He's put a lot of dogs back together; I've watched and admired as he stitched up friends' dogs on levees and hillsides. He is analytical, fast, direct, and generous—he's a vet's vet.

If you work your own dog frequently, his normal disposition, attitude,

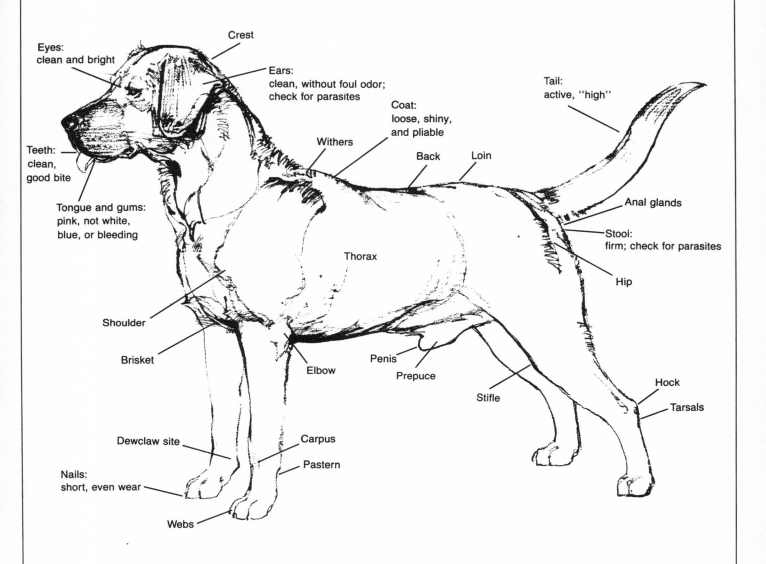

Diagram 41. A healthy dog's body parts. The normal temperature of your dog at rest is 100° to 102.5° F. Drastic deviation may indicate the presence of disease. A regular vaccination schedule is essential for the maintenance of good health. Have your pup vaccinated for distemper, hepatitis, and leptospirosis two weeks after weaning or at seven weeks, whichever occurs first, and again at two-week intervals until twelve weeks of age. Give him a booster for each disease annually thereafter. At sixteen weeks of age—not earlier—your pup should be vaccinated for rabies, and he should receive a booster every other year thereafter.

and vitality should be so readily apparent that when he's "not right" or "not his old self," you're immediately aware of it. But for any dog, there are certain key warnings that something is wrong.

1. Lack of appetite   4. Diarrhea
2. Poor color of gums   5. Abnormal breathing or coughing
3. Abnormal temperature   6. Vomiting

These symptoms, their likely causes and suggested cures, as well as development disorders and general care, are discussed in detail in the following text.

FOOD AND FEEDING

The soundest feeding rule I know is: Match the food to the dog and the amount of food to the work. This is especially important for the hard-hunted dog; for a day or two following a rigorous upland effort, I sometimes feed morning and evening both, supplying his normal daily portion in each. I know, and he shows, just how much we have taxed ourselves.

Feed a good-quality dry dog food. Many major brand suppliers have spent millions on nutritional research on a proper diet for working dogs. It is good food, yet the response to it will vary from dog to dog—even among litter mates. Matching an effective food to *your* dog is *your* job; when you find it, stick with it. You needn't try to entertain your dog's palate nightly in gourmet fashion. He may like that, but variety in foods can develop picky eating habits.

Canned food is handy for flavor only. It's 70 percent water, and serves mainly to entice your dog to eat a sufficient amount of dry food.

Certain "custom" foods are available through your vet, at extra effort and expense. These provide more protein or more fat, for growth, endurance, and stress situations. They're useful for athletes that hammer through the fields all day, but this diet would be wasted on a lapdog or a large housebound retriever. It can also lead to gut problems and disease in sedentary pets.

There are dog foods intended to help your animal reduce, but these represent sheer owner indulgence! You put that extra weight on him, and it's up to you to get it off. Feed less to overweight dogs. On the other hand, reluctant eaters are often helped by feeding six days a week only. "Fasting" one day a week makes food more precious, and your dog will usually eat more when it is available. Feed your dog yourself, and praise him while he eats. Make it a *privilege* to eat, a reward rather than a right.

Duck dogs sometimes need more fat for insulation and energy reserves.

Your aim in feeding should be a healthy but lean animal from age six months to two years, the critical maturation period. Truly fat puppies, tottering with their own weight, invite disaster—usually to their skeletons. Supplemental amounts of calcium *may* sometimes be needed, and should be furnished from the age of four months to one year, while bones are in their maximum growth phase. It's advisable to consult your vet regarding your dog's particular needs.

The amount of food to feed your dog should be dictated by the amount of work he does. Consider his size and weight and how often and how hard you train or hunt. Less work usually requires less food. The average frequency for feeding a mature dog is once a day. A pregnant bitch, or a dog recovering from illness, usually requires other programs—often up to four light meals a day, plus vitamins. Puppies must be fed three times a day, then twice a day as they grow.

Water should be available at all times in a dog's home kennel. Plenty of water in the food, as well as drinking water, should be provided when your dog is crated for travel; this helps prevent gastric problems due to crate confinement. (Using your own water while out on the road is a good idea; traveling and letting a dog tank up on branch or swamp water will usually upset his gut.)

Some serious duck hunters like to keep a bit more fat on their dogs during water-fowl season for insulation and energy reserves. These dogs may be sitting and working in very cold water from before dawn through the day. Their shivering is real. You may want to feed your helper tidbits during a dark and freezing November day, just as you fortify yourself with coffee or soup.

DEVELOPMENTAL DISORDERS

At the age of three to four months, a pup's bones and joints are still forming, and the skeleton's growth plates are still in the process of closing up. This is such a crucial stage that prospective young racehorses are examined radiographically before they are allowed to start training, to ensure that they are fully finished growing. While a precocious pup at this age may begin to find real speed, it is all too commonly a time when he may involve himself in accidents in the field. *Take it easy with a developing dog.* You've probably invested some effort and expense in acquiring him; don't ruin his future by racing him over rough ground too early.

Osteochondritis desiccans. The separation of cartilage from bone, most commonly seen in the shoulder. Big, eager young dogs from six months to a year old seem to be afflicted most frequently. The jammed shoulder "lameness" is often slight, but if it recurs, or persists for three days, see your vet. Other developmental disorders of the skeleton may also show up in lameness in pups of four months to two years. Any persistent evidence of lameness should be reviewed by your vet.

Hip dysplasia (poorly formed hips). This is common among retrieving dogs. It can be detected by radiograph as early as six months of age. There are many forms and degrees of dysplasia, and evidence of it does *not* always mean the dog will "break down." Some of the highest-achieving field-trial dogs—bitches and males—have had forms of hip dysplasia.

Diet (too heavy, too fat) and exercise (rough ground, deep mud) influence these joints. Recently, great effort has been expended by owners and the Orthopedic Foundation for Animals (OFA), Inc., to try to recognize and reduce the insidious disease of hip dysplasia in our dogs by registering hip X rays of each dog and supplying the owner an evaluation. It's a huge relief to learn that your animal is structurally sound.

It is generally accepted today that dogs of poor skeletal conformation should not be bred. Asking the dog if he is fit to go on retrieving is a mistake; many dogs actually are too big-hearted to stop their work because of pain. Dogs have gone on retrieving with their forequarters or hindquarters totally out of commission, dragging or pushing themselves forward. The handler who truly knows his dog will know when to keep working, when to stop, and when to see the vet.

EYE DISORDERS

Retinal dysplasia. Spots and blind zones may be detected as early as six months. Your puppy's eyes should be checked for this by an expert during his first physical exam. Some dogs with this disorder manage to function very well in spite of it. Breeding two retinally dysplastic animals can result in blind puppies.

Retinal atrophy. This is unhappily not so easily detected or so benign in its effects. A deterioration that usually results in blindness, it can take four or five years to be fully recognized—by which time vast amounts of training and attention have been wasted, as well as the animal itself.

COMMON HEALTH PROBLEMS

— *Eyes and Ears* —

Dog's eyes are remarkably tough and resistant to puncture. Handlers should be encouraged to examine them, especially after the animals have been running in thick-cover fields.

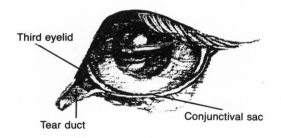

Diagram 42. Parts of a dog's eye.

Seeds and debris can enter and obstruct the tear ducts (in the nose-corner of the eye), resulting in infection. The conjunctival sac below some dogs' eyes hangs open more than in others; owners occasionally have this slack surgically tightened. This vulnerable region of the eye should be examined after working by pulling the skin down beneath the eyes to expose any foreign contents. The sac can be swept clean with a cotton-tipped applicator. Clean all debris from the eyes. You can remove seeds, plant awns, and other foreign matter from the eye by holding it open wide with thumb and forefinger; with a quick, hard breath, blow close to the eye from the outside corner to the nose. Or you may flush the eye gently with clean water or a mild boric acid solution. The third eyelid area, in the inner corner of the eye, can be another catchall for debris as well.

Eye infections. Remove matting, pus, and debris. Apply ophthalmic ointment three to four times a day. If the infection persists after three days, see your vet. Any deep corneal scratches or cuts from tules, barbwire, or thorns should be treated immediately by a vet.

Ear infections. Most commonly the result of foreign bodies in the ear canal. Some dogs don't drain water from their ears as readily as others. Constant head-shaking—sometimes to the point of splitting the tips of the ears—usually indicates the presence of plant awns, ear mites, or a yeastlike organism. Mites leave a dark, cheesy debris. Inspect closely. Clean and remove any debris you can see by means of a cotton-tipped applicator, then apply an antibiotic ointment once daily, working it thoroughly down the ear canal with thumb and fingers at the cartilaginous base of the ear. Any persistent odor, discharge, or irritation lasting beyond three to four days should be brought to your vet's attention, especially if the dog has recently been exposed to foxtails.

— *Feet* —

Pads. Pad cuts and gouges are common. They sometimes bleed profusely and are slow to heal. They are very difficult to keep closed with stitching; the damaged foot should be protected during healing. Usually the dog keeps the wound clean as it heals, but it should be wrapped or bandaged during working periods. Pad tougheners and conditioners are available and may be of benefit to tender-footed dogs. Frequent saltwater excursions sometimes help toughen feet.

Toenails. Torn and split toenails are painful and distracting enough to affect a dog's job performance. They often have to be completely removed to facilitate healing. The dog will easily grow a new nail. Exercise on concrete yields good, even nail wear.

Dewclaws. These are preferably removed by a vet at several days of age. Adult dogs may require removal of the dewclaw if it protrudes and is subject to tearing.

Traumatic Injuries: Bruises, Lacerations, and Deep Cuts

Clean superficial cuts and abrasions with mild soap and water, then treat with an appropriate antibiotic ointment. Bandaging is necessary only to prevent the dog's biting or licking the wound.

In the case of extensive skin tears or flaps, try to clean the wound and close it to protect the underlying tissues. As an emergency measure, safety pins can be used to hold the tear together until you can get to the vet for stitches.

With deep cuts, apply local pressure above the wound to control excessive bleeding; tourniquets in the form of rubber bands, duck ties, or surveyor's tape can be useful for this purpose. Try to protect the wound from dirt and further damage, and bandage with gauze, strips of cotton sheet, or towel until proper veterinary care is available.

Sprains and Lameness

Obvious fractures or dislocations must be attended to immediately. Lameness that lingers three or more days should be examined professionally. Good lameness diagnosis is difficult. It is advisable to consult an orthopedic specialist.

Carpal or wrist sprains are common. Apply a light support wrap and confine the dog to his kennel for a full week's respite from training. An aspirin tablet is sometimes temporarily helpful to a sore dog after training or a long hunting day. Swelling, or any obvious deviation in the wrist angle, should receive veterinary attention.

Shoulder sprains from jamming—jumping wide ditches with a crash into the opposite bank, for example—require rest and a respite from training. See your vet if the dog persists in favoring the joint.

Stifle or knee sprains of collateral ligaments usually heal with rest—often for several weeks. A ruptured cruciate ligament causes acute lameness; however, with surgical repair by an expert and six months of careful rest and therapy, the leg can recover.

A partially torn cruciate is tough to diagnose. The dog will use the leg during interesting work, forgetting discomfort, but will carry it up when the joint is cold. This is a dangerous disability; as much as you'd like to avoid surgery and let it heal naturally, an unstable knee has a strong tendency to develop arthritis. The crippling result is worse than the total cruciate break and repair. To help avoid tarsal or heel sprains, rupture of ligaments or tendons—which are particularly common in larger dogs—spare your dog unnecessary vertical leaps, like bouncing ball or Frisbee retrieves.

There is a natural tendency for a dog with one knee damaged to overstrain his opposite good leg and snap that ligament as well. Overweight dogs of all breeds, incidentally, tend to break down easily in the stifle area. After knee surgery, great care should be taken not to rush the dog back to work. Progressively longer swims are the best postoperative therapy. Avoid soft, muddy ground, fast starts, and tough angling conditions. Refrain from any marking until the leg is restored.

The risk of lameness in athletic dogs simply can't be avoided, any more than it can in football and basketball players or in other human contact sports. Pushing your dog too hard, without enough rest, will increase the hazards, often resulting in arthritis and early retirement.

— *Gastrointestinal System Disorders* —

Intestinal parasites. All young dogs probably have worms and should be given a fecal check during their early general physical exam. Your vet can issue specific oral drug treatment for each condition or parasite. All parasites are dangerous to good health and performance; lack of treatment may cause the death of your pup.

Roundworms. These are common in young dogs and are usually acquired from the mother. Weak, thin, dull-coated, potbellied pups are often hosts to roundworms.

Tapeworms. Segments are visible in the stool. Their presence is usually related to fleas. Rats and mice that may be ingested can also carry tapeworms.

Hookworms. These can severely debilitate a dog. Anemia and loss of blood can be associated with the presence of hookworm.

Whipworms. These can be a chronic problem, resulting in persistent diarrhea.

Coccida. Indicated by diarrhea with mucus and blood.

Giardia. Indicated by constant soft stool and blood. It is difficult to identify in lab tests. Ask your vet about treating *Giardia* with a product called Flaggell.

Parvo virus. Lack of appetite and listlessness, followed in twelve to twenty-four hours by vomiting, diarrhea, possibly bloody stool. See your vet—a delay may be fatal.

If diarrhea persists and you suspect intestinal parasites, a fresh fecal sample should be examined by your vet.

Gastric torsion. Abdominal distension and bloat add up to a potentially fatal condition. Avoid exercise, especially jumping, after the dog has eaten or consumed a large quantity of water—particularly on hot days. Some dogs inadvertently take in amazing amounts of water when swimming in with a retrieved article. Allow several hours for this water to move through the dog's system before continuing to train. Any rapid distension of the abdomen, accompanied by discomfort and weakness, should receive veterinary care.

Vomiting. Withhold food for twenty-four hours. Limit water intake to small quantities at a time; ice cubes may be given to the dog to lick. Pepto-Bismol is safe for canines, but if vomiting persists over three days, or temperature exceeds 103.5 degrees F., see your vet. (Normal temperature for an adult dog at rest is 101.0 degrees to 102.5 degrees F.)

Diarrhea. Allow access to water. Feed a bland diet, such as boiled rice. Avoid meat and fat supplements. Antidiarrhea medications like Kaopectate are available and should be given two to three times daily. Diarrhea owing to trial or hunting excitement and traveling is common, and usually stops when the action subsides.

— *Respiratory System Disorders* —

Kennel cough (infectious tracheobronchitis). This highly contagious disease of the upper respiratory tract is caused by a virus infection. It is characterized by a gagging cough, as if the dog had a bone caught in its throat. The cough can sound worse than it actually is. It is usually a self-remedied disease, much like a cold in humans. Relieve the irritation, suppress the cough, and prevent secondary bacterial invasion. Depressant-type cough syrups (such as Romilar, Vicks 44) obtainable from most drugstores can be useful in easing throat irritation. The dosage for a forty- to fifty-pound dog is approximately the same as for an adult human. Examine the mouth and oral cavity, especially around the tonsils, for foreign matter such as foxtails and other debris. Check the color of the gums and tongue for a blueness in the mucus membrane. Report such changes, and any cough that persists, to your vet.

Laryngo spasm. This acute, short-duration gagging and throat spasm is often accompanied by snorting and repetitive swallowing. Some dogs will have episodes throughout their lives; others will have a seasonal occurrence. Unfortunately little can be done except to wait for the condition to pass.

Heartworm. Persistent cough, shortness of breath, and weakness can indicate heartworm, an insidious mosquito-borne parasite that was once confined to the deep South. The affliction is now nationwide; it can incapacitate and permanently ruin your retriever. Preventive medicine is available from your vet; it can be given directly or mixed into the dog's food.

— *Heatstroke* —

Respect the heat. Retrievers are heavy-coated dogs. Black dogs, especially, absorb solar heat, which can raise their body temperature to 109 degrees F. and virtually fry their willing brains. Strenuous work in heat can lower the sperm count in males, thereby reducing potency. Keen dogs hunting game in the heat don't know when to quit—you should. Also, avoid confining your dog in closed, hot automobiles while shopping or working.

Heavy panting and convulsions are symptomatic of heatstroke. As an immediate treatment, cool the dog down by submerging his body in cool water; if that isn't possible, pack the neck area with ice. Water or any alcohol may also be applied to cool by evaporation. A rectal enema with cool water can be helpful in this very real crisis. A dog in convulsions should be attended by a vet.

Retrieving dogs are essentially explosive, dash-oriented athletes, not marathoners: a long land test in a trial rarely lasts over six minutes. While well-conditioned field dogs have great body strength and enormous athletes' hearts (whose size often amazes or alarms a vet unfamiliar with trial dogs), few of our heavy-coated dogs could keep up with working varmint hounds or well-conditioned pointers. It is unfair and dangerous to take your out-of-shape, soft, anxious dog out on opening day and be gung ho in excessive heat or cold.

OTHER HEALTH CONCERNS

Hypothermia. Ability to move well is limited. This condition usually results from exhaustion following prolonged heavy exercise in cold, wet conditions. Get the dog warm and dry. Feed him sugar or honey if he can swallow. If you hunt in freezing conditions for long periods, consider buying or making your dog a polyurethane wetsuit. Find a skin-diving or surfing shop to help you. Paint the suit in camouflage if you like. It's not "sissy stuff" to make your dog as comfortable and as effective as possible.

Hypoglycemia. Low blood sugar may be indicated by recurring periods of collapse, seizure, or convulsions following exercise. Consult your vet.

Anal glands. A low, limp tail position may mean that the scent glands alongside the anus are plugged and painful. See your vet. He may teach you to express these glands yourself.

Teeth. Stylish retrievers can, and occasionally do, break off their canines on rocks that they mistake for the breast of a hen pheasant. These teeth are the dog's tools of the trade. Several have been fitted with gold replacements by understanding dentists.

Dogs may develop a buildup of tartar on their teeth, which should be removed and controlled to prevent gum infection. Some dogs remove it by chewing dry food or by working out on large, nonsplintery bones. Bone chewing, however, may foster hardmouth or a bird-crunching habit (see pp. 152–153). Your vet can occasionally scale the tartar from the teeth.

Allergies. Some dogs are more prone to allergies than others. Insect bites (particularly ticks and fleas), pollens, grasses, and vegetation such as poison oak and poison ivy can seriously disrupt a dog's performance. Stinging nettles are dangerous and naturally avoided by a working dog, but a keen dog in hot scent may disregard his instincts and hunt in them anyway. My own dogs have done this and paid the price with sneezing and swelling. I've even heard of several light-coated pointers that died directly after a day of hunting pheasants in nettles. I now work my dogs around them as cautiously as I do myself.

A number of plants are dangerous or deadly if ingested: oleander, monkshood, castor bean, mistletoe, foxglove, autumn crocus, larkspur, daphne, lily of the valley, and hemlock root, to name a few.

Poison. There are often agricultural pest-control efforts going on where we like to train and hunt our dogs. Grain, with strychnine added, is used as bait for muskrats and ground squirrels along irrigation ditches and levees. A dog may easily pick up, mouth, or eat a poisoned animal. You may or may not see him do it, but the symptoms are convulsions. Your dog may eat a rat that has been poisoned by bait around houses or barns; his gums, anus, and prepuce will bleed and his gums will become pale to white. In either case, get him to a vet—it's an emergency.

Snakebite. Treating snakebite in canines is similar to treating a human victim: prompt medical attention is the first rule. Calm or restrain the dog; activity only helps spread the venom. Use a tourniquet above the wound if it's on an extremity. Don't loosen it until you have the vet's help or until two hours have passed.

Hot spots. This is a sudden, moist skin inflammation, caused by allergies, insect bites, and trauma. The spots are active bacterial growth on serum and skin debris. First, clip away surrounding hair, then thoroughly cleanse the site with soap and water. An antibiotic, anti-inflammatory, or drying agent may then be applied. An aggravated hot spot left unattended often enlarges and becomes a lick granuloma.

Lick granuloma. These open sores and thickened, irritated areas of skin, usually on the lower legs or tail, are most often associated with nervous or high-achiever dogs. Some dogs are content to eat their dog houses, chew up their water buckets, or dig holes; others (like people who bite their nails) actually prefer to lick or chew on themselves remorselessly.

The lick granuloma syndrome can begin with a scratch or an itch that develops from the dog's own irritating saliva as he drools on his paws while traveling or watching birds. Sometimes it's psychosomatic, the result of training pressure. Whatever the cause, this chronic, self-inflicted wound is disfiguring and a dangerous invitation to infections.

There are several remedies. Some dogs respond while others resist any cure, and many dogs outgrow the condition on their own. Remedies include:

• "Taste-bad" repellent ointments.

• Cortisone injection at site to relieve itching.

• Cobra-venom injections to anesthetize surface nerves (must be closely vet-supervised).

• Liquid nitrogen, similar to the above but disfiguring.

• Head restraint with a plastic bucket or Elizabethan collar to prevent the dog from reaching lick sites.

• Acupuncture by an experienced practitioner (side effects are possible).

• Palosein shots by a vet.

• Vitamin C added to food.

• Wound shield: a removable fiber-glass cast on the leg to protect the wound and allow uninterrupted healing.

• Remove training pressure or offer dog bones or toys to chew (can result in hardmouth).

— *Foxtails* —

Foxtails are the most common field hazard in the western states. There are several varieties of this grass, which resembles small wheat or barley heads. Their arrowlike awns, ranging in length from ¼ inch to 2 inches, propel themselves directionally and easily penetrate tissue within hours or days. Foxtails are no worry in the spring while still green and soft, or after the first hard summer or fall rains ruin their tensile springiness and ability to travel. But in the peak of summer they can kill your dog.

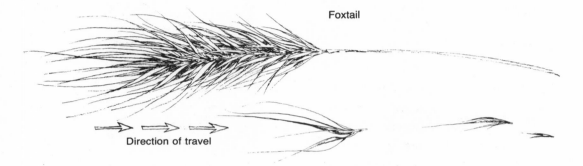

Foxtail

Direction of travel

Diagram 43. Foxtail and direction of travel.

Watch for foxtails, especially where a bird falls. When dogs inhale them, great sneezing results, but foxtails can still migrate through the lungs and damage the spinal cord. A dog's nose often bleeds if he inhales a large foxtail. To dislodge foxtails, old-timers recommend spitting into the nose (to lubricate it), and then blowing into the nose, as in artificial respiration. Sometimes it works. But alligator forceps and a vet are the most effective treatment. Foxtails can cause abcesses anywhere. Check your dog routinely after work in any foxtail country. Examine nose, ears, eyes, mouth (including the area under the tongue and the tonsils), underarms and flanks, prepuce of the male and vulva of the female. Don't overlook the webs between the toes or the pocket near the thumb pad and dewclaw. Swimming can remove foxtails, or hinder them from traveling. A carpet placed in your dog's crate will attract some of them from his coat. Have your dog carry a bird or bumper at heel when you absolutely must traverse a foxtail-laden field; this helps keep his nose off the ground.

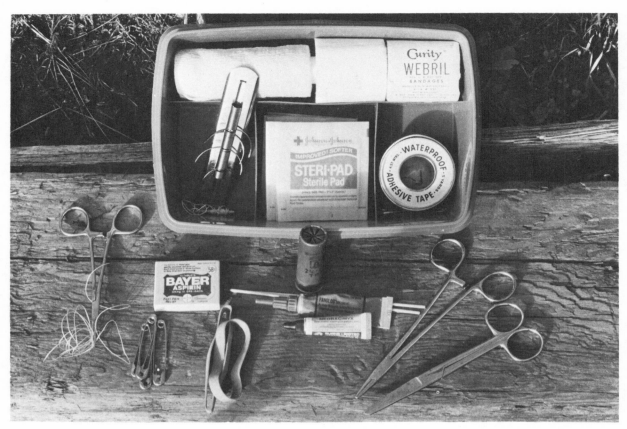

A medical kit carried in your vehicle with basic components is useful for field problems.

VETERINARIANS

I do not want to make new business for vets or a hypochondriac of your dog. The subject of vets, however, does deserve consideration. In my experience, really good, small-animal vets are hard to come by; some large-animal vets, on the other hand, find interest only in pigs, cows, and horses. Find a veterinarian on the recommendation of someone you trust, *before* your dog's life is on the line. All doctors are not created equal, and they are not all equally interested in your dog. The ideal situation is to have a competent vet who has actually seen your dog at work training or trialing, or who has hunted over retrievers himself.

Try not to pester your vet by crying "wolf" too often. But by all means call when you need him and make sure he understands that your animal is very valuable. Most animals he ministers to are pets, not working dogs, and while their owners may cherish them dearly, they have little marketable value. Many vets become hardened by treating daily dozens of dogs and cats that have been neglected, maltreated, starved, or abandoned; they may eventually come to handle them like millwork. Somehow you must convince your vet that *this* dog is different. Your veterinarian must *know* that he's got the equivalent of Secretariat lying on his worktable, not just another "HBC" (Hit-by-Car).

The good vet is generally busy and should be spared things you can learn to do for your dog yourself. Get a copy of *The Well Dog Book* by Terri McGinnis (Random House), or *First Aid for Pets* by R. W. Kirk (Dutton), for your own reference and guidance. A really good vet, if need arises, won't hesitate to consult a specialist or a human doctor on a close-call decision. Check with him before whelping pups; make arrangements to have him close by and available if you need him.

FIRST AID FIELD KITS

Now that you've waded through these everyday disasters and cures, you've probably figured out that it would be handy to keep a small medicine box in your vehicle when you're training, hunting, or trialing. You're right; most professionals carry them on their rigs and take pride in doctoring their string of dogs themselves. Good, comprehensive, preassembled kits, with instructions, are available. If you choose to put your own kit together, the basic components should include the following:

- Rectal thermometer
- Small flashlight
- Forceps
- Needles and thread
- Large and small safety pins
- Bandaging materials
- Medicines. See your vet for recommended antibiotic, anti-inflammatory, and ophthalmic ointments.

Keep your kennels and gear clean. *And know your dog.*

STUD DOGS AND OTHER MATTERS

If your male is handsome or a field genius (one hopes he's both), you may need a plan for dealing with his possibilities, potentials, and problems as a stud dog. If you decide to breed your male, remember that it's the girls who ask the boys for the waltz; the owner of the bitch must bring her to your dog. You should discuss and agree to all terms of the breeding *before* any exchange of services. These include stud fee, bitch lodging, vet care, hip and eye records and qualifications, definition of how many pups represent a litter, bitch arrival time, food, disposition, and travel details.

Because the bitch is brought to your male, it is a good opportunity to *compartmentalize* this experience by breeding him in the same place every time—whether in your garage, your yard, or his kennel. This provides him with a breeding territory, and helps differentiate his new sex role from his normal role as a retrieving dog.

All males react differently to bitch stimulus. If you insist on the perilous practice of breeding your stud haphazardly in trial or hunting situations, and he slobbers and eats dirt when he should be hunting up your bird, you have no one to blame but yourself.

You may emphatically wish your dog to become excited and to perform strongly with a valuable bitch that someone has shipped a long distance for this special purpose, but your good wishes can turn to exasperation when your dog is enchanted by similar bitch scent during his fieldwork. Even a dog who has been bred often in a correct area may get to thinking that any moving dot on the horizon is something else for him to breed. As a result, some trainers preclude all training while a bitch is there to be bred, while others will take their dog out and shoot a few easy flyers for him after he services a bitch, to help him separate the two pleasures. Another tactic is to put another, uppity, *cold* bitch in with him after a successful breeding. His amorous advances may be met with total boredom or a face full of snapping, indignant teeth—and this can show him that all bitches are *not* in heat.

One trouble-prevention theory holds that a young male should be bred early in his career, to define the real thing for him, and then reprimanded later for uninvited, nuisance courtships. Still other dogs are made to abstain like celibate monks for three or four years before standing at stud. Probably the best and most direct approach is a natural confrontation: running the males *after* the bitches have trained and aired in a field. Then if they hang up in a nonbird scent, they can be punished for their inattention to their bird work with an emphatic version of force-fetch. Work through these alluring areas, but remember, in this instance, that blind retrieves through bitch scent are more difficult than marks.

For many reasons, street dogs always seem to breed easily, while purebreds often need good assistance and careful timing. Breeding can be physically dangerous to both bitch and stud if improperly handled. For further insight on actual breeding and whelping procedures, I recommend *The Dog Breeder's Handbook,* by Ernest Hart.

—— *Choosing a Sire* ——

Finding a good sire to mate with a particular bitch is similar to finding a good vet; the research should be done long before you need him.

Trial- and hunting-oriented people should consult the *Retriever Field Trial News.* Show-minded people and those whose dogs are simply house pets should contact the American Kennel Club for the name of the current club secretary for the particular breed.

Ask questions! The owner of a potential sire will generally be too enamored of his own dog to accurately cite his weaknesses. Ask outside people who know the dog well. How is his water work? You may be able to observe his running style, but does he have any brains? What were his previous pups like? Has he ever bred a similarly blooded bitch to yours? What are his real failings and strengths, and are these inherent or taught?

Before you air-freight your little princess off to the current megastud, consider who his trainers and handlers have been. If you had bred to one of the great National champions when he was at his zenith, you wouldn't have purchased his handler's dexterity or benefited from an arduous, lavishly financed training and trialing schedule. These champions have demonstrated talent and trainability—but all you're purchasing is dog talent, not handler talent. This is not intended to discredit any National-quality dogs, since pups from recognized parents are surely easier to sell. But I am somewhat suspicious of blind, "stampede" breeding, whether to a National champ or to some backyard stalwart.

Is your bitch really worth breeding? A good sire can't save the bacon if she can't contribute a hell of a lot. English breeders and most knowledgeable Americans rely on the bitches for the most significant contribution.

Although very few dogs or bitches are "naturals," it's enlightening to watch the could-be greats as raw talent before they're altered by amounts and methods of training. If you see some hard-running, half-trained young maniac who is exceptional in his early marking, who will volunteer to swim extra water and accept an appreciable number of casts and whistles—make note of him. He may go untitled for a long spell, be ruined by his trainer's approach, or eventually be slowed by age or injury, but remember what he had as a rookie, when he was natural and his blood was talking. Look at the compatibility of his pedigree to that of your bitch.

Another aspect of stampede breeding—besides its unimaginativeness—is that great numbers of bitches are bred to a small handful of recognized studs. This seriously narrows the options for future match-ups. As time goes by, the individual family lines are smeared into a legion of cousins, uncles, and aunts with similar physical and mental deficiencies. Some extremely fine dogs have resulted from tight line breeding. However, myopically attempting to duplicate genetically a great dog of yesterday by an alignment of sons and daughters seems to me like lazy, wishful cloning or resurrecting the dead.

For those who imagine that breeding their bitches is a quick shot in the purse, don't rush to the head of the line until you've checked your motives and your market. What are you going to do with six or a dozen of these well-born creatures, once you and your bitch have them? Besides the stud fee, the space, and the *work* required for good litter care—medicating, feeding, worming, dewclaw removal, a possible cesarean section, and a possible bitch death—all are costly considerations. Knowledgeable, skilled, and respectable breeders may find profit enough to operate, and the high-volume, keep-'em-pregnant puppy mills are likely to be satisfied by the bottom-line results. But I've watched several beautifully bred and cared-for litters of high quality go begging for decent homes at any price, through poor timing and naïveté in planning and marketing.

If there is an opportunity to draw real revenue from your amateur canine investment, one avenue is the very narrow one of the Great Proven Stud Dog. He would be one of a half dozen that are national targets of stampede breeders, because he is potent enough to pass on some of his qualities. If you're fortunate enough to own such a male, you might be able to make back your dog-food money and pay your bird bill or put your kid through college or perhaps even buy yourself a small airplane to get you to more field trials and splendid hunting.

OLDER DOGS

As working dogs age, the incidence increases for many of the maladies of human old folks: weak sightedness, blindness, deafness, arthritis, cancer, and senility. Aside from forgiving and adjusting for changes in the healthy older dog, a knowledgeable dogman may extend his dog's working life by assuring him consistent physical fitness. Somewhere in the middle age of a trial dog (five to seven years), he will cease to require the copious amounts of drilling needed in a younger dog. He should be accomplished in most areas. Instead, review his *honesty* on water entries and angles. Watch for signs of boredom, jadedness, and laziness—for example, standing but not sitting on whistle-stops and loafing at half speed.

Attitude is now the most critical ingredient of your dog's training, and there are various ways to sustain or reawaken his ambition. If the dog is birdy, take advantage of it—shoot more flyers and increase the number of birds in all tasks. He should perk up with anticipation at hearing DEAD BIRD, MARK, or OVER into water. A slowed-down old-timer sometimes finds his speed again when a hot flyer is shot for him, he is told to LEAVE IT, and is sent off in another direction on a blind. His new haste may result from his desire to get the damned blind over with and get back to the hot bird—this mark is quite good for honing his memory as well. The workouts should amount to just enough mileage to keep his body well conditioned; precision rather than long distances is desired.

Many hunters and trialers work their white-muzzled partners through their ninth and tenth years and on, but inevitably the curve of accomplishment begins to descend. Stamina and abilities are lost. If you have trained and worked closely with your animal his full life, his loss or retirement is significantly more painful. Resignation and helplessness in the face of aging is hard to bear.

He looks as if he's gone fifteen rounds; his grinning face says he wants more hunt; an oblivious face sliced and scraped clean of half its hair from crashing miles of tule ditches, his lacerated nose a worn raspberry, puffy brows and skull spiked with wildrose and berry thorns—how can you replace this one?

You can't! The only solution that makes any sense for the ongoing dog-man was put into words by a thoughtful friend who himself had lost his three-year-old Field Champion to cancer: "I refuse to have my heart broken *again* by these creatures. I'll keep at least two, or I'll never have another one." When a dog reaches his fifth year and is in his prime, it is well to think of starting a pup—not during a burial. You may integrate the pup's training with that of the mature dog, while placing the burden of advanced tasks on the latter. In many cases gifted oldsters can teach and transfer bits of field and water lore to the young, green ones. For insurance against loss and heartbreak, a man should have a ten- or twelve-year-old to warm his memories, a five-year-old charger to handle his wishes, and a weanling to keep the flame alive.

"How can I replace this one?"

— *Eulogy* —

Her old eyes salute you through dimness; she joins you yet still hasn't moved. Lying across a shady patch in her run she doesn't rise, offering instead two dozen slow tail thumps. She seems to hope this is enough; she is too crippled to hunt for you.

Losing your friend of the fields, the pride of your eye, wears deeply into your own immortality. You blew away a whole damned decade together. Mind and memory busy themselves enriching, canonizing, protecting the good stuff; silver images become golden and lead turns to silver.

You remember the terrible cold, fastening you stiffly to a shoreline, an embarrassed spectator; you wish you hadn't shot. The dog crunches on, shattering green pond ice for half an hour. You both saw the hen mallard fold and plummet, punching a neat hole through the crust. You tell her to forget it and move away uphill. She finds your bird alive, wedged in tall cow parsnips, ashore, sixty yards from the ice.

Carefully etched is another time, in another marsh two thousand miles away. A freezing National Open gallery watches two dogs cruise through a devastating water blind on a single whistle. One was the mighty River Oaks Corky, twice the National Amateur Champion; the other was yours.

Dogs wear out. You knew this when you took her from her litter mates. The old campaigner is gone, leaving you snagged in the thorns of the present by your own longevity. Her final covey has exploded; the last sprig's been ferried in. Pick up a shovel and take her to rest. The partnership is smashed by time.

12

Buying and Selling

CANADA GEESE

There's another way than breeding to make a personal fund-raiser of your well-trained young field dog. Sell him! But if you should turn up with an absolutely stunning dog—one that draws gallery gasps and applause, one that can find his birds when none of the others can, one that keeps a crowd of fans lingering—and you suddenly decide to cut him loose for a handsome offer, remember: he or she may be your once-in-a-lifetime dog. You may spend the rest of your life searching for another, and punting yourself around in grief and contrition. And if you have trained the superdog yourself, you may be under the delusion that you can grab another lump of clay and shape it into something beautiful again. This doesn't happen often. What's more, if you added up your entry fees, gasoline, birds, travel and training time (even at a dollar an hour, let alone considering how you could have better spent your time), you might not find a very fat profit margin from the sale.

He may be your once-in-a-lifetime dog.

If you should turn down a wheelbarrow full of money for your dog, he should not be regarded or trained any differently. You might as well just say, "This is my dog," and give him the best life possible. If he hits a badger hole and is crippled, or is smacked by a car, you are not just out twenty grand. You've lost a good companion and a way of life.

As a professional trainer friend likes to say: "They're only flesh and blood."

If you *do* have a hot product and are *sure* you want to sell him, there are better and worse ways of going about it. Most potential buyers will want to be convinced that you're offering a worthy product. Generally, an evaluation of the dog's powers and potential is done with help from a competent and reputable professional. If the dog's price tag is considerable, I recommend accompanying him to any test evaluations that are planned for him. One of the items he must usually demonstrate is how he responds to a contrary problem and to follow-up pressure: in other words, can he "take a licking and keep on ticking"?

By being on hand, you know just how your dog has performed and what he experienced in terms of pressure. There are far too many horror stories of fine, expensive animals being trustingly sent out "on approval," kept for a month of "tire kicking"—if not run over by a truck—then sent home, psychologically scarred. Missing the virtues they had had when they left, they're worth considerably less in any future sale.

If you absolutely can't accompany your dog on an inspection and checking-out trip, one way of protecting the dog and yourself is to demand payment in advance of the evaluation and to draw up a comprehensive, binding contractual letter with your attorney. This letter, to be signed by the buyer or his representative, is designed to protect both you and your dog from any physical, psychological, or financial harm.

Naturally, there are as many ways to sell or buy a dog as there are different dogs for sale. The more money is at stake, the more thorough and cautious both buyer and seller must be. Below is an example of a legal sales agreement for a dog. It might seem long-winded and overdetailed, but it does protect both the seller and the dog.

AGREEMENT FOR SALE
OF DOG NAMED

_____

Come Now _____ of
_____ (hereinafter Seller), and
_____ of _____ (hereinafter
Buyer), through his agent _____ (hereinafter
Buyer's agent), and agree as follows:

Whereas Seller is desirous to sell and Buyer is desirous to buy that certain Retriever dog named _____ registry number _____ for the amount of _____ and,

Whereas Buyer is desirous of inspecting said animal at _____, prior to the finalization of the sale and,

Whereas Seller warrants that said animal is in excellent physical condition,

For consideration granted it is HEREBY AGREED that:

1. Seller will deliver said animal to Buyer's agent at _____ for the purpose of allowing a thorough examination and inspection of it,

2. Buyer's agent shall retain said animal for the purpose of examination and inspection for a period not to exceed twenty-one (21) days from the date of delivery to him,

3. Buyer shall have all risk of loss concerning the physical and emo-

tional well-being of said animal from its delivery to Buyer's agent until it is back in the physical possession of Seller,

4. Buyer's agent agrees that if said animal becomes ill while it is in his possession, said agent will seek prompt and professional veterinary care for it,

5. Within twenty-five (25) days of delivery of possession of said animal to Buyer's agent, Buyer or his agent shall deliver, in writing, to Seller at _____, an acceptance or rejection of said animal. Said acceptance or rejection shall be effective upon receipt. Failure to accept or reject in the allotted time will serve as a rejection,

6. Regardless of acceptance or rejection of said animal, Buyer will bear all costs incurred for the maintenance and/or transportation of said animal until its actual delivery to Seller,

7. Time is of the essence in this contract,

8. Should it be necessary to institute legal action to enforce the provisions of this contract, the losing party shall bear all reasonable court costs and attorney's fees as established by the Court. In any such action this contract shall be construed in accordance with the laws of the State of _____ in existence at the time of its execution.

Dated:

_____

AGENT

Dated:

_____

BUYER

Dated:

_____

SELLER

The buyer may come home proudly with his lightning bug in a jar—but he may never see it light up again: the one who writes the check takes a considerable risk because he buys no guarantees of allegiance. Neither does he guarantee the dog a master who commands respect, or speaks a comprehensible dialect of dog language. These dogs—these individuals—are not always like common trade goods that can be shuttled around with equanimity. I frankly enjoy the idea that dogs, like children, thrive under certain personal relationships, and not others.

Very few people run my dogs, yet other trainers believe in and practice an opposite approach. They want their dogs to be run by as many different people as possible. They want the dogs to respond to a system of *universal* commands, no matter who issues them, and like to regard the handler as interchangeable as a transistor. These dogs are probably a more trustworthy proposition for purchase, because they're prepared to respond like the canine equivalent of a rental car—the same for everybody—rather than as an individually attuned friend. Once purchased, some such dogs are expected to perform in a dollars-and-cents delivery fashion like a Kareem Abdul Jabbar or Reggie Jackson. This has always seemed a peculiar outside pressure to impose on a dog, and it often results in a miserable life for him.

An average hunter is sometimes bowled over at some of the values placed on retrieving dogs that appear to be just like his. To my knowledge, prices can run from a gift dog worth no monetary sum to the brink of infinity because some dogs are simply unavailable at any price. For reasons of discretion and security, owners usually prefer to keep any talk of the dollar value of their animals strictly private.

Why are field-trial retrievers so valuable and expensive? If the average-to-good dog is professionally trained—that is, boarded and trained with shot birds—his school bill can run roughly $3,000 a year. If he is also roundly campaigned—say, twenty trials a year in two stakes, plus a handling fee—you can add another $3,000 to $5,000. In any search for Perfection, dollar figures go far beyond function or sentimentality. Ultimately, the price rests on how much someone is willing to spend to own and enjoy anything that seems extraordinary. There's an analogy between dogs and diamonds. Even the world's most-prized and sought-after diamonds are "useful" for little more than scrawling your initials on the glass wall of a phone booth. Yet the ones that emit a fiery blue light are judged far better and more valuable than those of the same size that flash only yellow. There are plenty of rhinestone retrievers, but very few dazzle with blue light.

13

Hunting and Habitat

WADING SNIPE

My wife and child and I once lived in a plywood box on stilts. It was small, somewhat like a well-equipped duck blind, brushed by tall lupines and dune grass. Alone on five miles of gently curved beach near the cusp of Point Reyes, we were attended only by birds and the whims of the Pacific. I walked the empty beach daily and swam the shock-cold breakers. During fierce southern blows, the sea rose and smothered the beach, lashing the house around its concrete ankles with heavy coils of fresh kelp. My frail studio, built between the legs of the house, was in seasonal jeopardy from tons of surf-flung bridge timbers.

After most violent winter storms, the beach was peppered with broken birds. I picked up these protesting pilgrims by the coatful. Many had wing strains and others were merely exhausted. Most were gulls—Bonapartes, Ring-Billed, Western, Mew, California, and Heermann's. But occasionally there were injured ducks and plovers. Sometimes the open-sea birds—Murres, Loons, and Scoters—would scramble in and collapse in the dunes, having bucked too much big surf too long.

I provided them all a manner of hospitality—food, rest, and medical care—by building a "recovery room" next to my studio. When the injured birds were again full of fight, I sent them back to their everyday jobs. My most memorable patient was a delicate Mew gull. I amputated her smashed and rotting wing tip; she healed well. For most of a year, she paced freely in and out of my studio, critically eying my efforts as I drew and painted for New York clients. Eventually, she walked away north, toward Alaska, in a pathetic version of the migration urge.

We were certainly surrounded by the best marsh I had ever seen, far wilder and more striking than "the Flats" of my youth. Ours was a deliciously lonely place—mystical, always changing, and guarded by seven tortured miles of steep, narrow road and two locked gates. An ornithologist friend told me we lived in the world's second largest winter layover spot for migratory birds. We spent long evenings discussing the occupants of my hospital and the flow of visitors: wading and shore birds, brant, ducks, swans, songbirds, shrikes, hawks, and an occasional eagle. I mentioned that I had hunted this marshy estuary fifteen years before with my old Lab. He informed me that there was a thirty-acre hole in the new federal land acquisition, only two walking miles away and still legally huntable. Drawing me a detailed map, he added that he would enjoy tagging along sometime if the area proved rich in birdlife; unlike Audubon, he had yet to "collect" a single duck.

The "hole" he spoke of was a roadless drainage of baffled fresh water and salty tidal pockets. I broke down my 12-gauge Parker, dropping the barrels into one hip boot, the receiver in the other, then hobbled over the packed sand and sloshed through the estuaries. Clouds of teal, widgeon, sprig, and canvasback lifted and quickly settled again.

Motionless in a slick-grass swale, I delighted once more in watching tide, wind, and birds shift in the gilded evening light. A gray fox nimbly trotted the tide line, pausing and marking familiar addresses, sniffing for payoffs of sick and storm-doomed birds. Ducks and tattlers respectfully deferred their gossipy preening as he passed. I felt I was regaining an old and comfortable membership in the movement of the marsh—the shared participation of a predator, more intimately absorbing than that of a simple onlooker with paintbrush and canvas or a lens.

Across the weeks of that bird season I gained a number of fine ducks and a solitary landscape painting. Some days I watched color and bird shapes change and never touched the trigger. Other times I would pass shoot from high ground and send my small son, Dan, scooting happily after birds. He, too, liked their markings and soft plumage. I told him their names.

No decoys, blinds, or calls were needed, but eventually I found myself looped in a familiar time warp—I had ducks but no dog. Relief arrived with a borrowed Labrador brat named Hobbit.

Gradually the beach was "discovered." California was beginning to gush with the pulse of Neo-Ruralism. People streamed out of the cities, but instead of slowing for the once-vaunted suburbs, they now demanded the texture of tall grasses and the smoothness of clean wind. Many brought along their blighted, unbridled urban behavior, and their beloved canine symbols of freedom: Shepherd, Malamute, Setter, and Retriever crosses. Some newcomers were genuine and enthusiastic in their hunger for the outdoors; others sullied much of the open country with runaway fires, broken wine jugs, and spray-paint politics.

In January 1971, a pivotal and deplorable event took place. Two fully laden ancient oil tankers unwittingly gored each other in the dark waters inside the Golden Gate.

By morning, onlookers were appalled as thousands of barrels of crude and bunker oil sloshed out of the Gate and crept northward, darkly staining and fouling the pristine haunts of all marine life; most noticeably those of the shore birds. The undismayed oil company sat smug, then apologized during an unprecedented, unilateral public howl. It wasn't enough. Spontaneously, white-collar straights, hippies, rednecks, housewives, and hard hats (all exuding beams of holy wrath and energy) formed a fanatical work force to save the beaches.

Armies of chic bird-savers fanned out and scoured our beach for oil-soaked refugees. Flinging themselves at the bewildered, exhausted birds, they drove them back into the sea to drown.

As Hobbit and I glumly appraised the beach damage, I wondered if she could safely deal with the rapier bills of these birds. (My own eyes had always been in danger when handling them.) I aimed her at a smeared, struggling Arctic Loon and sent her. She sprinted across the hard sand, snatched it up with style and speed, laid the long neck and bill over her shoulders, sped back to me and presented it. The bird was a pitiful, hostile lump of adhesive black crude. I aimed her again. This time she brought back a fighting Western Grebe. Wiping the tar out of her mouth, I sent her again. Within half an hour, my arms were loaded with large, sticky, vicious birds. I considered taking them to my infirmary even though I lacked a clean-up plan. A passing hippie admired my holdings.

"Your dog's outta sight, man. I've been trying for one all day!"

He told me there was an official bird rescue station about ten miles away. I handed him the birds and told him he now had two Murres, two Western Grebes, and a Loon. Righteously he went forth, rich and satisfied, guaranteeing delivery to the cleaning station.

During the next three days, Hobbit and I scooped up scores of reeking, imperiled birds and gave them to the ardent, well-meaning hordes of collectors. The more they were pecked, the more profusely they bled, the more they became *birdmen,* having purchased for themselves red badges of ecology.

Almost all the carefully cleaned birds eventually died, in spite of us all. Many in the legions of people who volunteered their time and labored so heroically to save wildlife (in this and subsequent disasters) later emerged as trendy, lightly ordained environmentalists. In their new wisdom, they eventually came to hate bird dogs and hunters with the same vengeance they reserved for industrial polluters.

Ironically, many men who are unable to recognize themselves as predatory are the least likely to help maintain wild herds, flocks, and habitat. Two hundred and fifty million dollars are anted up each year by hunters for wildlife restoration and maintenance. Anyone genuinely concerned with the future of wild things should buy hunting and fishing licenses whether they shoot, hook, observe, or abstain. Ducks Unlimited and Trout Unlimited (among others) deserve similar attention because they, too, provide funds for habitat.

Unfortunately, working retrieving dogs and their people (often in white training coats) are cheap shots and easy targets in the war for jurisdiction of the remaining wild places, a struggle between hunters and other conservationists. The "barbaric" act of shooting barn pigeons (the same nuisance birds that defile public buildings and serve as a source of disease for people and livestock) often lands dog trainers on the opposite side of the ideological fence from many avid environmentalists/conservationists.

The fact remains that many retriever people hunt, many active environmentalists bird-watch, and a considerable number in each group do both.* The

* Balanced and enlightened reading on the subject of hunting in America may be found in *The Hunt,* by John G. Mitchell (New York: Alfred A. Knopf, 1980).

The author with 1977 National Derby Champion Dr. Davey, Ph.D., at home in California.

most informed, best educated, and most experienced members of each group recognize that they share nearly identical goals, and that the enemy is hardly one another. If the fears of both groups were analyzed and sorted, a single concern would emerge: *loss of habitat*.

Though polarized by mistrust and disgust, both factions share common enemies: the swamp drainers, marsh fillers, stream straighteners, river changers, dam builders, and the busy U.S. Army Corps of Engineers; the polluters, poisoners, wasters, and spillers of sewage, chemicals, oil, and nuclear wastes; the eroders who overgraze, overstock, overharvest, overlog, clear-cut, and clean-farm; the overtooled with Caterpillars, earthmovers, draglines, chainsaws, trail bikes, snowmobiles, four-wheel drives, and RVs; the developers and subdividers, farm killers, ranch breakers, and orchard flatteners; the slob fishermen, hunters, tourists, horsemen, and campers with wild fire and litter.

If responsible hunting and fishing interests (variously estimated at somewhere between 30 and 60 million people) could align themselves with responsible environmentalists (roughly another 30 million), misleading myths about each other would fade away and their combined political muscle for habitat protection and restoration would, in fact, be overwhelming.

Such hopes are not entirely unrealistic. Much fairy-tale prejudice and ignorance are being replaced by enlightened educational programs regarding the balance of nature, food chains, endangered species, predator/prey relationships, and ecosystems. I'm encouraged by efforts in some states to provide and demand environmental awareness of game patterns, population, cover, food, and pressure—as well as weapon safety—*before* a hunter is issued his first license.

The Germans have taken the environmental education of the hunter even farther. Each license applicant must pass a withering exam, somewhat akin to a naturalist's doctorate, before he is privileged to enter the forest. The result is a relatively sparse population of very intelligent users of a bountiful, sound, healthy habitat—without litter.

The English, who invented wing shooting (apparently bored by bushwhacking birds on the ground), have long recognized the value of providing habitat on their country estates, parks, and farms. Those who have the acreage, hunt. They are usually wealthy, educated, and conscientious about their land and game. Those without access to land simply do not hunt or own shotguns.

Whether it happens through pressure of consumerism, free enterprise, or pursuit of the American Dream, when wild habitat suffers or vanishes, we are all diminished. I wince when I see a pothole in a rural road, partly from the jolt, but mostly from the fear that if I turn my back, someone will fill it with a freeway.

Often this clash of dreams appears like the confluence of two rivers to me: On one bank there are the Disney-groomed environmentalists, many of whom have yet to advance beyond decades of entertaining myths about animal behavior and damaging morality plays concerning predator and prey. Entrenched on the other side are the beleaguered hunters, clutching at the specious vision of father and son plinking their way into the sunset. Both factions are marooned with their views of how it's all "supposed to be."

Fortunately, nature rarely gives a damn. A steady diet of Big Macs, or organically grown vegetation, or even caviar has yet to dull our canine teeth: They keep popping up with each generation.

Some modern philosophers and psychologists self-consciously admit to vestiges of caveman behavior in this age of space travel and software technology. Others, like myself, maintain that we are *all* still rather primitive, despite a veneer of vinyls and satellite communications.

Ten thousand years is only a spit on the hot stovepipe of evolution. Man continues to look wistfully behind him. Every day, 20 million people scheme to reduce their workload, get away from the office or kitchen, pull off their clothes, and go jogging. Future behaviorists may contend that jogging was partially a reawakening of the chase, a rediscovery of a primary hunter's drive—to pursue something—without a tool or much of a quarry. (Appetite, health, fitness, and figure are all secondary goals.) When a lone jogger pulls into my view, I mentally salute him—especially if his dog is along.

Good hunting and dog trialing or training are among the few remaining unpackaged pastimes. Results are a surprise and never guaranteed. Unlike theater and programmed sports, there are no computerized ticket sales, artificial illumination, fast-food slingers, or fears of changing weather.

I can't say that I like dumping myself out of a warm bed into a dark frosted murk, or skidding a tinny boatful of decoys over half a mile of knee-sucking black mud, or squishing down into a rank duck blind. Peering through a tule fog, my blurred Labrador is hardly perceptible. While we wait and sit, usually with his hindquarters submerged, I hear tiny rhythmic swishings. There he is, watching and hoping and wagging his tail *under* the numbing cold water. I like that a lot. That's probably why we are here.

Some time ago I spent a year stashed in a hospital bed. Unable to walk, I entertained myself with remembrances of my teen-age legs running and my summer-tanned arms lofting whippy bamboo frog gigs, then shouldering ponderous winter shotguns. Years later, my legs came back. So did my lungs. So did the fingers that couldn't open a pocketknife or a tube of paint.

Today, hunting well over my dogs means a great deal to me. Even when we get skunked, I feel good after a hunt. Sometimes better than good: improved, replenished, restored. When the bird season ends, I try to spread the ceremony of it over the rest of the year by training and trialing. This keeps us in the laps of swamps and the beauty of birds, and offers enough morning exercise to get our hearts started.

I'll probably always hunt. Who but a hunter or an ornithologist can tell you where to look for a snipe's ears and how his bill hinges and why there are spots on it, or how he sends his eerie spring music through the thick evening air? Who but a savvy retriever can find him when he is down? And if this exquisite creature should fall before the diminutive barrels of a .410, how much more appropriate! Often only my dogs and I are there to appreciate it if the shot does connect. As with much of my retriever training, I usually hunt without the company of other people. I like the solitude and freedom to change my direction and go where I will . . . but without the companionship of my dog much of the richness of the hunt would be gone.

Glossary

air to provide a dog with a period to empty his bladder and bowels.

airing, to air the period so provided for a dog to empty his bladder and bowels.

Amateur an individual who has not derived or attempted to derive any part of his livelihood from the training, handling, or showing of field or hunting dogs (as defined by the National Amateur Retriever Club).

Amateur All-Age Stake for dogs over six months of age, if handled in that stake by persons who are Amateurs (as determined by the Field Trial Committee of the trial-giving club).

Amateur Field Champion, AFC a retriever who has won fifteen points, including a first place at an all-breed retriever trial, in Open or Limited stakes when handled by an Amateur, or in Amateur stakes at licensed retriever trials; or one who has won a National or National Amateur Championship Stake.

angling diagonally traversing terrain or entering water other than on perpendicular lines.

"back" 1. a term meaning "farther away from the handler"; 2. a directional signal given with the raised arm and hand, directing the dog away from the handler; 3. the verbal command issued to the dog to direct him away from the handler, or to release him from the heel-sit position for a blind retrieve.

baseball primary drill for teaching directional casts, right or left "over" and "back" casts.

bench show a dog show, judged on conformation and beauty according to breed standards.

bird bagged retrieving condition in which the dog allows the scent of bird crates to interfere with his hunt.

bird boy a trial worker who places the bird for a blind retrieve, or a person who throws the bird or bumper for the dog to retrieve.

birdiness high appreciation of feathers, a desirable quality in dogs.

blind retrieve (land or water) any retrieve in which the dog does not know the location of the bird or bumper, but the handler does.

bolter a dog who runs away from the trainer and training area.

break an attempt to retrieve without the handler's command to do so.

bumper, dummy a plastic or canvas boat fender, usually cylindrical, and approximately the size of a bird; most have a throwing rope attached.

bumper gun a gas-powered training aid capable of mechanically throwing bumpers long distances.

call backs an announced list of dogs remaining in the field trial after each series of tests.

cast a directional hand and/or voice signal from trainer to dog.

cast refusal, C.R. a dog's unwillingness to respond to handler's direction or cast.

CD Companion Dog, first obedience title.

C.D.X. Companion Dog Excellent, second obedience title.

channeling swimming a long, deep, narrow body of water.

CNFC Canadian National Field Champion.

cold blind any blind retrieve that the dog has never run or practiced before.

compartmentalizing a system of separating diverse training methods.

controlled break in the Derby and Qualifying stakes, when a dog makes a slight break and is brought immediately under control. He may not necessarily be eliminated, but rather penalized for unsteadiness.

cover any grass, brush, vegetation, or trees that may conceal the bird or dog and affect scenting conditions.

creeping a dog's forward movement from the line while marking; just short of breaking.

cue an audible reminder or instruction to the dog.

cunningness a defiant, unwilling attitude.

Derby Stake a stake for retrievers over six months of age who have not yet reached their second birthday.

delay bird any mark shot after one or more birds of a multiple are retrieved.

diversion an accompanying mark or blind that adds difficulty to a following mark or blind.

double mark two marked-fall retrieves.

dragback trail of incoming scent left in the field by preceding dogs and birds.

dry gun or **dry pop** a gunner who fires without an accompanying dead bird throw or flyer.

Field Champion, FC a retriever who has won ten points, including a first place in an all-breed retriever trial, in Open or Limited stakes at AKC-licensed retriever trials; or has won a National Championship Stake.

flat throw see **square throw.**

force-fetch a method that teaches the dog he *must* retrieve when commanded.

forty-nine-day theory canine behaviorists' belief in the optimum time (seven weeks after birth) for the developing puppy to leave the litter.

"fountain" or **"momma and poppa"** a gun station that throws two marks, one to each side of the position, in sequence.

freezing   a dog's total refusal to give up the bird to the handler.

gallery   main body of field-trial observers.

"grocery list"   a system of assessing the difficulty of terrain in marks and blinds.

gunner or **guns**   positions or people who throw and shoot birds as marks.

handle   a directional cast or gesture from the handler.

happy bumper   a frivolous fun mark.

hardmouth   to rough or abuse the retrieved game.

holding blind or screen   a fabric enclosure for dog and handler to stand behind, intended to obscure the dog's view of forthcoming tests.

honoring   a dog's remaining seated in alert readiness on the line while another dog works.

indented bird   term used to describe angle of throw, such as ninety degrees, square, or "flat" throw.

JAM   Judges' Award of Merit: a green ribbon given to any unplaced dog for excellent work.

kennel   a dog run; or a trainer's or breeder's facility.

kennel walker   a nervous, high-strung dog who paces his kennel.

key bird   the most difficult mark of a multiple.

Licensed Trial   a trial licensed by the AKC where championship points are given.

Limited All-Age Stake   a stake for dogs over six months of age that have previously placed or been awarded a Judges' Award of Merit in an Open Stake, or that have been placed first or second in a Qualifying Stake, or placed or awarded a JAM in an Amateur Stake carrying championship points.

line   1. in a field trial, the specific spot designated by the judges from where the handler works his dog; 2. the acceptable straight path of travel from the handler to a blind retrieve.

line manners   a dog and handler's demeanor on the way to the line and while working under judgment.

lining   the handler's adjustment in setting up the position of his dog before running a blind or mark.

lining the blind   executing a perfect line of travel between the handler and blind without whistles or casts.

mark, single   a shot flyer, thrown dead bird, or bumper that the dog watches and retrieves; a multiple mark can be a double, triple, or quadruple.

National Amateur Retriever Trial   the trial for dogs who have qualified during the previous year, held each year to determine the National Amateur Champion of that year. Dogs may be handled by Amateurs only.

National Retriever Trial   the trial for dogs who have qualified during the previous year, held each year to determine the National Champion of that year. Dogs may be handled by Amateurs or professionals.

NFC   National Field Champion.

old fall the place where another bird has previously been retrieved, leaving a scent that may divert a dog in a subsequent retrieve.

Open All-Age Stake a stake for all dogs over six months of age.

"over" 1. a term denoting "in a lateral direction"; 2. a signal, given with the arm and hand, directing the dog in a lateral direction; 3. a verbal command issued to the dog to send him in a lateral direction; 4. a movement of a dog in a lateral direction.

"over and under" a configuration of marks in which a long deep bird falls on the same line as a shorter mark.

outcross a breeding made between unrelated family bloodlines.

pattern any familiar or memorized drill.

permanent blind a memorized pattern blind made to teach line running and build confidence.

pick up 1. the physical act and the dog's style in picking up his game; 2. "Pick up your dog"—judges' request of the handler to call in or remove his dog from the field.

pin, pinpoint mark a direct, faultless, accurate retrieve.

"poison" or **"leave it" bird** a marked bird that the dog is instructed to ignore before executing another task.

poison ground or **point** an area deliberately scented or "salted" with bird scent by the judges.

pop 1. the dog stops his hunt or line of travel and looks to the handler for assistance on a mark or blind; 2. firing a gun to accompany a thrown mark.

pull or **suction** attraction to a certain area because of scent or previous mark or geographic enticement.

quartering orderly method of questing for game, employing the nose.

rat trap tool for holding and floating a bird for a water blind.

recast a second attempt to send the dog from the line.

retired gun a gun that disappears from sight after throwing and shooting a mark.

running in British term for breaking.

sanctioned trial an informal trial, sanctioned by the AKC, in which dogs compete but not for championship points.

selection any method of retrieving multiple marks out of the sequence in which they fall.

series a trial test.

shore break teaching process that forces the dog not to avoid water.

sluice added shooting of a downed bird on the water.

spooky shy or apprehensive; said of a dog.

square throw a bird thrown at an angle of 90° from a line from the dog's starting position for the retrieve to the thrower's position. See diagram 3.

stake event or contest.

staunch or **steady**   not moving to retrieve until commanded to do so.

sticking   a hesitation or reluctance on the dog's part to give the retrieved bird to the handler.

studdiness   sexy behavior in a male dog.

style   a dog's willingness, ability, and manner of retrieving, as characterized by desire, speed, courage, and attitude.

switch   to leave the area of one mark after hunting for it and go to another, more easily remembered mark.

walk-up   a trial test intended to simulate actual hunting: The handler, with dog at heel, judges, and gunners, all advance together in the field before the birds are thrown and shot. See page 13.

water refusal   a dog's unwillingness to go into the water after being directed to do so.

whistle commands   repeated short toots means "come in"; one long blast means "sit."

whistle refusal   a dog's failure to respond to the whistle command; often called a "slipped whistle."

Acknowledgments

It has always been fascinating to me that there are many different methods of correcting dogs for the same error in the same situation—and as many different answers to the problem may be correct. Finding the best of these "correct" ways is one of the chief tasks confronting the trainer.

In writing this book, I have called upon a number of retriever people whom I have admired. All of them enriched the book by their cooperation. In this book I have often quoted these people in order through their insights to help the reader find the particular way of handling the problem that is "correct" for him. These people are listed below. Professional trainers among them are designated with an asterisk; the dogs listed are among the trainers' most successful "students." (*L.* designates Labrador, *Ches.* Chesapeake, *Gold.* Golden; *M.* male and *F.* female. Abbreviations for championships are explained in full in the Glossary.)

John Anderson, D.V.M., Winters, California
>   AFC Winroc's Ripper (L.M.); FC AFC Wild Hearted Dinah (L.F.); FC AFC T. R. Tucker (L.M.)

Joe Boatright, Pleasanton, California
>   FC AFC Midge of Greenwood (L.F.); FC AFC Paladin VII (L.M.); FC AFC Clipper VI (L.M.)

*Dana Brown, Santa Barbara, California
>   Dual Ch AFC Royal Oaks Jill of Burgundy (L.F.); FC AFC Tigathoe's Mainliner Miriah (L.F.); FC AFC Volwood's Abby (L.F.); FC AFC Royal Oaks Something Super (L.M.)

*Rex Carr, Escalon, California
>   NFC NAFC Super Chief (L.M.); FC NAFC Carr-Lab Hilltop (L.M.); FC AFC Mount Joy's Bit O'Ginger (Ches. F.); FC AFC Trumarc's Raider (L.M.)

Eloise H. Cherry, Sonoma, California
>   FC AFC Nelgard's Baron (Ches. M.); Dual Ch AFC Tiger's Cub (Ches. M.); FC AFC Baron's Tule Tiger (Ches. M.)

Sal Gelardi, Woodland, California
  FC AFC Chuk Chukar Chuk (L.M.); FC AFC Chukar's Big Jake (L.M.);
  AFC World Famous Sweet Pea (L.F.)
*Jim Gonia, McKenna, Washington
  NFC NAFC NCFC Wanapum Darts Dandy (L.F.); FC CNFC Wanapum
  Darts Garbo (L.F.); NFC AFC Risky Business Ruby (L.F.)
*Roy Gonia, McKenna, Washington
  CNFC FC Rip of Holly Hill (L.M.); NFC FC Massie's Sassy Boots (L.M.);
  NFC FC Brignall's Gringo (L.M.); FC AFC Misty's Sungold Lad, C.D.X.
  (Gold. M.)
A. A. Jones, Hillsborough, California
  FC AFC Dairy Hill's Night Watch (L.M.); FC AFC Dairy Hill's Night
  Cap (L.M.); FC AFC Dairy Hill's Michikiniquia (L.F.)
*Ed Minoggi, Portland, Oregon
  FC Leroy III (L.M.); FC AFC Shamrock Acres Super Value (L.M.); FC
  Michel (L.F.); FC AFC Alaska's Fall Blizzard (L.M.)
Barbara Ornbaun, Suisun, California
  FC AFC Ornbaun's Diamond Lil (L.F.); FC AFC Amazing Grace of Orn-
  baun (L.F.); FC AFC Ornbaun's Raucous Riley (L.M.)
*Doug Orr, Seattle, Washington
  FC Carnation Butter Boy (L.M.)—highest Open point yellow Labrador;
  CNFC FC Washington's Lucky Minerva (L.F.); FC Anzac of Zenith
  (L.M.); FC Moby Dick (L.M.)
*Tom Sorenson, Wentzville, Missouri
  NFC AFC Baird's Centerville Sam (L.M.); FC AFC Win-Toba's Majestic
  Lad (L.M.); FC AFC Sunshine Rockabye Mickie (L.M.); FC AFC Toni's
  Blaine Child (L.M.)
*J. J. Sweezey, Chestertown, Maryland
  FC Sassy Sioux of Tukwila (L.F.); FC Zipper Dee Do (L.M.); FC Floodbay
  Baron (L.M.); FC Zipper's Dapper Sapper (L.M.)
Jay and Val Walker, Medford, Oregon
  FC AFC Misty's Sungold Lad, C.D.X. (Gold.M.)—all-time high-point
  Golden; FC AFC CFC Triven Thunderhead (L.M.); FC AFC Ern-Bar's
  Twinkle Boots (L.F.); FC AFC Sungold Lad's Talisman (Gold.M.)

Chapter 2 was written with the help of Mr. and Mrs. Guy Cherry, and Mr. and
Mrs. Andrius A. Jones, Mrs. Rosita Wraith, and Mrs. Marianne Foote.

Selected Bibliography

Cherry, Eloise Heller. *The Complete Chesapeake Bay Retriever.* New York: Howell Book House, 1981.

Fisher, Gertrude. *The Complete Golden Retriever.* New York: Howell Book House, 1974.

Free, James L. *Training Your Retriever.* rev. ed. New York: Coward-McCann, 1963.

Gaines Dog Research Center. *Basic Guide to Canine Nutrition.* New York, 1971.

Kelley, R. B., D.V.Sc. *Sheep Dogs.* 3rd ed. Sydney: Angus & Robertson, 1958.

Kirk, Robert W., D.V.M. *First Aid for Pets.* New York: E.P. Dutton, 1978.

McGinnis, Terri, D.V.M. *The Well Dog Book.* New York: Random House, 1974.

Mitchell, John G. *The Hunt.* New York: Alfred A. Knopf, 1980.

Morgan, Charles. *Charles Morgan on Retrievers.* Edited by Ann Fowler and D. K. Walters. Stonington, Conn.: October House, 1968.

Roslin-Williams, Mary. *All About the Labrador.* Salem, N.H.: Michael Joseph, Inc., 1980.

Walsh, Harry M. *The Outlaw Gunner.* Centreville, Md.: Tidewater Publishers, 1971.

Walters, D. L., and Walters, Ann. *Training Retrievers to Handle.* Order from authors, Route 1, La Cygne, Kansas 66040. N.d.

Warwick, Helen. *The Complete Labrador Retriever.* New York: Howell Book House, 1965.

Wolters, Richard A. *The Labrador Retriever: The History . . . The People.* Los Angeles: Petersen Prints, 1981.

———. *Water Dog.* New York: E.P. Dutton, 1964.

Index

Page references for illustrations are in **boldface** type.

Illustration Credits

— *Color* —

Chesapeake Female Lotta: Courtesy Mr. and Mrs. Donald Ongaro
Two Drake Pintails with Nut Grass: Courtesy Mr. and Mrs. Charles Schwab
Swimming Canada Gander: Courtesy Mr. and Mrs. Gary Schmidt
Walking Canada Gander: Courtesy Mr. Harold Ruth
Tipping Sprig: Courtesy Mrs. Barbara Ornbaun
Resting Snipe: Author's Collection
Golden Male FC AFC Right On Dynamite John: Courtesy Mr. and Mrs. Robert Klicker
Dr. Davey, Ph.D., at Speed: Photograph by Tupper Ansel Blake
Hen Quail in Grasses: Courtesy Mr. and Mrs. Douglas Jones
Appletree Quail: Courtesy Mr. and Mrs. Guy Cherry
Bobwhites and Broom Weed: Courtesy Mr. Martin Wood
Mallard Hen and Ducklings: Courtesy Mr. and Mrs. Joseph Boatwright
Labrador Female Teal: Courtesy Dr. and Mrs. Maurice Smith
Drake Cinnamon Teal: Courtesy Ms. Mary Beth Walker
Virginia Rail: Courtesy Mr. and·Mrs. John Lail
Chesapeake Male Dual Champion and AFC Tiger's Cub CD: Courtesy Mrs. Eloise Cherry
Labrador Male FC AFC Paladin VII: Courtesy Mr. and Mrs. Joseph Boatwright

— *Black and White* —

Page v: Bill Hillmann Photo
Pages 14, 16: Edwin Levick Photos; courtesy the Labrador Retriever Club
Page 19: Photo by Harold Mack, Jr.
Page 19: Courtesy Roy and Wanda Gonia
Pages 28, 98: Jeri Nichols Quinn
Pages 28, 38, 45, 48, 52, 58, 60, 61, 64, 66, 78, 79, 94–96, 110, 115, 118–121, 127, 139, 147, 154, 157, 160, 168, 186, 203, 214, 220, 223, 234: Photos by Hal Lauritzen
Pages 44, 72–76, 191: Tom Quinn
Page 231: Photo by Art Rogers

— *Chapter Headpieces* —

The chapter headpieces are from paintings and drawings by Thomas Quinn, courtesy of Dr. and Mrs. John Bennhoff, Chapter 1; Mr. and Mrs. Wendel Mackey, Chapter 2; M. J. Mowinkle, Chapter 3; Martin Wood, Chapter 4; Barbara Ornbaun, Chapter 5; Hayden Hays Gallery, Chapter 6; Mr. and Mrs. John Lail, Chapter 7; Mr. and Mrs. Ted Sherman, Chapter 8; Mr. and Mrs. Gary Schmidt, Chapter 9; Creekside Gallery, Chapter 10; Frank Stout, Chapter 11; Caroline Brooke, Chapter 12; Martin Wood, Chapter 13.

A Note about the Author

Both as a professional artist of distinction and as an unusually successful trainer of retrievers for hunting and field trialing, Tom Quinn's work is marked by originality and careful attention to detail. His home area in northern California provides an ideal environment for his painting and work with dogs.

During the past thirteen years no fewer than eleven high-ranking retrievers with whose training Tom Quinn has been associated have won major National, Open, or Amateur championships. Among them have been Amateur Field Champion Rip Snortin' Good Times (1982); National Open Champion Risky Business Ruby (1980), who also achieved her Amateur Field Championship and Canadian Field Championship; Field Champion and Amateur Field Champion Amazing Grace of Ornbaun (1980); National Derby Champion Dr. Davey, Ph.D. (1977); Field Champion and Amateur Field Champion Ornbaun's Diamond Lil (1976); and Field Champion and Amateur Field Champion Nakai Anny (1974).

In addition to his work as breeder, trainer, and painter who often selects dogs and game birds as his subjects, Tom Quinn holds a high rating as a field-trial judge. In this capacity he has officiated at many trialing events throughout the country.